WAGE RIGIDITY & UNEMPLOYMENT

WAGE RIGIDITY AND UNEMPLOYMENT

edited by

Wilfred Beckerman

The Johns Hopkins University Press
Baltimore

First published in 1986 by
The Johns Hopkins University Press
701 West 40th Street
Baltimore, Maryland 21211

Library of Congress Cataloging-in-Publication Data

Wage rigidity and unemployment.

Bibliography: p.
Includes index.
1. Wages—Congresses.   2. Unemployment—Congresses.
3. Inflation (Finance)—Congresses.   I. Beckerman, Wilfred.
HD4909.W26 1986   331.2′1   86-45446

ISBN 0-7156-2081-9

Printed in Great Britain

Contents

Introduction

As in the 1930s, the major issue confronting most industrialised countries is the persistence of very high unemployment. And, as in the 1930s, one of the explanations often advanced has been the alleged rigidity of wages. The crucial importance of this hypothesis for economic policy cannot be over-emphasised, and all the papers in this volume have been designed to throw light on one or other aspect of it.

In the first paper Frank Hahn and Bob Solow question the widespread assumption that wage flexibility is desirable to begin with, and demonstrate, in the context of a dynamic model, not merely that Keynes was right but that he was perhaps not categorical enough in asserting that the paths followed by an economy with flexible nominal wages were likely to be far less attractive than those followed by one with rigid wages.

In the next paper Wilfred Beckerman and Tim Jenkinson challenge the validity of existing measures of wage flexibility and propose a new method of measuring it.

There follows a group of three papers which consider—from different points of view—the causes of wage rigidity. Dan Mitchell provides a comprehensive survey of various explanations (as well as a concluding comparison of the relative merits of greater wage flexibility and a profit-sharing policy of the type proposed by Martin Weitzman in a later paper in the volume). Andrew Oswald studies in detail the widely held view that lay-offs by seniority aggravate wage rigidity. This is closely related to the hypothesis advanced by Assar Lindbeck and Dennis Snower, that wage rigidity is increased by 'insider-outsider' conflict, in the context of a paper that also discusses the macroeconomic implications of this form of wage rigidity and the policy consequences.

George Perry surveys macro-economic policies followed in the post-war world with special reference to the degree to which the costs of anti-inflationary policies have been increased as a result of wage rigidity.

Richard Jackman and Richard Layard, recognising that most governments are inhibited from adopting expansionary policies by fear of the resulting inflation, consider a particular policy proposal—

namely, a form of wage-tax and worker-subsidy scheme—designed to reduce what is generally known among economists as the 'natural' rate of unemployment.

A completely different policy for reducing unemployment is set out by Martin Weitzman, namely the 'share economy' proposal. Some form of profit sharing has been operating for some time, of course, in many companies—particularly in Japan. But the objective has generally been to improve industrial relations. Professor Weitzman, however, has now set out the full theoretical case for a profit-sharing economy as a means of ensuring full employment by, in effect, introducing greater flexibility in wages without this having a perverse influence on demand.

Finally, Pierre Dehez and Jean-Paul Fitoussi examine formally and in detail the macro-implications of a dynamic three-generation model in which the degree to which nominal wages are indexed to prices varies from period to period according to variables describing the conditions of the labour market.

All the papers are based on contributions to a symposium held, in April 1985, at the University of the South, Sewanee, Tennessee.

Grateful acknowledgment is made to the American Economic Association for kind permission to reproduce Martin Weitzman's contribution to the December 1985 issue of the *American Economic Review*.

Oxford, August 1985   W.B.

Contributors

WILFRED BECKERMAN, Fellow of Balliol College, Oxford

PIERRE DEHEZ, Professor at the European University Institute, Florence

JEAN-PAUL FITOUSSI, Professor at the Fondation Nationale des Sciences Politiques; Director of the Research Department, Observatoire Française des Conjonctures Economiques, Paris

F.H. HAHN, Professor of Economics, University of Cambridge

R. JACKMAN, Senior Lecturer in Economics, London School of Economics

TIM JENKINSON, Fellow of Merton College, Oxford

R. LAYARD, Professor of Economics and Director of the Centre for Labour Economics, London School of Economics

ASSAR LINDBECK, Professor of Economics, University of Stockholm, and Director of the Institute for International Economic Studies, Stockholm

DANIEL J.B. MITCHELL, Professor, Graduate School of Management and Director of the Institute of Industrial Relations, University of California, Los Angeles

ANDREW J. OSWALD, Senior Research Fellow, Centre for Labour Economics, London School of Economics

GEORGE L. PERRY, Senior Fellow, Brookings Institution, Washington D.C.; Director of the Brookings Panel on Economic Activity

DENNIS J. SNOWER, Reader in Economics, Birkbeck College, University of London

R.M. SOLOW, Professor of Economics, Massachusetts Institute of Technology

MARTIN L. WEITZMAN, Professor of Economics, Massachusetts Institute of Technology

1. Is Wage Flexibility a Good Thing?*

F.H. Hahn & R.M. Solow

1. *Introduction*

It sounds blasphemous even to ask the question. But that cannot be the appropriate reaction: economics is not, after all, a religion. Well, then, *is* wage flexibility a good thing? That depends on what you mean by 'wage', by 'flexibility' and by 'good'. (There seems to be no point in quibbling about the definition of 'thing'.)

We shall focus on the nominal wage. There would no doubt be general consensus that a market economy can easily find itself in trouble if real-wage rates are not free to move. The real wage (or structure of real wages) compatible with full employment – it may be unique – can change as tastes, technology and external circumstances change. An economy that has no good way to adapt its real wages to such events may be unable to achieve a desirable market equilibrium. Even this more or less static statement may actually concede too much to wage flexibility. There are perfectly reasonable circumstances, with a heavy dose of increasing returns to scale, in which equilibria with higher employment have *higher* real-wage rates. In such economies, when the dynamics are taken into account, even real-wage flexibility may create more problems than it solves. (See the definition of 'flexibility' in the next paragraph.) In any case, the normal way to achieve a flexible real wage is through flexible nominal wages, and that is what we propose to study. The question is whether that is the best way.

Nominal-wage rates are flexible if they rise pretty promptly and rapidly when there is excess demand for labour and fall pretty promptly and rapidly when there is excess supply of labour. There is excess supply of labour when there are more than a handful of workers for whom the marginal utility of leisure in terms of goods is less than the going real wage in jobs for which they are qualified. (This covers the case of under-employment as well as pure joblessness.) In these days no

---

* This paper rests on the preliminary stages of a larger work on macroeconomic theory on which we are engaged.

one doubts much that nominal-wage rates will rise amply when there is excess demand for labour, i.e. when the marginal product of labour in many jobs exceeds the marginal utility of leisure to the occupants of those jobs. This presumption suggests that the degree of nominal-wage flexibility may be asymmetric with respect to direction. It is rather remarkable that empirical-econometric studies usually find it impossible to confirm the existence of this asymmetry, however 'natural' it may seem. We shall be speaking about downward flexibility of the nominal wage, just for concreteness and relevance.

Finally, how does one judge whether nominal-wage flexibility is a good thing? There must be a standard of comparison, an alternative to which the flexible-wage system can be compared. Here the historically obvious choice appears to be a good one. One imagines two otherwise identical economies that start in a situation of general excess supply of labour. In one of the twin economies the nominal wage is flexible, so it falls. In the other the nominal wage is inflexible; this economy responds to unemployment with a policy-induced increase in the money supply, whose purpose is to create an appropriately higher real money supply without the need for intervening deflation. The idea is to compare the paths traced out by the two economies. If the first one does better, traces out a Pareto-superior or otherwise-superior path, then nominal-wage flexibility is a good thing. Otherwise it is not, and there are better ways to handle generalised unemployment.

It will not do, by the way, simply to say that the second economy may well undergo a certain amount of inflation and, since inflation is by common consent a bad thing, must be worse off than its flexible-wage twin. The point is that the flexible-wage economy will undergo a certain amount of deflation, and that is not especially a good thing either. In fact the usual casual presumption has been that deflation is perhaps a bit the worse of the two on the ground that it is hard on debtors, among whom progressive entrepreneurs are disproportionately represented. That is too casual by half; and anyway the usual caveats about anticipations apply. No matter; the point is that there is no short cut – the flexible-wage and inflexible-wage paths must be compared and judged explicitly.

2. *Keynes*

Some of the complications associated with the whole idea of nominal-wage flexibility are illustrated in *The General Theory*. Keynes certainly believed that his doctrine did not rest on the hypothesis of rigid nominal wages. His contemporaries all understood that nominal-wage rigidity could entail prolonged unemployment. Had Keynes merely agreed with them, he could hardly have claimed to be making a revolution in economic thought. That does not mean that he believed wages to be flexible. He did not; he even gave what is still a cogent explanation for the fact that workers resist nominal-wage cuts, to the point of allowing themselves to be laid off, whereas they accept rising prices passively. Keynes argued that workers cared a lot about traditional relativities among occupations. (To achieve explanatory power, this argument requires a utility-kink at the traditional relative wage.) In a decentralised wage-making system, to accept a lower nominal wage is to accept a lower relative wage, with no guarantee that other wages will follow one's own down. So this solution is resisted. Furthermore workers cannot 'bargain over the real wage', not even the product wage. A rise in prices is the one way the system has to reduce real wages without disturbing relativities.

Keynes did not think that nominal-wage ridigity was the sole or main cause of unemployment. Indeed, and this is our direct concern, he was at pains to argue that wage cuts were not the proper cure for unemployment, and might be no cure at all. One reason he gave is now a commonplace and need not detain us. His contemporaries tended to emphasise the favourable substitution effects of wage cuts and to ignore the unfavourable effects on nominal aggregate demand. If prices were merely to follow wage rates down, only the weak reed that later came to be called the 'Keynes effect' would be left; and monetary policy would be an excellent and quick substitute. (The dependence of current expenditure on current income has been clarified, of course, since Clower's writings.)

In chapter 19 ('Changes in Money Wages') Keynes comes to the dynamic effects of downward wage flexibility. There he argues (a) that the effects of *falling* wages are likely to be, on the whole, depressing; (b) that whatever good effects there might be could more easily be achieved by an increase in the money supply; and (c) that a policy of stable wages – with prices gently falling as productivity improves – is probably the best macroeconomic environment.

Here are some of the key passages.

> If the reduction of money-wages is expected to be a *reduction relative to money wages in the future*, the change will be favourable to investment, because . . .

it will increase the marginal efficiency of capital; whilst for the same reason it may be favourable to consumption. If, on the other hand, the reduction leads to the expectation, or even to the serious possibility, of a further wage reduction in prospect, it will have precisely the opposite effect. For it will diminish the marginal efficiency of capital and will lead to the postponement of both investment and consumption.

He mentions the increase in the real burden of business debt associated with general deflation. And then:

> When we enter on a period of weakening effective demand, a sudden large reduction of money-wages to a level so low that no one believes in its indefinite continuance would be the event most favourable to a strengthening of effective demand. But this ... is scarcely practical politics under a system of free wage-bargaining. On the other hand, it would be much better that wages should be rigidly fixed and deemed incapable of material changes, than that depressions should be accompanied by a gradual downward tendency of money-wages, a further moderate wage decrease being expected to signalise each increase, of, say, 1 per cent in the amount of unemployment. For example, the effect of an expectation that wages are going to sag by, say, 2 per cent in the coming year will be roughly equivalent to the effect of a rise of 2 per cent in the amount of interest payable for the same period.

Finally:

> Except in a socialised community where wage-policy is settled by decree, there is no means of securing uniform wage reductions for every class of labour. The result can be brought about by a series of gradual, irregular changes, justifiable on no criterion of social justice or economic expedience, and probably completed only after wasteful and disastrous struggles, where those in the weakest bargaining position will suffer relatively to the rest. A change in the quantity of money on the other hand, is already within the power of most governments by open-market policy or analogous measures. Having regard to human nature and our institutions, it can only be a foolish person who would prefer a flexible wage policy to a flexible money policy, unless he can point to advantages from the former which are not obtainable from the latter.

Keynes, of course, thought that monetary policy by itself was an inadequate tool for macroeconomic management, because moderate-sized actions might be inadequate and large-scale ones destructive of confidence. But that is neither here nor there in the present context.

3. *The emergence of second thoughts*

The dominant reading of *The General Theory* – though not the only one – seems nevertheless to have ticketed Keynes as the theorist of sticky-price macroeconomics. His suggestion, documented above, that wage and price flexibility, if they were possible, might be a poor or even self-defeating way to achieve equilibrium at full employment, seems more or less to have disappeared from professional consciousness. Just recently, however, in what is either a great coincidence or the start of a groundswell, several economists – including ourselves – have begun to re-explore the notion that wage and price flexibility might not be an unambiguously good operating mechanism for a market economy subject to occasional contractionary shocks, especially real shocks. As an aid to discussion, we want to describe several recent essays along this line, before we come to our own current research. The first two are Charles Schultze (1985) and J. Bradford DeLong and Lawrence Summers (1984). We shall then briefly review separate efforts by each of us that preceded and prefigured the analysis that is our main subject. This revival of interest was anticipated by James Tobin (1975). He remarks that Keynes 'was well aware of the dynamic argument that *declining* money wage rates are unfavourable to aggregate demand. But perhaps he did not insist upon it strongly enough, for the subsequent theoretical argument focused on the statics of alternative stable wage levels.' One of the mechanisms recalled by Tobin will play a role in our own model: that deflation, by raising the real interest rate, may discourage both consumption and especially investment expenditure.

The reflex belief that wage and price flexibility must be good for an economy undoubtedly traces back to the desirable static properties of Walrasian equilibrium, Pareto-efficiency and all that. Even this goes too far, as we shall point out, when some standard assumptions, like non-increasing returns to scale and its customary twin perfect competition, are abandoned for what may well be more realistic alternatives. But an equally important point, as Tobin saw, is that the dynamic properties of a flexible-price system may be perverse. When an economy is disturbed from a good equilibrium by a real shock, say, it is not enough to remark sagely that a new good equilibrium can be supported by a new vector of prices. One must also ask if the economy will be driven promptly to such a new good equilibrium if wages and prices respond freely to excess supply and demand in the natural way,

or if they move instantaneously to clear markets given the immediate –
and perhaps now inappropriate – inheritance from the past.

DeLong and Summers begin by confirming the common casual
judgment that the US economy has exhibited less business-cycle
variability in the years after the Second World War than in the first
half of the century.[1] There is an element of paradox in this observation,
because there is also reason to believe that wages and prices have
become less flexible during the same period. Almost anyone would
agree that the economy of the 1960s and 1970s was 'less Walrasian'
than the economy of the first three decades of the twentieth century.
The extension of regulation and unionism are the causes most often
cited, but there is independent evidence that prices and wages have
become less flexible.

DeLong and Summers consider a number of 'structural' explanations of this correlation: the relative decline of agriculture (a
notoriously unstable industry), the avoidance of financial panics, the
fall in the multiplier induced by automatic stabilisers like the income
tax, the wider availability of consumer credit which reduces the
dependence of current consumption expenditure on current disposable income, etc. They find that these factors, while no doubt working
in the right direction, seem unable to account for a gain in stability as
large as that suggested by the time-series history. Their own preferred
account runs in terms of the real interest rate, and is quite compatible
with Tobin's brief remarks already cited and with our own work to be
described below.

The main point is that deflation following a contractionary shock
must increase the real rate of interest, or prevent it from falling as it
might otherwise do. In other language, deflation favours the holding of
money as compared with claims to real capital. The resultant drop in
interest-sensitive expenditures is a force for further contraction; and it
may outweigh any Pigou-effect expansionary consequences of a lower
general price level. The important distinction need only be pointed out
to be understood: lower prices may be favourable, but falling prices are
unfavourable. It is the essence of real-time dynamics that one cannot
have the first without the second.

DeLong and Summers illustrate this point by formulating a simple
IS-LM model that takes seriously the dependence of the demand for
money on the nominal interest rate and the dependence of investment

[1] This reading of history has been powerfully challenged by Christina Romer in a
1985 MIT PhD thesis. The DeLong-Summers thesis can stand on its own, however.

on the expected real rate. They append a price equation in which the price level is driven by long-term wage contracts, with the wage embodied in currently negotiated contracts dependent on current market conditions. Greater wage-price flexibility then corresponds to either (a) shorter contract length and/or (b) increased sensitivity of the currently negotiated wage to current market conditions. Simulation of this model with a white-noise disturbance to aggregate demand and a non-accommodative monetary policy leads to three interesting conclusons: (1) such a model is unstable for some parameter values that are not extreme; (2) when it is stable, shortening the contract length generally increases the variability of aggregate output; (3) when it is stable, increasing the flexibility of current wages seems usually but not always to increase the variability of aggregate output.

In his presidential address to the American Economic Association, Schultze approaches the problem of sticky wages and prices from a quite different point of view. Since it has much less to do with our own work, we report his argument only very briefly. Schultze follows Okun (1981) in arguing that long-term customer relationships and employment relationships are in fact an efficient solution to some of the problems of modern economic life. Market institutions, including those involved in setting wages and prices, evolve to preserve those relationships. These institutions will generally encourage sluggish adjustment of wages and prices, because there are important real costs when price changes cause long-term buyer-seller relations to be broken off in response to what turn out to be transitory shocks, soon to be reversed.

But now the individual market has no way of knowing whether an initial observed reduction in sales, say, signals the need for a real reallocation of resources or merely the occurrence of a reduction in aggregate nominal demand. If it is the first, then the 'correct' response is a slow and cautious adjustment of prices with much of the burden of adjustment transferred to inventories, delivery times, intensity of work, temporary layoffs, and other such mechanisms. If the source of the impulse is falling aggregate demand ' . . . an opposite response is wanted – large changes in wages and prices and small changes in quantities or slack.' There is a slight inexactness here: Schultze really means *instantaneous* changes in wages and prices. It would not be enough if prices moved, say, twice as fast in response to changes in aggregate demand as they do in response to real shocks, because then the real-time dynamics come into play and one must explicitly analyse the economy's path to wherever it is going. But Schultze's main point stands: 'excessive' wage and price flexibility, even if it improved the economy's adaptability to aggregate demand disturbances, might be destructive of the complex fabric of customer-supplier relations and the behaviour patterns that have evolved to preserve them. (One could, we suppose, deny Schultze's premise and hold to a completely atomistic view of the modern economy; but that case can hardly be taken as proved, nor can the burden of proof be fairly shifted to the Okun-Schultze view.)

Even within a more traditional neo-classical framework there are circumstances in which the naive equation of 'higher employment' with 'lower wages' can be misleading or worse. Two different routes to this conclusion are illustrated in earlier work of ours.

Hahn (1985) analyses a model economy exhibiting constant returns to scale and satisfying the dynamic non-substitution theorem. Consider two copies of such an economy; call them *A* and *B*. Equip them with the same constant stock of money and imagine them to be in steady-state equilibrium with constant prices. *A* and *B* have access to the same technology and the same underlying demand conditions. They are not quite identical, however. Suppose that economy *B* has more employment than *A* and that therefore the money wage and the price level for goods are lower in *B* than in *A*. Real cash balances will thus be higher in *B* than they are in *A*. If that is the case, the interest rate in *B* will have to be lower than that in *A* in order to generate the required asset-demand for real money. The lower interest rate must induce a substitution of capital for labour. The marginal product of capital will be lower in *B* and the marginal product of labour higher than in economy *A*. So *B* must have the higher real wage.

In this comparison, even the comparative-static connection between employment being too low and the real wage being too high seems to be less than self-evident. The dynamics are even less transparent. Think of *B* as a later stage of *A*, and imagine a possible transition from *A* to *B*. If money wages fall initially, the path must be very complicated, perhaps too complicated to come about. In the initial stages falling wages and prices will tend to drive up the real interest rate above its steady-state level in *A*. At the end, however, when the economy clicks into the *B* steady state, the real interest rate must be lower than it was in *A*. There is certainly a potential for overshooting, cycles, and perhaps worse.

The naive view is in even worse trouble when one gets away from the simple but unrealistic picture of constant returns to scale and perfect competition. As Weitzman – and before him Kaldor – have pointed out, this sort of environment is utterly unsuited to the discussion of unemployment. In such a world there would be no non-trivial firms, because the very notion of a firm involves some sort of set-up costs that give it its existence. No 'coordination' problem could ever arise. Any potentially unemployed workers could simply create their own firms of negligible size and join the market economy.

An economy characterised by U-shaped cost curves and imperfectly competitive firms of finite size can behave quite differently from the naive picture. Suppose the market form is such that full equilibrium requires zero profits. (Free entry is the usual story, of course.) Now compare two equilibrium economies, say *C* and *D*. Once again they are structurally identical; but once again *D* has more employment than *C*. Under perfectly reasonable specifications of the demand conditions, *D* will have more firms than *C*, and each firm in *D* will produce a larger output than its counterpart in *C*. (One can generate exceptions to this statement, but they are on the whole peculiar.) The combination of lower unit costs and zero profits implies that *D* will have the higher equilibrium real wage. This positive correlation of employment and real wages across equilibria is analysed in Solow's (1985) Mitsui Lectures.

In this set-up too the dynamics offer still further complications. There is first of all the obvious fact that a real-time transition from *C* to *D* is likely to be problematical. Think of *C* as exhibiting some unemployment. It is not easy to see how it can find its way to a higher-employment equilibrium with a higher real wage. Falling nominal wages is not an obviously useful prescription. Worse is still to come. The comparative-static proposition just stated is a comparison of long-run – i.e., zero-profit – equilibria. Any real-time transition will give rise to profits and losses. They are an indispensable part of the process, providing signals for entry and exit. In the short run, however, with profits not necessarily zero, the correlation between real wages and employment will generally run the other way, higher real wage rates accompanying lower employment. It is not clear that wage flexibility will work at all as a way of getting from *C* to *D*. Even if it does, one suspects there must be better ways.

4. *A specific model*

To make a start on the detailed study of transition paths, we revert to a simpler and more conventional model without the complications just discussed. Even so, as will be seen, the analysis is not without difficulties of its own. We provide an overview in this section and leave technical detail to an Appendix.

The model we use is one of overlapping generations in which agents live for three periods. There is a single producible good. The technology exhibits constant returns to scale with two inputs: the good itself and labour.

We have chosen the overlapping-generations model in preference to the main alternative (infinitely long-lived agents) for the following reason. At the level of aggregation and simplicity that can be handled in practice, the infinite-lifetime model leads one to look at the economy as if it were guided by a Ramsey optimiser. This in turn means, when there is no discounting, that the economy, starting from historically-given initial conditions, will follow a unique perfect-foresight path to the appropriate steady state. This is indeed what happens in many of the models now fashionable as rigorous foundations for macroeconomics. The infinite-life model thus forecloses the answer to the very question we want to ask. So drastic a closing of analytical doors requires more justification than it ever gets. It does not seem to us that anything in common observation or in serious theory requires that the Invisible Hand be given quite that much credit by assumptions that rule out of court so many questions that ought to concern the macroeconomist.

If not infinite lives, why not a finite-horizon economy? The answer is that we want to include fiat money as a valuable asset and that, combined with perfect foresight or rational expectations, is not possible in a finite economy. It is for this reason also that the agents in our model live for three periods instead of the conventional two. If there is an asset with a positive return, no one would willingly hold fiat money with a zero return. Our device is to resort to a version of a 'Clower constraint'. We suppose that agents who invest in productive capital when they are young can use it to produce saleable goods when they are middle-aged; but the profits of this production become available for spending only when they are old. If they want to consume at all when they are middle-aged – and they always do – they will need to transfer money from the first to the second period of their lives.

The demand for money is thus a transactions demand imposed by the need to bridge the gap between productive investment and access to profits. A model from first principles would presumably deduce this structure from transactions costs; but that is no part of our business here.

The simplest case arises when the production function has the form

$$y_t = \beta k_{t-1} + \gamma L_t.$$

Here y_t is output in period t, k_{t-1} is investment undertaken in period $t-1$ for use in period t, and L_t is employment in period t. We assume that goods can not be stored, and that goods used in production are used up in production. Then we must take it that $\beta > 1$, so that investment can have a positive net return in the steady state. The linear form of the production function is for convenience only.[2]

A household which is young in period t and consumes amounts of the good equal to c_t, c_{t+1}, c_{t+2} in the three periods of its life achieves the lifetime utility level

$$V(c_t, c_{t+1}, c_{t+2}) = \alpha^{-1}(c_t^\alpha + c_{t+1}^\alpha + c_{t+2}^\alpha)$$

where $\alpha < 1$. We shall generally assume that $\alpha < 0$ in order to guarantee without further ado that households will seek positive consumption in every period. Only young households are able to work. We shall assume initially that a young household can offer one unit of labour. Our aim is to discover how this economy adjusts to the news that the household supply of labour jumps to $h > 1$ from a certain date on; this is a neat way of asking how the economy reacts to potential unemployment. Leisure does not enter the utility function, so the household's whole capacity to work is supplied inelastically to the market. Households are not impatient; if they were, we would have one more parameter to carry along, but nothing much would change.

A young agent who invests in k_t units of productive capital at time t will be able to sell the output resulting from k_t and employment of L_{t+1} when he is middle-aged. The gross return on investment is given by

$$R_t = \beta P_{t+1}/P_t$$

where P_t is the nominal price of output in period t. If $R_t > 1$ investment is more profitable than holding money and the young will plan to hold only enough money to finance their planned consumption in middle

[2] A more complicated analysis with a Cobb-Douglas technology will appear in the larger work mentioned earlier.

age. When $R_t < 1$ no investment is undertaken. (This drastic statement is a consequence of the linearity of the production function. With Cobb-Douglas, for instance, investment would never fall below the positive level that makes $R = 1$ for positive price of output. Notice that $\beta > 1$ guarantees $R_t > 1$ when $P_{t+1} = P_t$.) It is worth noting explicitly that when $R_t < 1$, on our assumptions, the household simply spends its wage income in equal instalments over its lifetime. When $R_t = 1$, the household is indifferent between money and capital as assets.

There are now two matters of interpretation to be considered. First, we have not modelled firms as separate entities. That is not a matter of any significance in this kind of model. We could imagine that firms – of indeterminate size, given constant returns to scale – sell bonds to the young to finance their investment. The gross yield R is determined in the usual way by the maximising behaviour of firms and the willingness of the young to save for old age. The firms pay out gross profit when the bondholder is old.

Secondly, our model does not allow borrowing for consumption purposes. In principle there could be a market for loans between the middle-aged and the young. But the young would only plan to borrow when middle-aged (and repay when old) if that is cheaper than borrowing from themselves when young, by buying less capital. In steady-state equilibrium the exclusion of consumption loans is therefore innocuous. Outside the steady state we are not so sure, but we have not investigated the matter. We must simply exclude the additional possibility that the currently middle-aged might sell rights to next-period profits to the currently young. *Something* in the transactions technology must require the holding of money.[3]

There is a fixed stock of fiat money in this economy. At the end of any period it is held in part by the young (an amount equal to their planned nominal consumption expenditure in middle age) and in part by the middle-aged or their firms (their sales revenue in the period just ending less wage payments to the young). At the beginning of the next period, the money is held by the middle-aged (who have carried it over and will spend it) and by the old (who can and will now spend the profits of their middle-aged economic activity).

An equilibrium of this economy is a sequence of prices and wages known to agents when young which induces them to take and to plan actions which lead to the clearing of all markets at these prices. There

---

[3] This possibility is investigated in the longer work.

are three markets: for goods, for labour, and for money. As usual, Walras' Law allows us to focus on any two of the three, usually the first two.

It is easy to show that the economy just described has a unique stationary equilibrium in which prices are constant at P^* (and $W^* = \gamma P^*$) and the young invest a constant amount k^* in every period. We choose units so that one unit of labour is supplied and employed in this initial stationary equilibrium.

The story begins with the economy in stationary equilibrium. Now suppose that it becomes known at the beginning of period t that the labour supply will increase to $h > 1$ in period $t + 1$ and remain at h thereafter. We think of this as an exogenous decision of existing agents to supply more labour (so that we do not have to account for an increase in population when calculating consumption). It is no trick to see that there is a new steady state in which investment is hk^* and the nominal price of goods is $h^{-1}p^*$. The interesting questions are different. Will the economy get to the new steady state assuming that the price sequence is such as to clear all markets at all dates, and that this sequence of market-clearing prices is perfectly foreseen? And, whether it does so or not, what do production, investment and prices look like during the transition? Answers to those questions will tell us whether wage flexibility is a good thing, at least for this simple economy.

The necessary calculations lead to a non-linear third-order difference equation in the price level and stock of capital. Like any such equation, this one requires three initial conditions to be set in motion. But two of these are necessarily arbitrary. The initial stock of productive capital is predetermined by decisions made in period $t - 1$. But the difference equation will tell us P_{t+2} only if we feed it P_t and P_{t+1}. That is because current actions always depend on three prices: today's, tomorrow's and the next day's. When the projected increase in labour supply first becomes known there is nothing which ties down the first two prices. Given them, P_{t+2} can be calculated from the difference equation, i.e. from the necessity to clear the market for goods in period t. From then on, the dynamics take over, but it is fundamental that the whole sequence hangs from the bootstraps of P_t and P_{t+1}.[4]

---

[4] The fundamental mathematical structure is well known in the theory of overlapping-generations models (e.g. T.J. Kehoe and D.K. Levine, 1985). Our concrete example has the particular interest of introducing capitalistic production as well as money.

We do not yet know exactly what sorts of histories the model will trace out for different choices of the first two prices after the initial surprise. Even so simple a model has sufficiently complicated dynamics that we will apparently have to find out by a series of computer simulations. We intend to pursue that trail, but have not yet done so. We know, however, from local analysis of the linearised equation, that this sort of economy can have many different futures, some of which may be very unattractive prospects even if the initial shock is small. We have both specific and general reasons for thinking this, among them the following.

(a) For concreteness, think of t, $t+1$, and $t+2$ as 1, 2, 3. We can prove a definite comparative-static result: for given P_2, a lower P_1 implies lower P_3 *relative to* P_1 and lower k_1. That is to say, the more deflationary the initial impact of the surprise, the more deflationary it remains and the more investment is discouraged. The mechanism appears to be precisely the one that operates through the real rate of interest to increase the opportunity cost of investment. It does not add to one's confidence in rapid deflation as a sovereign remedy for unemployment.

(b) There is no steady state with $k=0$, because $\beta > 1$. But a path may encounter price sequences that force R below the critical value of 1. Then investment stops altogether. We have not yet calculated the continuation of the process; there may be a discontinuous regime-switch. It remains to be seen whether such 'depression' episodes are self-correcting. We know that under some conditions they can last only for a finite length of time.

(c) The linear approximations to our difference equations are badly behaved. With 'reasonable' parameter values, for instance, there can be three real characteristic roots: one larger than unity, one smaller than -1, and one between -1 and 0. Since the model allows 'bad' paths to go on forever, without hitting axes or other barriers, there is no legitimate case for supposing that 'the economy will choose' initial conditions that excite only the convergent characteristic root. We would not accept that as a legitimate way to do descriptive macroeconomics even if the steady state were a saddle-point. Here it is not even that.

(d) Recent work on the mathematics of first-order non-linear difference equations has shown that they can generate a quite remarkable diversity of paths, including cycles of different periods and 'chaos'. It seems unlikely that higher-order systems have any smaller repertoire of possible behaviours. The 'bootstrap' phenomenon may then belong at the centre of attention, not at the periphery.

Much of the detailed work remains to be done, so these remarks are tentative. But so far there is strong indication that Keynes was right, and for the right reason, when he argued that wage-flexibility, in the sense of continuous market-clearing, could propel the economy along quite undesirable paths. He may have been equally right in his belief that the worst of such paths could be avoided by well-chosen policies.

Our support for this last remark is the following conjecture.

(e) If *h* is small enough, then the dynamics of the model permits a transition to the new steady state quickly; even if *h* is large, such a quick transition can always be made possible by an appropriate choice of money stocks, to be achieved by giving to the young or taxing them.

Where Keynes may have been wrong is in thinking that 'possibility' was enough. In the model, monetary policy can make smooth transitions possible but cannot enforce them. It can always be frustrated by perverse expectations that lead the economy to a 'bad' bootstrap path. This suggests to us as a 'practical' matter the desirability of nipping deviations in the bud, before adverse expectations take hold and make matters more difficult. It may even be an advantage if nominal wages are sluggish, so sluggish as to create a valid expectation of their sluggishness.

We emphasise that this is work in progress. Even so it casts (further) doubt on the naive proposition that wage-flexibility automatically delivers a stable economy. Our results so far also suggest that it is the implications of flexibility for real investment that play the central role – as Keynes said they did.

Appendix

The model is one of overlapping generations in which each agent lives for three periods and, in the first instance, supplies one unit of labour inelastically when he is young. He can not work in middle or old age. There are no bequests, so labour is the only endowment.

Let c_{Tt} be the consumption at t of an agent born in $T < t$. Let M_{Tt} be the money balances demanded by an agent born in T in period t. Also k_t is the capital investment of an agent born in t. (There is only one subscript because only the young invest.) Lastly P_t is the money price of the single produced good and W_t is the money wage, both at t. The analysis proceeds by means of a 'representative' agent and firm; as noted in the text we take the two to be integrated into a single decision unit.

The young agent born in t forms his plan by maximising

$$\alpha^{-1} \sum_{i=t}^{t+2} c_{ti}^{\alpha}$$

subject to the constraints

(1) $$P_t c_{tt} + P_t k_t + M_{tt} \leqq W_t$$
(2) $$P_{t+1} c_{tt+1} + M_{tt+1} \leqq M_{tt}$$
(3) $$P_{t+2} c_{tt+2} \leqq P_{t+1} y_{t+1} - W_{t+1} + M_{tt+1}$$

where M_{tt}, M_{tt+1}, and k_t are non-negative. The structure of the constraints has been explained in the text. Investment of k_t at t gives rise to output at $t+1$ according to

$$y_{t+1} = \beta k_t + \gamma$$

where, as explained, it is assumed that $\beta > 1$, and one unit of labour is employed. However the proceeds, net of wage payments, cannot be spent until $t+2$.

It follows easily that $R_t = \beta P_{t+1}/P_t > 1$ implies $M_{tt+1} = 0$; and further that $R_t > 1$ implies

(4) $$k_t = \gamma / \phi \, (P_t, P_{t+1}, P_{t+2})$$

where

$$\phi \, (P_t, P_{t+1}, P_{t+2}) = 1 + \beta^{\alpha/a} (P_{t+1}/P_{t+2})^{\alpha/a} (1 + (P_{t+1}/P_t)^{\alpha/a})$$

and

$$a = \alpha - 1.$$

Thus, in a steady state when the price of goods is constant,

(5) $$k_t = k^* = \gamma / (1 + 2 \, \beta^{\alpha/a}).$$

We must now impose market-clearing at each date. We have already set $L_t = 1$, the given supply of labour. It remains only to clear the goods market. Observe that those who are middle-aged and old in t hold all the money in t. But the money received by the middle-aged during t can not be spent by them: it amounts to $P_t y_t - W_t$, hence

(6) $$P_t (c_{t-1t} + c_{t-2t}) = M_t - (P_t y_t - W_t)$$

where M_t is the total stock of cash in the economy.

Market-clearing at t, in nominal terms, requires

$$(7) \qquad P_t \left(\sum_{j=t-2}^{t} c_{jt} + k_t \right) = P_t y_t$$

Combining (6) and (7), one gets

$$(8) \qquad M_t/P_t = 2y_t - (c_{tt} + k_t) - W_t/P_t.$$

After a lot of arithmetic, (8) can be written in the form

$$(9) \qquad [M_t/P_t - 2\beta k_{t-1}](P_t/P_{t+1})^{\alpha/a} = \beta^{\alpha/a} k_t (P_{t+1}/P_{t+2})^{\alpha/a}.$$

It is a straightforward implication of (9) that the only possible steady state (for $R > 1$) with a constant nominal money stock is that with $P_t = $ constant and $k_t = k^*$ satisfying (5). Then (9) and (5) can be used to calculate the unique steady-state value of the real money supply $M/P^* = m^* = (2\beta + \beta^{\alpha/a}) k^*$. But then P^* is obviously proportional to M.

Now (4) and (9), complicated as they are, form a pair of difference equations in k and P, second-order in P and first-order in k, thus third-order in all. To solve them, or even to iterate them numerically, one needs three initial conditions. The initial capital stock is given, inherited from past investment. One can choose trial values for P_t and P_{t+1} and, if all goes well, solve (4) and (9) for P_{t+2} and the next value of k. (It is, fortunately a bit easier than it looks, because of the special ways the price-ratios enter.) It is this system that we plan to simulate for a choice of initial values, subject to the conditions that $\beta P_{t+1}/P_t > 1$ for all eligible t.

For the present it is enough to say that linearisation of (4) and (9) around their steady state leads to a system whose characteristic equation is

$$\lambda^3 - [\delta + 2(1 + 2\beta)]\lambda^2 + [b\beta + \delta + 1 - a\alpha^{-1}\delta^{-1}(1 + 2\delta)(2\beta + \delta)]\lambda - 2\beta$$
$$= 0,$$

where $\delta = \beta^{\alpha/a}$. From the fact that the product of the roots is $2\beta > 2$, we know that this can not describe a stable system under small perturbations. In fact, if $\beta = \delta = 1$, and $\alpha = -\frac{1}{2}$ the equation is

$$\lambda^3 - 7\lambda^2 - 19\lambda - 2 = 0$$

with roots approximately equal to 9.11, -2.00, and -0.11, i.e. one stable (with saw-tooth oscillations) and two unstable (one monotone and one saw-tooth). Obviously the qualitative picture would be unchanged if β and δ were slightly larger than unity. The set of rational expectations or perfect-foresight paths is very badly behaved. For reasons given in the text, there is no good reason to emphasise the stable root.

Now suppose the economy has been in steady until t when it becomes known that each agent's supply of labour will be $h = 1 + \varepsilon$, $(\varepsilon > 0)$, from $t + 1$ onwards. The new steady state value of k is $k^{**} = \gamma h / (1 + 2\delta)$. Consider the following policy:

(a) Give to the generation born at t an amount of money Δm^t where

$$\Delta m^t = \varepsilon (R^* - 1)k^* + \varepsilon w^*$$

(b) Take the generation born at $t - 1$ an amount $\Delta m^t - 1 < 0$ where

$$-\Delta m^{t-1} = \varepsilon c_{\tilde{u}}^*$$

(c) Announce a subsidy to the generation born at a $t - 1$ to be paid at $t - 1$, of

$$\Delta m^{t-1}(t + 1) \text{ where}$$

$$\Delta m^{t-1}(t + 1) = \varepsilon k^* (R^* + 1)$$

Then at $t + 1$ the new money stock m^{**} is given by

(10)
$$m^{**} = m^* + \Delta m^t + \Delta m^{t-1} \Delta m^{t-1}(t + 1)$$

$$= m^* + \varepsilon (y^* - k^* - c_{\tilde{u}}^*) + \varepsilon R^* k^* = m^* + \varepsilon m^* = h m^*$$

To understand (10) recall that $y^* - k^* - c_{\tilde{u}}^*$ is the demand for money by the young and $R^* k^*$ is the demand for money by the firms.

Now notice that the policy has been so arranged as to make the demand for goods at date t equal to its supply (which depends on k^* and the supply of labour before the postulated increase at constant prices). The assumed utility function implies that the demand for consumption and investment of the young will, at constant prices, increase in the same proportion as their wealth is increased by (a). The taxation (b) of the middle-aged ensures that room is made for this increase by an equivalent reduction in the consumption of the middle-aged. Part (c) ensures that in the next period demand is high enough to absorb the now higher output.

Provided ε is not too large there thus exists a policy which can get the economy to the new steady state in one step *provided all agents (rationally) believe that the steady state prices will persist.* Such a belief could be fostered by past experience or even by price controls. The policy is to be compared with letting the market increase real balance by lower money wages. That, as our analysis has shown, may lead to the economy following a possibly tortuous path which may or may not lead it to the steady state.

The policy we suggest is somewhat complicated while the model is highly simplified. But we are here concerned with the qualitative lesson which we believe will survive more elaborate modelling and policies which allow for longer transition periods.

References

Delong, J.B. and Summers, L., 'The changing cyclical variability of economic activity in the United States', *National Bureau of Economic Research Working Paper* 1450 September 1984.

Hahn, F.H., 'Wages and employment', in Collard, D.A., Helm, D.R., Scott, M.F.G. and Sen, A.K. (eds.), *Economic Theory and Hicksian Themes* (Oxford: Clarendon Press, 1984).

Kehoe, T.J. and Levine, D.K., 'Indeterminacy of relative prices in overlapping generations models', *MIT Working Paper* 313 (1982).

Okun, A.M., *Prices and Quantities* (Washington D.C.: Brookings, 1981).

Schultze, C.E., 'Microeconomic efficiency and nominal wage stickiness', *American Economic Review*, 75 (March 1985), 1–15.

Solow, R.M., *Consequences of Unemployment Equilibrium* forthcoming (tentative title) (Oxford: Blackwell, 1986).

Tobin, J., 'Keynesian models of recession and depression', *American Economic Review*, 65 (May 1975), 195–202.

2. How Rigid are Wages Anyway?

Wilfred Beckerman & Tim Jenkinson

1. *Introduction*

The central issue in macroeconomic policy today, as in the 1930s, is the massive unemployment in most of the Western world. This has not quite reached the proportions of the 1930s in most countries, but in some it has not fallen far short of those levels. And, anyway, it had been believed until relatively recently that the large-scale unemployment of the pre-war years was a thing of the past and that economic policy had progressed to the point where such scourges had been brought under control, like many hitherto widespread and dangerous diseases. As in the 1930s, there is a widespread belief that this unemployment is largely the consequence of wage rigidity preventing wages from moving enough to restore equilibrium in the labour market. This has aroused renewed intense interest in the whole problem of wage flexibility. Robert Gordon (1982) begins a recent article on the subject with the proposition that 'if a poll were to be conducted among American academic economists to select "The Most Mystifying Phenomenon of Our Time", surely the sticky nominal wage rate would emerge at or near the top of the list'.

Of course, the widespread view that inflexible wages are responsible for much of the unemployment is the subject of intense controversy, as it was back in the 1930s. The fact that the same basic issues reappear in economics without, apparently, much progress having been made in reaching definitive solutions illustrates the enormous obstacles encountered in attempting to provide a sound empirically-based understanding of exactly how the economic universe operates.

At the theoretical level the situation is somewhat better, though some people would question whether this is such a big deal if it is not helping us add to our positive knowledge of the workings of the economic system. There has been much progress in clarifying various aspects of the concept of equilibrium and the development of 'disequilibrium' economics. More particularly there has been con-siderable interest during the last decade not only in the consequences of wage rigidity but also in attempting to formulate hypotheses to explain wage rigidity using models of the optimising behaviour of workers, firms or trade unions.

One of the obstacles to progress on the empirical front is probably the difficulty of measuring wage (or price) flexibility in the manner that we believe is appropriate for purposes of testing rival hypotheses concerning either the causes or the consequences of wage rigidity. From a methodological point of view the selection between rival hypotheses would presumably require comparisons to be made between situations that differ with respect to the degree of wage flexibility in order to see how far these differences can be correlated with alternative variables. It would seem, therefore, that an obvious starting point in the empirical testing of alternative hypotheses would be some reliable method for comparing degrees of wage flexibility between different situations – as between countries, or over time, or between industries, and so on.

But, alas, not enough progress has been made in this connection. In this paper we begin by discussing what we consider to be among the most important representative examples of such estimates of wage flexibility that are available. We argue that some of these estimates are conceptually inappropriate for the purposes in hand and that others, while along the right lines, do not go far enough. We go on to set out what we believe is a preferable concept of wage flexibility for the purposes of the questions that are being asked, and to provide some tentative empirical results.

But some fairly elementary ambiguities in the concept of wage flexibility need to be mentioned at the outset. First, which wages are we interested in – real wages or nominal (i.e. money) wages? As Stiglitz (1984) rightly points out, traditional Keynesian economics has tended to fudge the issue. Presumably, much depends on whether one is concerned with equilibrium in the labour market or equilibrium in the money market. For example, if attention is focussed on the latter, it is money-wage flexibility that matters, since this is more likely to lead to price flexibility and hence to the adjustment of real-money balances required to restore macroeconomic equilibrium via some form of real balance effect.

On the other hand, if one is concentrating on labour-market equilibrium and attaches little importance to the role of money-market adjustments, it will be the real wage that matters, since it is this that enters into the demand and supply functions for labour. Of course, to get behind the reasons for such real-wage flexibility, or lack of it, that may be found, it may be necessary to analyse the amount of flexibility that is found in nominal wages (as, for example, in Gordon (1982) and Sachs (1983)). Since in this paper we concentrate on the labour market and are not directly concerned with how wage contracts are negotiated, we shall focus primarily on real wages. But this still leaves other ambiguities that need to be cleared up.

In particular there are two main alternative concepts of the real wage, namely the real wage received by the employee, which is sometimes referred to as 'real wage income', and the real product wage. The former is defined as the employee's nominal wage deflated by the cost of living (or whatever is regarded as 'wage goods') and the latter is defined as the nominal wage deflated by the price of the value added in the productive activity in question. In the simplest model of a profit-maximising firm under conditions of perfect competition, it is obvious that even without any change in real-wage income the profitability of employing a given amount of labour will vary if there is a change in the price of the firm's output or of its non-labour inputs. One can go further and allow for taxes paid by employees in order to get closer to the real wage that enters into their labour supply curves, or allow for the taxes on labour borne by firms in order to approximate more closely to the real wage cost to the firm.

The next step follows from the fact that we are concerned with analysing wage flexibility in the context of its relationship to labour-market disequilibrium. In this connection we must emphasise that we are adopting the narrow Marshallian and Walrasian concept of 'equilibrium', according to which equilibrium prevails when demand and supply are equal (as also in Keynes' (1936) *General Theory*, page 64) rather than some non-Walrasian equilibrium in which, even though demand and supply may not be equal, there is no tendency for the variables in the model to change (as in Keynes' *General Theory*, page 249).[1] Hence, what is needed, presumably, is some measure of the degree to which changes in the 'warranted' real wage, where this is the real wage that would equate supply and demand in the labour market, are related to differences between the demand and supply of labour.

Clearly, if real wages fluctuate considerably, but still do so less than would be required to match changes in the other variables influencing labour demand (such as productivity or the prices of other inputs) or

---

[1] See also the recent discussion of this distinction in Benassy (1984).

labour supply (such as employees' leisure/income trade-off), disequilibria in the labour market are still likely to emerge in spite of the wage variability. Conversely, the absence of much movement in real wages may not matter at all for labour-market equilibrium if there has been no movement in these other variables and hence no changes in the 'warranted' real wage (assuming that we were starting from a position of equilibrium).

This leads to the central point of this paper, which is the best way to define wage flexibility for the purposes in hand, namely its contribution to reducing labour-market disequilibria. For, given the choice of a real wage concept, there are still various statistical measures that could be used for purposes of measuring its flexibility. In this paper, before setting out our own definition of, and possible techniques for estimating, wage flexibility, we discuss first one crude method that has been used – which is basically an analysis of the variability of wages – and then two other approaches which we believe are in the right direction but which are still subject to important limitations.

2. *Wage variability*

Robert Gordon must be given credit for pioneering much of the work on the measurement of wage flexibility and for insisting on the importance of analysing inter-country and inter-temporal variations in wage and price flexibility in order to understand better the causes and consequences of different degrees of flexibility. Some of his earlier estimates, particularly those contained in a paper presented to the Royal Economic Society meeting in London in 1981, are used here to illustrate one common method used in this area. In this particular study, Gordon (op. cit.) used two 'measures of volatility' of each of the variables he was studying (wages, hours and employment), namely the standard deviation of the rates of change, and the coefficients of response of each variable to changes in nominal GNP. A more recent contribution by Metcalf (1984) used only the former measure, so we shall not discuss this contribution separately; our comments on Gordon's use of this measure will apply equally to Metcalf's.

Although the theme of Gordon's work in this area is wage and price 'flexibility', the standard deviation measure would appear to be more a measure of *variability*. A similar tendency to equate the two concepts is apparent in Metcalf (op. cit.) which contains a table (Table 7) showing the standard deviations of annual per cent changes, 1960–82, in both real and nominal wages, and from which he concludes that 'it is interesting to note in passing that Britain and Japan have the longest job tenures and the most flexibility of wages' (page 65).

But variability and flexibility are two totally different concepts. For example, a steel spring may exhibit no movement whatsoever, but this is nothing to do with the degree of flexibility that it would display when subjected to different amounts of force. The concept of flexibility is concerned with the degree of response of some variable to a given force exerted on it. In our view it is not any old force or shock that matters. What matters is how far and how fast wages adjust to the disequilibrium in the labour market.

From this standpoint the simple standard deviation analysis of Gordon and others is clearly unsatisfactory. It may well be true, as Gordon's estimates show (row 8 of Table 1 and the addendum table following it) that ' . . . the volatility of both real and nominal wage rates is greater in Britain and Japan as compared to the United States' (op. cit., page 19), but it is far from obvious that this has any bearing on wage *flexibility* as an aid to equilibrating labour markets. As for the particular choice of the standard deviation which Gordon and Metcalf have used to measure variability, this seems to be no more appropriate – and probably less appropriate – than many others. The standard deviation is a concept derived from probability theory and that can be shown to have a precise mathematical relationship to the probability of a sample mean approximating closely to a population mean. But in the present context this is irrelevent. Nobody is asking how far the mean of wage changes in any particular period in any particular country can be taken as a good approximation to what the mean of wage changes would be in some broader sample.

Of course, it might be argued that insofar as one does want to measure variability – leaving aside the relevance of this concept – the standard deviation is as good a measure of central tendency as any other. Whether or not this is true, it would not imply that it must give the same results as any other. As the following estimates show, it does not. In Table 1 below alternative statistical concepts are used. Some of them are used largely because Gordon's estimates (like Metcalf's) take no account of trend changes in wages. Hence it is quite possible that his estimates of flexibility (which are the standard deviations of four-quarter overlapping rates of change of wages) will be higher in countries such as Britain and Japan, which were experiencing much higher rates of inflation, than in the USA. One way of overcoming this

Table 1: Alternative statistical measures of the variability of real wages in manufacturing, 1974.I to 1981.IV; for the USA, UK and Japan
(estimates relate to logs of basic series)

	USA	UK	Japan
(i) *4 quarter changes*			
[a] Standard deviation	0·020	0·026	0·034
[b] Coefficient of variation	5·092	1·677	1·873
(ii) Variance of series (× 100)	0·056	0·208	0·090
(iii) 'goodness of fit' to trend (R^2)	0·101	0·048	0·117

would be to use the coefficient of variation of the series (i.e. the standard deviation divided by the mean). Another would be simply to test the goodness of fit of the data to fitted trends. A further concept used below is the variance of the series, particularly since the variance is at least decomposable into the variance and covariance of the constituent series. That is, the variance of real wages, with which we are primarily interested here, can be analysed exhaustively in terms of the variances of nominal wages and prices and the covariance of wages and prices.

It can be seen from the table that different statistical measures give different results. The Gordon method (4 quarter overlapping changes) does, of course, give the result he finds, namely that the variability in the USA is less than in the other two countries. But using the coefficient of variation measure, the USA exhibits more variability in real wages than the UK and Japan. To confuse matters even more, when we use the goodness of fit measure the USA ranks in between the other countries, and the variance of the series measure indicates that the UK has the most flexible wages, and the USA the least flexible wages! Hence, as far as real wages are concerned, in the absence of any clear theoretical reason for selecting one measure of variability rather than another, one is free to draw whatever conclusion one likes from the estimates. The same result – i.e. differences in the degree of variability according to which particular measure of central tendency is used – was also obtained for nominal wages, but they are not shown here since the limitations of these measures of 'flexibility' have, we hope, been sufficiently demonstrated. Thus, taken all round, it appears that even if estimates of wage flexibility could legitimately be based on measures of variability, existing estimates of this kind provide no support for the hypothesis that is often encountered to the effect that the lower level of unemployment in the USA (in 1984) reflects the greater degree of wage flexibility in that country.[2]

3. *The wage-gap approach*

A contribution to the measurement of wage developments that is much more in line with our central point, namely the need to relate flexibility to equilibrium, is the approach embodied in certain attempts to compare actual changes in real wages with 'warranted' changes. 'Warranted' is usually taken to mean the change in the real wage that is matched by the change in productivity and that, therefore, would leave wage costs per unit output constant. The concept of the real wage implicit in this definition of the warranted real wage is the real product wage (which, as indicated earlier, is not the same as the real wage that employees receive, which is sometimes defined as the 'real wage income'). For a given sector, the real product wage may change as a result of a change in the relationship between the prices of the goods it sells and the prices of the inputs into that sector from outside it, as well as changes in the relative increases in consumer prices as compared with the general price index of national product as a whole. The warranted change in the real wage income is thus equal to the change in productivity adjusted for the changes in the terms of trade of the sector in question. This approach thus recognises that what matters is not just how much wages change, but how much they change in line with such changes as are needed in order to preserve, or restore, equilibrium in the labour market.

Of course, there are great difficulties involved in estimating changes in the warranted real wage, but some studies, notably those by Jeffrey Sachs (1983) and Jaques Artus (1984), have made great progress in this direction. As in other similar studies, both authors assume that the labour market was in equilibrium at some date, or dates, in the past,

[2] It should be pointed out that in Professor Gordon's later work in this area, notably in Tobin (1983), he concentrated on estimates of the coefficients of nominal and real wages in equations that include nominal and real GNP (and changes in their levels) as explanatory variables. However, quite apart from the statistical problems encountered in explaining price changes in terms of explanatory variables that include nominal GNP (as Barry Bosworth pointed out on page 123), the relationship between levels and changes in GNP, on the one hand, and the gap between the demand and supply of labour, on the other hand, is far too indirect and unspecified for the coefficients of wages on GNP in these equations to be regarded as acceptable approximations to the concept of wage flexibility that we are advocating here.

and then try to estimate how far the subsequent change in the real wage differs from the change that was warranted in each of the countries that they study.

This procedure raises various problems that the authors are well aware of and that they attempt, by various methods, to solve. In particular the choice of the base period in which the market was assumed to be in equilibrium is somewhat arbitrary. For example, during the 1950s and 1960s there was full employment in Britain but the wage share was rising. If full employment is taken as a criterion for equilibrium and at the same time a change in the wage share is taken as a criterion of disequilibrium, it is impossible to find a reference period that satisfies both criteria. Other difficulties include the problem of allowing adequately for the feed-back on productivity growth of reductions in activity either caused by deflationary policies or other factors reducing output, or the problem of estimating the degree to which a change in the wage may be warranted on account of changes in the technical conditions of production, and so on.

But even if these difficulties are satisfactorily overcome, these studies only go some of the way to providing an input into the estimation of wage flexibility. This is basically because they are asking a different question, namely how far has the rise in unemployment in different countries been the result of different degrees of deviations of the real wage from the warranted real wage (as defined by them)? What they measure, therefore, are the deviations of actual wages from warranted real wages over varying time periods – usually of a few years – in different countries, and these deviations are then compared with different levels of unemployment in the countries concerned over these time periods. In this approach unemployment is the dependent variable, and the real wage deviation is the force that acts upon it. In our approach the relationship is the other way round. Also, since they are not concerned with flexibility *per se*, the concept of the time period within which the variables are changing does not play a crucial role, whereas from our standpoint of concentrating on wage flexibility the dynamics of the adjustment process of the wage in response to labour market disequilibria are of central importance. Hence, while both studies make most valuable contributions to the methodology of measuring the wage disequilibrium, they are not designed to provide inputs into measures of wage flexibility that can be used in correlations with any other economic variables believed to be either the causes or the consequences of the flexibility.

4. Wage flexibility and wage equations

As indicated at the outset, the concept of wage flexibility has to be seen as a response to the forces acting on wages. The 'response' side of the story is not difficult. It is just the speed of wage change measured as the amount of change per unit of time, though, as will be indicated later, the dynamics of the adjustment process are probably complex, and in fully articulated models the response is likely to be measured in terms of mean or median lags.

The force side of the story is more difficult. The force acting on wages is conventionally measured by unemployment, on the grounds that this was a measure of the disequilibrium acting on wages – as in the original Lipsey (1960) interpretation of the Phillips Curve. It corresponds to orthodox concepts of excess demands and supplies influencing prices, as in a Walrasian setting. As succinctly set out by Oskar Lange (1945) forty years ago, the basic assumption of stability analysis is:

$$\text{sign } dp_r = \text{sign } X_r$$

where X_r is excess demand in the rth market and p_r is the price of the rth good. Lange adds that if we let $dp_r/dt = F_r(X_r)$ ' . . . when the functions on the right hand side (of these equations) are taken as linear in X_r, the basic assumption of stability analysis necessarily implies that the speed of increase of price is greater the greater the excess demand. F_r' ( ) may serve as a measure of the flexibility of the price p_r.'

Now this is all perfectly consistent, as far as it goes, with the approach that we have been advocating. Clearly the greater the first derivatives of F_r, the greater the adjustment of price per unit of time for a given X_r. Another way of looking at this is simply to recognise that although, as Hahn (1984) has pointed out, in some contexts it might be better to abandon the notion of wage flexibility and to discuss instead how far wages are endogenous, it is also useful in many contexts simply to refine and clarify the concept of flexibility that one is using. Two possibilities seem to be available. First, one can define flexibility in terms of the time lag required for wages to change by the amount needed to restore equilibrium (if at all). Secondly, one can define flexibility in terms of the amount of equilibrating change in wages that takes place in any given time period – such as a year. This is essentially the concept of wage flexibility underlying the wage equation approach. Here, although we adopt a similar concept we apply it in a way that differs significantly from the conventional wage equation approach.[3]

The major methodological problems surround the estimation of the extent of any excess demand in the markets in question. However, to determine X_r it is necessary to have some estimate of, in the case of the labour market, the 'equilibrium' employment level, and its evolution over time. This is a problem that will inevitably recur at the empirical level. In the wage-gap approach equilibrium was *assumed* to exist over certain time periods based on casual observation and, in the analysis of Artus (op. cit.), an argument in terms of the Beveridge Curve, i.e. the relationship between vacancies and unemployment.

In the simple wage equation approach, the variable that measures excess demand is unemployment. Increases in unemployment over time are, in simple models, interpreted as increases in (negative) excess demand, with no account being taken of changes in the 'equilibrium' level of employment.[4] Any increase in registered unemployment is taken as an increase in involuntary unemployment. In addition, many recent theories of wage determination, produced in the wake of Trade Union models, assume that the firm retains the 'right to manage', which implies that, given the wage, the firm will always fix employment so as to be on its labour-demand curve. The firm is thus always optimising in its use of labour, given the wage, and so no demand-side pressures are exerted on the wage.

Using such a procedure, however, may result in a rather strange definition of flexibility. Numerous factors affect both the demand for labour and the quantity of labour supplied at the market wage, and these in turn will influence the 'equilibrium' wage and employment level. For example, consider a fourfold increase in the price of oil. The impact of this shock on the equilibrium employment level will be rather complicated. There will be a substitution effect away from the use of oil towards other factors of production, including to some extent labour, but there will also be a decrease in the value added of labour. Which of these effects dominates will determine the change in the

[3] For example, in Grubb, Jackman, Layard (1983), the coefficient of unemployment in the wage equation is the basis of their estimate of wage flexibility. Clearly, given the responsiveness of wages to unemployment, one can also estimate – as they do – how much extra unemployment is needed to achieve any given reduction in the rate of wage increase in order to offset any adverse supply shock, which is the essence of their definition of wage flexibility.

[4] Although lip-service is occasionally paid to this criticism by the inclusion of some trend terms.

market wage necessary to keep the labour market in equilibrium. Suppose the latter dominates, and the demand for labour falls at the existing wage rate, then if the wage were flexible it would fall in response and there would be no increase in unemployment. On the other hand, if the wage did not fall in response to the rise of fuel prices, unemployment would result, and, using the wage equation approach, only then would we consider the effects of the shock, in terms of the impact of the increased unemployment on wages. In a rather important way the initial shock, and reaction to that shock, will be ignored, and only the subsequent reaction of the wage to unemployment considered. But in reality what we mean by a flexible wage is not only how quickly the wage reacts to unemployment, but more generally to any disequilibrium pressure caused by changes in either labour demand or supply.

The use of wage equations to measure wage flexibility thus relies upon the simple relationship between wages and unemployment. Herein lies a major problem with this approach. Much evidence has recently been forthcoming to suggest that any time series relationship that exists between unemployment and wages is at best very tenuous in many countries. Ashenfelter and Card (1983), using US data, conclude that there is no evidence to support the claim that unemployment 'Granger causes' either nominal or real wages. Beckerman and Jenkinson (1986), using pooled data on twelve OECD countries, are unable to find any simple unemployment effect on wage dynamics, and Jenkinson (1986), using time series data for seven EEC countries, finds insignificant unemployment effects on wages in six of them. In addition, Geary and Kennan (1982) have presented evidence that unemployment and wages are statistically independent in twelve selected OECD countries.

The wage equation approach does not, therefore, appear to be suited to studying wage flexibility, and indeed wage equations are usually estimated as part of a system to explain the behaviour of major macroeconomic targets such as inflation and unemployment. Registered unemployment is a very imprecise measure of the many complex pressures acting on wages, and therefore it is hardly surprising that major empirical problems are encountered during attempts to measure flexibility using wage equations. In the following section we present an attempt to model the disequilibrium pressures acting in the labour market more explicitly, and provide some illustrative empirical results.

5. *Towards a new method of estimating wage flexibility*

If the definition of wage flexibility that appears of most relevance is the speed with which the wage moves in response to disequilibrium in the labour market, we are faced with the problem of estimating empirically the extent of any disequilibrium on either or both sides of the labour market. The determinants of equilibrium employment are many, of which the wage is but one. In theory, any variable that could enter into the labour demand or labour supply functions will be a determinant, to some degree, of the equilibrium level of employment. Energy and raw materials prices, the rate of interest, and the level of demand in the goods market are all likely, therefore, to affect the 'equilibrium' wage and level of employment. How quickly the wage reacts to changes in its equilibrium value in such a complex dynamic environment when the only observable manifestation of disequilibrium may be rationing of labour is the crucial issue.

Within the context of equilibrium models such questions never arise, and indeed the notion of what constitutes a flexible wage is rather difficult to define. If the wage, by assumption, attains its equilibrium value at all instants, then the whole question of whether the wage efficiently performs its allocational role in the labour market is ignored. The dynamic adjustment processes which may push a market towards equilibrium are not explicitly considered, although in the context of wage flexibility these are likely to be of primary interest. A popular approach to modelling the labour market which acknowledges the restrictions imposed by the equilibrium approach has been to assume that if a market does not clear then the 'short' side of the market will prevail. That is:

$$N_t = min \ (L_t^d, \ L_t^s)$$

where L_t^d and L_t^s are labour demand and supply respectively. While a definite improvement on the simple equilibrium approach, there are a number of problems with such models. The usual assumption that is made in order to interpret this rationing scheme is that the wage is fixed, and ex-post rationing occurs. In reality, however, neither the wage nor the level of employment are fixed independently of the other, although some popular trade-union models assume that the union only bargains over the wage and not the level of unemployment. Indeed, if we are to examine the empirical measurement of wage flexibility, such simplifying assumptions cannot be made. In such a situation there can be no presumption that the economy is necessarily on either L^d or L^s in any period. The relevant question to answer is how quickly does the wage react to the gap between the plans and realisations of both the workers and the employers.

As Malinvaud (1977) remarked about the macroeconomic 'disequilibrium' models, 'In most cases the analysis is not dynamic in the sense that it would consider a process of adjustment; it is in fact plain equilibrium analysis, but operating with a specific concept of equilibrium.' This is equally true of the labour-market literature. Consequently a disequilibrium model is proposed which focuses on the forces behind the dynamic data-generating process, rather than the static equilibrium states. This approach is very much in the spirit of Frisch's (1949) suggestion of attempting to model pressures.

For example, if there is excess supply of labour, in the form of involuntary unemployment, the important question is how quickly the observed wage rate reacts to the gap between the 'bid' and 'offer' wage. Intentions and realisations clearly do not coincide out of equilibrium, and the speed with which plans are revised is the important notion. A fundamental distinction is that there is no presumption that the 'market' has operated so as to establish an equilibrium in each period. The plans of individuals are clearly based upon their conjectures, and it is possible that even when agents' plans prove to be inconsistent, each individual may conjecture that it is not in their interest to change the 'bid' or 'offer' price or quantity quickly, if at all. The speed with which the labour market moves towards reconciliation of intentions is the concept of 'flexibility' proposed. Flexibility of wages is only important to the extent that it moves the labour market towards an equilibrium. This is in stark contrast to the equilibrium approach which assumes pre-reconciliation of all actions at all instants.

Equilibrium is an unobservable, or latent, variable. In many cases the observed values for a variable, such as employment, cannot reasonably be taken to be identical to equilibrium values. But without some estimate of the equilibrium relationships between the variables determining employment it is not possible to estimate the extent of any disequilibrium pressures. Two possible approaches to this problem are, first, to construct equilibria from theory and/or casual observation (as, for example, in Sachs (1983)), or, secondly, to examine whether the data reveal any such equilibrium relationship. We pursue the latter route, attempting to identify 'equilibrium' labour-demand and labour-supply relationships from the quarterly time series data for the UK. Once such relationships are estimated any gap between the observed levels of employment and their equilibrium values will be our measure of the extent of the disequilibrium pressures in the labour market.

The basic model from which our estimates are derived consists of the following three equations:

(1) $$L_t^d = a_0 + a_1 w_{ft} + A' X_t + u_{1t} \ldots$$

where X_t is the vector of variables, other than the real product wage w_f (in terms of producer prices and allowing for any taxes on labour borne by the firm), that influence labour demand.

(2) $$L_t^s = b_0 + b_1 w_{ct} + B' Z_t + u_{2t} \ldots$$

where Z_t is the vector of variables, other than the real wage w_c, expressed in terms of consumer prices, that influence labour supply.

(3) $$w_t = f\{w_{t-1}, (L_d^t - N_t), (L_s^t - N_t)\} \ldots$$

where N_t is the actual number of people employed in period t. Equation (3) simply says that the current wage will be a function of the wage in the previous period and the extent of any excess demand or supply in the labour market. A specific form for estimation which only allows disequilibrium pressures in the previous quarter, rather than a more complex dynamic correction process, to influence the current wage is given in equation (4) below.

(4) $$w_t = c_0 + c_1 w_{t-1} + c_2 (L^d - N)_{t-1} + c_3 (N - L^s)_{t-1} + u_{3t} \ldots$$

Equations (1) to (3) define a simple disequilibrium model of the labour market. (1) and (2) describe what factors influence the demand for, and supply of, labour. Both these correspondences are unobservable in reality. Only when markets clear in all periods will L_t^d and L_t^s become observable in the simple sense that

$$L_t^d = L_t^s = N_t$$

Since we do not maintain any assumptions regarding market clearing, L_d^t and L_s^t need to be estimated, and we adopt a purely time series approach to this problem, based on the cointegrated variables techniques introduced by Granger (for details see Granger (1983)).

The basic idea is that most economic time series are non-stationary and hence require differencing to induce stationarity.[5] But if over a long period of time two time series are linked by some stable relationship, this is a reasonable notion of an equilibrium relationship existing. In practical terms, this means that if some linear combination of a vector of time series is stationary, even though the individual series do not satisfy stationarity, then the long run evolutionary behaviour of those series are linked over time. Equilibrium is thus treated as a statistical property of the time series, whose putative existence can, and should, be tested. This is in sharp contrast to models where 'equilibria' are derived from theory or assertion.

The second stage is to take the differences between the observed levels of employment and the estimated 'equilibrium' values of labour demand and supply. These residuals are then of prime interest[6] since they represent our estimates of the disequilibrium pressures. It is clear that much depends in our analysis on the ability to estimate the long-run labour demand and supply relationships accurately. In this respect work is very much in its infancy, but a disequilibrium approach to such questions will always require an estimate at some stage of the extent of the disequilibrium, and once we drop the exceedingly restrictive assumption that the observed data series actually corresponds to the equilibrium values of a variable we are faced with the problem of *estimating* and *testing* an equilibrium relationship. The arguments advanced in this paper suggest that even though such questions do not have easy answers, until we attempt to answer them we will not obtain meaningful results.

The labour demand relationship that we estimate is of the form:

$$L_t^d = f\,(w_f,\, m,\, K,\, POP,\, Q,\, \mathcal{Z},\, c)$$

where m represents the real price of raw materials and fuels (in terms of producer prices, K is the capital stock, POP is the working population, Q is real GNP, $\mathcal{Z}$ is a productivity index, for the manufacturing sector, c is a constant term. This is a fairly general labour demand specification which includes most of the explanatory variables suggested by, among others, Nickell and Andrews (1983), Beenstock et al (1983), and Minford (1983). The next stage is to determine the evolutionary behaviour of these variables individually. In other words, assuming that the time series have an Autoregressive Integrated Moving

---

[5] A variable x_t is stationary if (i) $E(x_t) = $ constant, for all t, and (ii) var (x_t) is finite for all t.

[6] In practical terms they include all the complex dynamics of the wage-setting process.

Average (ARIMA) representation, it is necessary to determine the order of integration, that is, how many times the series require differencing to induce stationarity. This we perform by running a simple regression of each variable on a constant and observing the behaviour of the residuals. The null hypothesis we test against is that the residuals follow a random walk, which, if accepted, would imply that the series were non-stationary. Test statistics for the Durbin-Watson test under the 'random walk' null have been computed by Sargan and Bhargava (1983). Without going into details, the result of this testing is that the time series individually appear to be integrated of order 1, or require differencing once to induce stationarity. This is a fairly common finding in economic time series.

The next stage is to estimate, and test the existence of, a long run or 'equilibrium' relationship between the variables under consideration. This amounts to searching for a cointegrating vector between the labour demand variables. A cointegrating vector simply defines a linear combination of the individually non-stationary variables that is stationary. This is the nature of the equilibrium relationship that we are searching for in the data. The details can be found in Granger (op. cit.) but amount to running an Ordinary Least Squares regression of employment on the labour demand variables and observing the behaviour of the residuals. The existence of such an equilibrium relationship is then a testable proposition, since if the residuals from this long-term relationship (which include all the short-run adjustment dynamics) do not move systematically about the equilibrium, then we have not found the correct long-run relationship.

The long-run parameters that are estimated from the above model, using quarterly data for the UK, are presented in Table 2.[7] The parameters generally have the signs we would expect a priori, although productivity enters with a negative coefficient. One tentative explanation for this result could be that if the labour market is for substantial periods output-constrained, then productivity could be negatively related to employment, since fewer workers would be needed to produce the (constrained) output. The capital stock also enters with a negative coefficient, suggesting perhaps that over much of the sample period capital has been substituted for labour in the production process. The value of the Durbin-Watson statistic is

[7] An interesting result is that simultaneity bias is of second order in regressions of this form, i.e. all variables expressed as current levels and with no lags, in the case of variables that are integrated of order unity.

Table 2: An equilibrium labour-demand relationship
Dependent variable: employment

Explanatory variable	Parameter estimate
w_f	−0·15
m	0·02
K	−0·20
POP	0·11
Q	1·05
Z	−0·47
c	7·63
T	96
s.e. (100)	1·33
DW	0·44
time period	1960:I–1983:IV

between the upper and lower critical values given in Sargan and Bhargava (op. cit.). The question of what inference to draw in such situations is moot, but the existence of an equilibrium relationship is at least not refuted.[8]

We now turn to the labour-supply relationship, and pursue a similar method of analysis. We take as our theoretical basis a labour-supply function of the form:

$$L_t^s = g(w_c, r, POP, t, c)$$

where r is a measure of the real interest rate (in terms of consumer prices), and t is a trend term to pick up trended changes in unobservable variables. There are many other factors that could affect the supply of labour, such as trade unions, unemployment and social security benefits, effective marginal rates of tax on the unemployed upon taking up employment, the extent of the 'work ethic', etc. For some of these factors it is difficult to obtain data on a quarterly basis, and for some it is not at all obvious how they should be measured. In the present estimates the trended components of these factors have been relegated into the trend term, which is not really very satisfactory, and it is hoped in future work to improve on the specification of the labour-supply relationship. The evolutionary behaviour of all the variables individually suggests that, as in the case of labour demand, they require differencing once to induce stationar-

---

[8] The same cannot be said of more restrictive models such as a strict neoclassical labour-demand relationship, where the existence of an equilibrium relationship is easily refuted.

Table 3: An equilibrium labour-supply relationship
Dependent variable: employment

Explanatory variable	Parameter estimate
w_c	0·39
r	−0·03
POP	1·56
t	−0·29
c	−7·72
T	96
s.e. (100)	1·29
DW	0·32
time period	1960:I–1983:IV

ity, and hence we search for a cointegrating vector over the levels of the variables. The results are presented in Table 3.

The DW statistic again satisfies the minimum requirement that it is above the lower bound of the test statistic under the null that the residuals follow a random walk. The explanatory variables are signed as we would expect a priori.

Having derived simple 'equilibrium' relationships from the data, we are able quantitatively to estimate the extent of any disequilibrium on either, or both, sides of the labour market. These excess demand and excess supply estimates will simply be the residuals of the fitted values for labour demand and supply from the actual observed level of employment. We take these residuals and use them in a wage adjustment model in the form of equation (4). The choice of such a simple one-period adjustment model is purely for expository purposes. In reality, the adjustment of the wage in response to disequilibrium pressures is likely to be a complex dynamic process. Since our main purpose here is not to provide definitive estimates of mean lags of response of the wage to the disequilibrium pressures we limit ourselves to a simple one period lagged wage adjustment.

To recapitulate, we have now estimated long-term 'equilibrium' labour-demand and supply relationships using the time series data available. Equilibrium, however, is a *process* rather than a *state*, and in the short run points on either equilibrium relationship are unlikely to be observed. The extent of any disequilibrium is estimated by the residuals of the fitted labour demand and supply relationships from the observed level of employment. The responsiveness of the observed real wage to these disequilibrium pressures is the notion of flexibility proposed, and in Equation 4a we present the response coefficients obtained using our simple model.

(4a) $dw_{et} = 0.0047 + 0.151 \ (L^d - N)_{t-1} + 0.318(N - L^s)_{t-1}$
         $(3.26) \qquad (2.35) \qquad\qquad (2.79)$
    s.e. $= 0.0139 \quad DW = 1.7 \quad \zeta_3 = 0.64 \quad \zeta_4 = 2.62$

The figures in parentheses are t-statistics, ζ_3 is the Chow test for parameter constancy, and ζ_4 is a Chi-squared test for predictive accuracy. The normalisation of the wage to the consumers price index is essentially arbitrary, and the results are virtually unchanged if w_f is substituted. The excess demand and excess supply terms are both signed as we would expect a priori, with excess demand tending to raise wages and excess supply tending to reduce the real wage. The response coefficient on the supply side is about twice as large as the demand-side response, which would suggest that there is some asymmetry between the two types of disequilibrium pressures. However, as noted throughout, these results are more suggestive than definitive since at the very least it would be necessary to allow for the possibility of more complex dynamics in the wage-adjustment process.

6. *Conclusions*

In this paper we have stressed the difference between measures of wage variability and wage flexibility. The relevance of the former to questions of the efficiency of the allocational role of wages in labour markets is, we have argued, minimal. Even if such measures of variability are interpreted as the 'stylised facts' of the wage-setting process, which answer one obtains simply depends upon which measure of variability one chooses. In the absence of theoretical reasons for preferring one measure to another the evidence on variability is without economic interest. The concept of flexibility of wages puts the emphasis back into the labour market, and concentrates on the pressures that may act on the wage rate to perform its market-clearing role. In the context of such models there can be no presumption that equilibrium is attained on either or both sides of the labour market, since it is the responsiveness of the wage to the disequilibrium pressures that is of prime interest. The model suggested in Section 5 is an initial attempt to put the emphasis back on modelling pressures explicitly, and it is hoped in future work to apply some of the techniques used to data from other major economies.

Appendix: Quarterly data for the UK

Abbreviations of sources:

BB   'Blue Book', National Income and Expenditure
DEG   Department of Employment Gazette
ETAS   Economic Trends Annual Supplement
BLSYB   British Labour Statistics Yearbook

1. E: Employees in employment, seasonally adjusted. Source: ETAS.

2. $(1 + t_g)$: Tax rate on goods and services. Computed as the ratio of 'GNP at market prices' (source: ETAS) to 'GNP at factor cost' (source: ETAS).

3. $(1 + t_L)$: Tax rate on labour borne by the firm. This series was computed, following Layard and Nickell (1985), as the ratio of 'Total labour costs per unit of output for the whole economy, 1975–100' (source: BLSYB and recent DEG) to 'Wages and salaries per unit of output for the whole economy, 1975–100' (source: ETAS). This gives an index with 1975–100 and thus, taking logs, gives

$$\log c(1 + t_L) = \log c + t_L$$

and we assume $\log c$ is included in the constant term.

4. P: Consumer price index. Source: OECD Main Economic Indicators.

5. P_f: Output price index. Defined as $P(1 + t_g)^{-1}$.

6. W: Wages. There are two main candidates as a measure of labour remuneration. The first would be a measure of wage rates, such as is measured in the series 'Basic weekly wage rates, manual workers: All industries and services' which could be adjusted to allow for changes in working hours. The second is some measure of earnings, in order that the wages/salaries of non-manual workers are also included. A major problem with the official wage rate data is that it only relates to national collective agreements of minimum wage rates for manual workers, and thus is not influenced by locally negotiated wage rates, or the wage settlements of non-manual workers. In the light of these objections an earnings data series was constructed. A slight problem is that the official earnings data provided by the Central Statistical Office was revised in 1976, when the coverage was increased significantly. Before 1976 the most general earnings data was provided in the series 'Index of average earnings, all industries covered' (source:

ETAS) which included production industries and some services. In 1976 the new series 'Index of average earnings, whole economy' (source: ETAS) was introduced which covered virtually the whole economy. These two series have been chained together. Calculations of earnings data only actually started in 1963, and so figures for 1960–62 inclusive are questions based on extending the series back using weekly wage rate data for all industries and services (source ETAS).

7. K: Capital Stock. Capital Stock data is only available on an annual basis, as 'Gross Capital Stock at 1975 replacement cost' (source: BB), so a quarterly series was constructed using the investment series 'Gross Domestic Fixed Capital Formation at 1975 prices, Total' (source: ETAS) which is available on a quarterly basis. Assuming a constant quarterly rate of depreciation, the change in the capital stock from one year to the next was allocated to the proportion of investment undertaken in each quarter.

i.e. $C_{t+1} = C_t + I_{t+1}(I_{t+1} + I_{t+2} + I_{t+3} + I_{t+4})^{-1}(C_{t+4} - C_t)$

8. M: 'Materials and fuels purchased by manufacturing industry'. Source: ETAS.

9. R: 'Treasury Bill Yield'. Source: ETAS.

10. Z: 'Output per person employed, manufacturing industries', seasonally adjusted. Source: ETAS.

11. GNP: 'Gross Domestic Product at Factor Cost, at 1975 prices, average estimate'. Source: ETAS.

12. POP: 'Working Population', source: ETAS.

References

Artus, J. 'The disequilibrium real wage hypothesis: an empirical evaluation', *IMF Staff Papers* 31 2 (1984).
Ashenfelter, O. and Card, D. 'Time series representations of labour market models', *Review of Economic Studies* 49, special issue on unemployment, 761–781.
Beckerman, W. and Jenkinson, T. 'What stopped the inflation? Unemployment or commodity prices?' *Economic Journal* 96 (381) (1986).
Benassy, J-P. *Macroeconomie et theorie du desequilibre* (Paris: Dunod, 1984).
Beenstock, M., Warburton, P., Lewington, P. and Macromatis, T. 'A medium-term macroeconometric model of the UK economy 1950–82', mimeo., City University, London.
Frisch, R., 'Prolegomena to a pressure-analysis of economic phenomena', *Metroeconomica* (1949), 135–160.

Geary, P.T. and Kennan, J. 'The employment-real wage relationship: an international study', *Journal of Political Economy* 90 (4) (1982), 854–871.

Gordon, R.J., 'Why US wage and employment behaviour differ from that in Britain and Japan', *Economic Journal* 92 (1982), 13–44.

Granger, C.W.J. 'Co-integrated variables and error correcting models', *mimeo*, University of California, San Diego, 1983.

Grubb, D., Jackman, R. and Layard, R. 'Wage rigidity and unemployment in OECD countries', *European Economic Review* 21 (1983) (International Seminar on Macroeconomics), 1130.

Hahn, F.H., 'Wages and employment', *Oxford Economic Papers* (Nov. 1984, Supplement on 'Economic theory and Hicksian themes'), 47–58.

Jenkinson, T.J. 'International Comparisons of NAIRUs: A Critique' (mimeo. Oxford University, 1986).

Keynes, J.M. *The General Theory of Employment, Interest and Money* (London: Macmillan, 1936).

Lange, O. *Price Flexibility and Employment* (1945) Cowles Commission Monograph, Wisconsin.

Layard, R. & Nickell, S.J. (1985) 'The causes of British unemployment', *National Institute Economic Review*, February.

Lipsey, R.G. (1960), 'The relationship between unemployment and the rate of change of money wage rates in the UK, 1862–1957: a further analysis', *Economica* 27 (1960) 1–31.

Malinvaud, E., *The Theory of Unemployment Reconsidered* (Oxford: Basil Blackwell, 1977).

Metcalf, D., 'On the measurement of employment and unemployment', *National Institute Economic Review* 109 (1984) 59–67.

Minford, P. (1983) 'Labour market equilibrium in an open economy', *Oxford Economic Papers* 35 (1983), 531–568.

Nickell, S.J. and Andrews, M., 'Unions, real wages, and employment in Britain 1951–79', *Oxford Economic Papers* 35 (1983), 507–530.

Sachs, J.D. 'Real wages and unemployment in the OECD countries', *Brookings Papers on Economic Activity* 1 (1983), 255–284.

Sargan, J.D. and Bhagava, A., 'Testing residuals from least squares regression for being generated by the Gaussian random walk', *Econometrica* 51 (1983), 153–174.

Stiglitz, J.E., 'Theories of wage rigidity', in Butkiewicz, Koford and Miller, *Keynes' Economic Legacy* (Praeger, 1986).

Tobin, J. (ed.), *Macroeconomics, Prices and Quantities*, Brookings Institution, Washington D.C. and Basil Blackwell, Oxford, 1983 (chapter by R.J. Gordon on 'A century of evidence on wage and price stickiness in the United States, the United Kingdom, and Japan').

3. Explanations of Wage Inflexibility: Institutions and Incentives

Daniel J. B. Mitchell

Introduction

Whenever a market doesn't clear, economists look for an influence which is hindering price adjustments. In introductory microeconomics classes, professors delight in demonstrating that farm 'surpluses' are really artifacts of government price supports and that there can really be no such thing as a 'shortage' of engineers, since employers would simply raise salaries if there were one. These are micro tales of demand-supply analysis. Yet they raise conceptual problems at the macro level.

The prime market that has trouble clearing at the macro level is the labour market. Yet it is difficult to point to government-imposed wage floors or ceilings as the primary causes of the surpluses and shortages that develop cyclically. In the US context minimum wage floors affect only the lowest paid and cannot have a direct effect on the employment (or unemployment) of most workers. Ceilings on wages have been imposed only on rare occasions as components of anti-inflation policies.

Even after acknowledging warnings that micro models may be misleading at the macro level, economists have looked for elements of 'rigidity' as the source of the aggregate economy's tendency to adjust to variations in demand through quantities rather than prices. And since the quantity variation tendency shows up most notably as variations in unemployment and job vacancy rates, rigidity of wages becomes the natural suspect.

But what precisely is meant by 'wage rigidity'? Nominal and real wages certainly change over time; they are not literally rigid. Hence, the word 'rigidity' has a relative connotation. Wages are seen as rigid relative to something else, but not completely inflexible.

The central theme of this paper is that there is no unified theory of wage rigidity (however defined) and there probably cannot be one. Both the historical and the cross-country evidence suggest that wage-setting practices are influenced in an important way by institutional factors. While the definition of economic endogeneity can be stretched to encompass such factors, there is little to be gained by doing so. Recent theorising on wage rigidity has provided insights into incentives which reinforce institutions. But these incentives by themselves would not have brought about contemporary wage setting practices.

Much of the analysis that follows is based on American data and economic history. The author apologises in advance for this ethnocentrism. He suspects, however, that the story could be told – with different details but similar conclusions – for any industrialised market economy.

1. *The classical auction market*

The standard demand-supply analysis of the textbooks is really a representation of an auction market in which alternative prices are tried until the market clears. There are markets which approximate such conditions, mainly in the financial and commodity sectors. It hardly requires acute perception to observe that labour markets do not function with the price flexibility which characterises the markets for stocks, bonds, precious metals or agricultural products.

In the context of the classical auction market, there is little meaning to the obvious question of whether by 'rigid wages' one is describing the nominal or real wage rate. With an auction market, a whisper of excess supply would quickly cause the price to plummet, until the excess was removed.[1] With labour as an important element of costs, such a plummeting in the labour market would most probably be associated with *both* real and nominal wage declines.

Under an auction-market model, an excess supply of labour would signal the auctioneer quickly to drop the real wage. But this would lead to nominal price declines in auction product markets, so that ultimately a real-wage decline would have to be a nominal-wage decline, too. The real versus nominal distinction is likely to be meaningful only when there are already departures from auction markets in the model.

It may seem unfair to pose the auction market's flexibility as a standard for wage setting. But consider the economic analyst who

---

[1] This statement does not imply that falling wages would *necessarily* relieve the excess supply. But as long as the excess supply remained, wages would continue to fall.

puzzles over why a worker with appropriate credentials and willing to work at a wage at or below the level paid by a given employer may be told that there is 'no help wanted'. Such an analyst is implicitly comparing the real world labour market with a classical auction system.

2. *Wages and real world product markets*

Of course, surpluses and shortages are found outside the labour market. There are examples of product markets which do not immediately clear, i.e. which are not characterised by auction-style price adjustments. Yet wage-setting seems rigid, even when compared with 'typical' product markets.

One measure of this characteristic can be seen from American data on Figure 1. The figure compares the standard deviation of December-to-December changes in a broad-based wage measure (the hourly earnings index – HEI – for production and non-supervisory workers) with the standard deviation of changes in various aggregate price

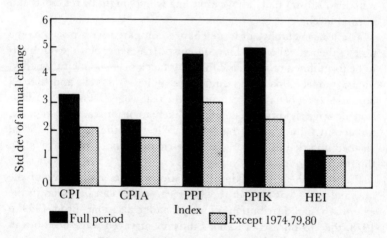

Figure 1. Wage and price variation

Sources of data: US President, *Economic Report of the President 1984* (Washington: GPO, 1984), pp. 283, 290; US Bureau of Economic Analysis, *Business Statistics 1982* (Washington: GPO, 1983), pp. 57, 171; *Current Wage Developments*, vol. 36 (November 1984), p. 33. See also Data appendix on pp. 73–74.

indexes during 1968–83: the Consumer Price Index (CPI), the CPI adjusted to exclude energy, shelter and food (CPIA), the Producer Price Index for finished goods (PPI), and the PPI component for capital equipment (PPIK). Wage change over this period exhibited a substantially lower standard deviation than price change, even after the price indexes are purged of 'volatile' components and the influence of 'abnormal' periods is deleted.[2]

This difference in price and wage setting has its counterpart in the degree to which product and labour markets rely on quantity rather than price adjustments. At the bottom of a recession, firms may well find themselves with excess inventories. But they liquidate these surpluses through distress sales, rebates and other price adjustments after a relatively short period. The labour market has some similar phenomena, but their scope is much more limited and the duration of the adjustment seems much longer. Thus, by the end of 1983, the inventory to sales ratio in US manufacturing and trade suggested that the excess supply of goods which had built up during the severe 1982 recession had been dissipated. But the national unemployment rate remained substantially above anything which might be regarded as a normal level.

The lesser volatility of wage change compared with price change poses a theoretical puzzle for economists. If a model of wage rigidity is to be formulated on the basic building block of economic rationality, such a model is likely to assume that money is a 'veil' and that all labour-market behaviour centres on the real wage. Thus any justification for wage rigidity that emerges is likely to be for real wage rigidity, not nominal. But the fact that wages are less volatile than prices (even cleaned up prices) suggests that wage-rigidity models need to explain the stickiness of nominal wages.

Perhaps the most striking illustration of the importance of the nominal wage – at least in the American case – can be found in the examination of distributions of wage-change decisions. From 1959 to 1978, the US Bureau of Labor Statistics surveyed wage decisions in manufacturing. Table 1 compares the distribution of wage decisions in 1961, a year in which the CPI rose by only 0.7 per cent and the unemployment rate stood at 6.7 per cent, with 1978, a more inflationary and buoyant year with a 9 per cent inflation rate and 6.1 per cent unemployment rate. In the later year there were no reported

---

[2] The years excluded as 'abnormal' are those of particularly high inflation. In addition 1974 may have been influenced by the lapsing of wage-price controls.

**Table 1. Wage decisions in US manufac-
turing, 1961 and 1978**
(Percentage of workers covered)

Type of decision	1961	1978
Wage decrease	0·2%	0·0%
No wage change	23·8	8·8
Wage increase		
0·1–1·9%	18·7	1·5
2·0–2·9%	20·3	1·9
3·0–3·9%	17·7	4·3
4·0–4·9%	6·4	4·3
5·0–5·9%	7·0	7·5
6·0–6·9%	1·5	11·0
7·0–7·9%	0·6	19·1
8·0–8·9%	0·3	15·7
9·0–9·9%	0·1	8·6
10% and above	2·5	17·2
Unknown	0·8	—

Note: Wage adjustments exclude escalator
and deferred increases. Details need
not sum to 100% due to rounding.
Source: *Monthly Labor Review*, 85 (September
1962), 1005; *Current Wage Developments* 33 (May 1981), 54.

wage cuts; in the earlier year the proportion of workers experiencing
wage cuts was only 0.2 per cent.

Table 1 demonstrates the unusual nature of nominal-wage decreases, even in periods of virtual price stability. During years of low
inflation, the wage-change distribution drifts down – as might be
expected – but does not retain its bell-shaped form. Rather it bunches
at the zero level and just above. Real-wage decreases are not
uncommon; nominal-wage cuts rate newspaper headlines.[3]

3. *International variation*

The evidence of Table 1 might be dismissed as a peculiar American
characteristic of wage setting. Some analysts have argued that the US

[3] The episode of US union wage concessions to management in the early 1980s, in
which wage freezes and cuts occurred on a dramatic scale, will be discussed in the final
section.

is particularly prone to nominal-wage rigidity due to multi-year union contracts (an issue addressed below) while other countries exhibit real wage rigidity (see Grubb, Jackman and Layard; Sachs; Gordon). This view developed after the experience in the mid-1970s of the OPEC oil price shock/recession. While US real wages showed some decline, those in certain other industrialised countries did not.

In principle, an external price shock of the OPEC type should not have the same impact on nominal wages as a bout of price inflation induced by domestic monetary expansion. An external price shock does not increase the 'ability to pay' of domestic employers. (It does not raise the marginal revenue product of labour of the typical firm.) Indeed, if the price shock involves a major input to production such as oil, it may reduce the 'ability to pay' of non-energy-producing firms. Moreover the OPEC shock triggered restrictive macroeconomic policies in most countries for anti-inflation reasons, still another reason to expect a real-wage decline.

Table 2 shows the diverse responses of manufacturing real wages in ten countries to the mid-1970s episode and the later oil shock/recession of the early 1980s. It indicates whether or not real wages declined in at least one year during 1972–78 or 1979–82. The US exhibited a real-wage decline in both periods, as did Canada (with a lag), Japan,

Table 2. Manufacturing real compensation per hour in ten countries

	Mid-1970s decline?	Early 1980s decline?
US	Yes	Yes
Canada	Yes	Yes
Japan	Yes	Yes
Denmark	Yes	Yes
France	No	No
Germany (FR)	No	No
Italy	Yes	Yes
Netherlands	No	Yes
Sweden	Yes	Yes
United Kingdom	Yes	No

Note: Mid-1970s refers to 1972–78; early 1980s refers to 1979–82.
Source: US Bureau of Labor Statistics, *Handbook of Labor Statistics* 2175 (Washington: GPO, 1983), 439.

Sweden, Denmark and Italy. On the other hand, Germany and France did not experience a real-wage decrease in either episode. Real wages did not decline in the Netherlands during the mid-1970s period but did so in the later one. Britain exhibited the reverse pattern: a decline in the earlier period, but not in the later.

The variegated reactions of national wage-determination systems pose a further challenge to any attempt to formulate a unified theory of wage rigidity. Variation in response to common phenomena suggests that institutional arrangements peculiar to each country play a role in explaining wage outcomes. While balance of payments constraints under fixed exchange rates may have once been important common determinants of these outcomes under fixed exchange rates (Nordhaus), the floating rates of the 1970s and 1980s provided more scope for such national differences to intrude on the wage-setting process.

4. *Variation over time*

Historical evidence also poses a challenge to proposed theories of wage rigidity. There is evidence that the degree of wage sensitivity to market pressures has changed over time. Unified theories must be capable of explaining such variations; a model which applies only to a single period is inherently suspect.

Some studies have analysed long-term series of wage change at the aggregate level and have found that earlier periods were characterised by more wage responsiveness than during the post-war period.[4] Some recently developed American data from the 1920s confirms this impression in graphic terms. For example, Figure 2 shows the distribution of wage-change decisions, as reported by the US Bureau of Labor Statistics' establishment surveys, for 1924 and 1925, years in which consumer prices reportedly changed by − .2 per cent and + 4.0 per cent, respectively. While these data must be interpreted with care (see Mitchell 1985), they give dramatic evidence of an earlier era in which both real- and nominal-wage decreases were well within the realm of employer discretion.

Figure 2 is even more impressive when compared with the wage distributions of Table 1. The wage-change distributions of the 1920s showed substantially wider variance than those of the post-war period.

[4] A survey of such studies may be found in Mitchell (1985).

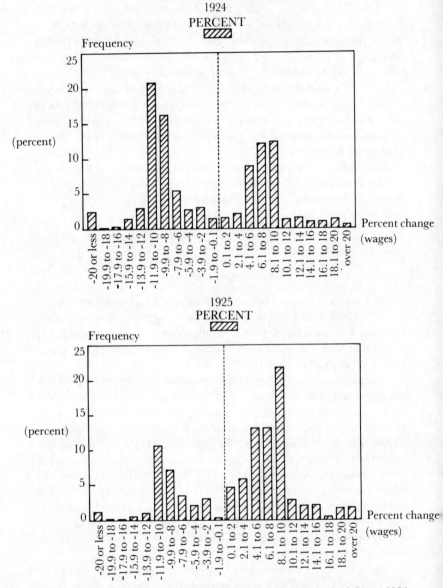

Figure 2. Distribution of wage increase or decrease decisions, 1924 and 1925

Source of data: See Figure 3; Mitchell, 1985b. See also Data appendix on pp. 73–74.

While the possibility that the difference in the two periods simply reflected a change in worker 'preferences' of the type likely to figure in a wage-rigidity model, there is historical evidence that wage cuts were not gladly received in the 1920s or before. Where unions existed, strikes over wage reductions were not uncommon.[5]

The evidence of Figure 2, and of other historical studies as well, is that wages were once more flexible than is currently the case. If the source of this flexibility is not on the supply side of the labour market, i.e. worker preferences, is it on the demand side? Are employers situated today so that they need less wage flexibility than their predecessors? Undoubtedly there are differences in economic structure that could be cited between the 1920s and the contemporary period. Probably the most outstanding difference is the lesser stability of the economy in the earlier period. In the 1920s prices were as liable to rise as to fall and the possibility of severe depression – not just recession – lurked in the background. Government was not expected to play a stabilising role. In such a world, greater flexibility of wages might be expected.

In short, theories of wage rigidity need to take some account of the general background of macroeconomic performance and policy. It is more difficult to fix a wage (or a price) in a world of substantial uncertainty than in one in which reasonable projections of the future can be made. This observation does not explain why one might wish to fix a wage or price; only that some circumstances make the attempt more difficult and potentially more costly.

5. *Pressures for new theories of wage rigidity*

One of the key elements in Keynesian thinking was a diminished emphasis on wage rigidity as a cause of unemployment and the business cycle. Keynes himself devoted a chapter of the *General Theory* to a discussion of nominal wage rigidity (chapter 19). He noted that nominal-wage cuts might well be followed by price cuts of similar proportions, thus leaving real wages – and, hence, the demand for labour – unchanged. And he cited various destabilising dynamic adjustments which might be set in motion by general wage-cutting, as well as others which might restore full employment. Generally, however, the Keynesian message was that it was unwise to await

[5] Mitchell (1985).

restoration of full employment through wage flexibility, which probably was not present in sufficient degree to do the job anyway.

By the early 1960s, this viewpoint had made its way into textbook economic orthodoxy (see Ackley, 377–93). It was recognised that in theory a freely-falling nominal wage in the face of a constant money supply would stabilise the economy through the 'Pigou' or real-balance effect (Pigou, 96–130). Falling nominal wages with a constant money supply would have the same real stimulatory effect as a rising money supply with constant nominal wages. But this theoretical observation was not considered an interesting result.

Nominal wages were not viewed as sufficiently flexible actually to perform the stabilising function in a reasonably short period. Early econometric work on the 'Phillips curve' and its variant (Phillips) – while providing a climate of optimism for macroeconomic management – indicated that wage change did not resemble the auction model, although it was somewhat responsive to real-demand conditions and price inflation. There was more interest in showing the empirical truth of this assertion than in developing a theory explaining it.

Various forces converged by the 1970s to stimulate theoretical work on wage rigidity to complement the outpouring of empirically-based wage equations. First, the 1960s produced a literature on 'internal labour markets' within firms. A pioneering work by Doeringer and Piore noted that large firms with formal personnel practices (or unions) offered high wages, good benefits and internal promotional opportunities to their workforces in contrast to smaller firms operating in the secondary sector of the labour market.

Reasons for the dualism in the labour market were not precisely specified, although costs of turnover were included as an explanation.[6] Firms in the primary sector obtained quality workforces with good work habits; those in the secondary sector could tolerate unreliable workers with high absenteeism and quit rates. The internal labour market model was used initially to address problems of structural unemployment, especially among minority workers who were being given increasing emphasis in federal public policy. But the significance for wage determination was not immediately emphasised.

A second influence contributing to theoretical work on wage rigidity

[6] Other economists have interpreted the Doeringer and Piore findings as a reflection of turnover costs and have been critical of the sharp dualism of their model (Wachter). Piore, however, rejects this interpretation as simplistic (see his comments on the Wachter paper, 684–8).

was the observation – inspired partly by the internal labour markets literature – that many workers had substantial job tenures, sometimes of twenty years or more, with a single employer (Hall; Akerlof and Main). Not only were the employment spells long, but when related to an earlier literature on employee turnover (see Ross), they suggested that there were differences between the contemporary economy and those of the pre-war period with regard to worker attachments to employers. Specifically, workers were less attached to their employers in the earlier period. High employee-turnover was the norm.

The observation of contemporary long-term attachments in the labour market suggested to analysts in the 1970s and 1980s that short-term fluctuations in demand might not be major wage determinants. Perhaps strongly attached employers and employees would simply agree on a fixed stream of payments regardless of external conditions in the employer's product market. After all, when a firm signs a long-term lease to rent a warehouse, the rental payment typically is not contingent on the renter's short-run business conditions.

A third motivator of research in models of wage rigidity had its roots in the seeming collapse of the Phillips curve in the 1970s. The notion that wage inflation and unemployment were locked in a fixed trade-off, while it raised analytical questions, enjoyed reasonable empirical confirmation until the late 1960s. Thereafter, the Phillips curve seemed to 'shift' to a less favourable position and the coefficient on the unemployment rate began to fade in magnitude and significance. The empirical observation of wage insensitivity to business fluctuations now demanded theoretical analysis.

Along with the empirical puzzle came the growing public policy preoccupation with inflation and its causes. This public policy concern became a fourth factor stimulating theoretical analysis of wage rigidity. Theories began to be developed suggesting that inflation had a certain momentum – that it was difficult to stop once it had continued for an extended period – because 'inflation expectations' were engendered by the observation of past inflation.

The resistance of inflation in the 1970s to demand restraint, and even formal wage and price controls and guidelines, contributed to this view. Yet expectations as an explanation for inflation momentum made sense only in a world of long-term contract-type arrangements. An auction labour market would not be much influenced by inflation expectations in setting today's spot wage rate.

A fifth observation which contributed to theoretical work on wage rigidity was the observation in the US that long-term union-management contracts seemed to be largely immune to demand fluctuations (Mitchell 1978). Indeed, during the 1970s union wages in the US seemed to be generally adrift from the majority non-union sector of wage determination. The union/non-union wage differential rose throughout the decade and into the early 1980s.

Some analysts noted that such behaviour of wages under collective bargaining could be explained by 'median voter' models in which senior workers dictated union wage policy (Freeman and Medoff, chapter 8). But the possibility that it was the union contract itself which caused the problem lent credence to the developing literature on contracting in the labour market as an explanation of wage rigidity and even led to public calls for bans on multi-year union agreements.[7]

6. *Implicit contract theories*

There are two strands of implicit contract theory; one is based on differential employer-employee risk preferences while the other is based on costs of employee turnover.[8] In reality, both are closely related. The central idea is that a cost is attached to breaking the employer-employee relationship. In such circumstances, an incentive is created to establish a long-duration relationship through an 'implicit' contract defining pay and other conditions of employment. The task of the theorist is then to explain why such contracts should feature rigid wages and quantity adjustments in labour utilisation in response to demand fluctuations.

(i) *Risk aversion models*

The risk-preference models tend to be the most elegantly presented. Employers in essence 'insure' workers against income fluctuations by offering steady employment. But there is a certain circularity involved. Risk in the labour market is primarily a matter of uncertainty about layoffs. But layoffs will be costly to workers only if the labour market is not characterised by auction processses. Otherwise a 'laid off' employee would merely amble to the nearest auctioneer and obtain

---

[7] For examples, see Jacoby and Mitchell (1984), 216–17, note 6.

[8] The literature has become so vast that complete references are not possible. For reviews (with references), see Riordan and Wachter, Stiglitz.

another job at the market wage. Risk preference models cannot really be used to explain the lack of auction markets: they already assume it!

Because they are elegantly presented, risk-preference models are most likely to be grounded in strict economic rationality and therefore to purport to explain *real*-wage rigidity rather than nominal. Moreover, as a result of their abstract nature such models are not well-adapted to consideration of cross-country variations or differences in wage behaviour in alternative periods. To the extent that authors of such models consider such matters, the treatment is often in the 'verbal' part of their papers.

A final difficulty with the risk-aversion approach to implicit contracting is its failure to address two key fundamental issues squarely. First, it is unclear why – at the abstract level at which the analysis usually proceeds – workers cannot deal with risk and uncertainty through saving and dissaving behaviour (Welch and Topel). Second, even if the worker finds it necessary to form an attachment to an insurance agent, it is unclear why the insurance agent and the employer must be one and the same entity (Haltiwanger).

(ii) Turnover cost models

The alternative strand in the implicit contract literature emphasises costs of voluntary employee turnover to the employer. Arthur M. Okun's presentation is probably the best example of this approach (chapters 2 and 3). Turnover is postulated as imposing a 'toll' on the employer. This toll might be viewed as the sum of employer search costs, screening expenses and investment in specific training.[9] To reduce such costs, the employer offers the worker a long-term association.

Under the Okun model, the employer must make the long-term arrangement attractive to the worker. Since there are costs of turnover, potentials will arise for either party to 'exploit' the other, depending on the tightness of the external labour market. To avoid such problems, the employer offers the employee 'fair' treatment – the 'invisible handshake' instead of the invisible hand.[10]

---

[9] Actually, the distinction between specific and general training erodes with long term worker/employer attachments. For example, if the worker received general training from the employer, the employer could expect that the increased productivity would be captured by the firm due to the strength of the attachment.

[10] A review of the Okun approach can be found in Solow.

The difficulty with (and strength of!) the Okun model is its imprecision. How is 'fair' to be defined? Is it obviously fair to have a rigid nominal wage and to adjust to declines in demand through layoffs in reverse order of seniority? The methods of adjustment may seem fair, but only because they are common contemporary practices. And the reason for an implicit contract rather than an explicit one is obscure. Until recently in the US, implicit promises created no legal obligation on the part of the employer.[11] Why should employers not compete for labour by offering legally binding explicit contracts spelling out the fair treatment to be provided?

At one extreme a permanent attachment between an employer and employee could give rise to a wage payment stream totally unrelated to demand. Under this model the worker effectively sells himself into slavery for a lump sum which he takes as some kind of annuity. But the insights provided by such models are limited by their unreality. Firms are unlikely to staff at peak levels, so that there would have to be a class of workers who were subject to demand fluctuations. The wages of these marginal workers should be flexible, even if the wages of the 'slaves' are not.

(iii) Historical insights

Recent historical analysis raises important questions about the implicit contracting approach. The essential element of implicit contracting analysis is its attempt to make wage rigidity (and other anomalies of the labour market) the natural result of rational profit and welfare maximisation. Yet, as already noted in Section 4, labour-market practices have changed over time.

In a pathbreaking new study Sanford Jacoby traces the development of personnel practices in US manufacturing firms. At the turn of the century these firms were content to leave personnel decisions to foremen. They had no personnel departments or professionals and saw little reason to have them. However, external social reformers perceived a need for uplifting the working class through career ladders

---

[11] Under American common law (and often in state labour codes), absent a written agreement or union contract, the 'at will' doctrine applies to employer/employee relationships. The worker is free to quit and the employer is free to discharge for any reason or no reason. No 'just cause' for discipline applies. In recent years, this doctrine has been eroded by court decisions and 'wrongful discharge' litigation has proliferated. However, it is unlikely that any court would infer norms of wage-setting in the absence of a written agreement.

and other such devices. Since these reformers were not especially interested in the profitability of their suggestions, their proposals for centralised, professionally-managed personnel policies initially made little headway. The reformers' lack of success might be compared with that of the initial advocates of quality of worklife programs in the early 1970s, who also were socially-minded rather than profit-oriented.

But during the First World War employers were faced with a massive labour shortage. Unions – fostered by government policies aimed at maintaining military production without strikes – became a substantial threat. Employers suddenly looked to professional personnel managers to cultivate worker loyalty through 'fair' treatment. Personnel departments were established and the authority of foremen was downgraded. Prominent employers found virtue in what was termed 'welfare work' among their employees, a term with obvious parallels to the external activity of social workers of the period.

During the 1920s, when the labour shortage abruptly ended and a large-scale anti-union campaign ended the union threat, employers reversed these policies. Personnel departments were downgraded and in some cases abolished; authority was returned to foremen. But personnel management experienced a renaissance in the 1930s, when the union threat re-emerged (with the backing of pro-union government policies). Subsequently the Second World War provided further impetus for centralised, bureaucratic personnel management by reviving the pressures of the First. Additionally, wartime wage controls required firms to have staff experts who could deal with the complex regulatory system.

Although employers had legislative success in their efforts to diminish the union threat, the union movement had become far more institutionalised than after the First World War. Thus the union element as an incentive to retain strong personnel departments remained. In addition other public policies came along during the post-war period to reinforce the union effect. These included tax incentives for employer-paid fringe benefits which required expertise to administer, programs of equal employment opportunity for women and minorities in the 1960s, and other regulatory policies in the 1970s.

In short, external pressures – rather than risk-aversion and turnover costs – seem to account for the personnel practices of modern employers, and certainly for the changes over time in those practices. It may be that the presence of risk-aversion and turnover costs reinforced the external factors. (Holding down turnover costs is a common justification of personnel managers for their activities.) But it is doubtful that in the absence of the external factors, US employers – on their own – would have established the internal labour-market practices which are now commonplace.

7. *Explicit union-management contracts*

As already noted, multi-year union contracts in the US were pinpointed in the empirical literature as being particularly insensitive to demand fluctuations in the 1970s. However, the degree to which explicit contracts offer insights into implicit, i.e. non-union, contracts is limited. To some extent, features found in union contracts are helpful in spotlighting otherwise unobservable worker preferences. For example, 'unionesque' seniority considerations have been shown to play a role in non-union personnel practices in the US (Abraham and Medoff). But as Jacoby and Mitchell (1983) have pointed out, much of what is observed in union contracting is explainable by strategic considerations rather than preferences.

(i) Multi-year contracts and wage rigidity

There are substantial questions raised by the proposition that American wage-setting peculiarities are explained by overlapping multi-year contracts. First, only a minority of American employees are organised. In the private sector – where wage data are typically drawn – unions represented less than a fourth of wage and salary workers by the late 1970s. The vast majority of private workers were covered by annual non-union wage decision-making or simply decision-making at the convenience of non-union employers. Second, even within the union sector, Taylor has shown that the stickiness in wages which might be associated with multi-year contracts is not substantial, precisely because of their overlapping nature.

It should be clear that contracting *per se* does not theoretically prevent wages from being flexible and responsive to demand. American union contracts have often included escalator clauses, requiring wage adjustments in response to price inflation. A few contracts have provided for wage adjustments in response to community wage surveys or other specified collective-bargaining settlements.[12] Thus a long duration contract can specify a contingent wage adjustment formula rather than a fixed wage. Nothing prevents such a formula from being geared to a demand-sensitive measure, as occurs, for example, under a profit-sharing plan.

The preference in the collective-bargaining sector for two- to three-year contracts is explainable by strike-avoidance motivations. Pressure for such contracts in the US appears to have come largely from the management side. Long-term contracts were expected to reduce strikes by reducing the frequency of negotiations. It is not clear that American management in fact obtained a reduction in time lost to strikes, but it did gain greater control over the *scheduling* of strikes. A three-week strike every three years is preferred by management to an annual one week strike (Jacoby and Mitchell (1983), (1984)). If the duration of the contract reflects management preferences, then it appears that the wage schedules and formulas reflect the preferences of senior unionised employees. Except in cases where the entire plant or firm is in danger of being closed, senior workers are insulated by seniority systems from displacement. Flexible wages might be helpful in providing job security to those junior employees on the margin of layoff. But such flexibility would imply 'subsidies' from senior workers (in terms of unwanted income fluctuations) for the benefit of their juniors. Median voter models of union decision-making preclude such behaviour (Medoff).

(ii) Bargaining models and wage rigidity

Other models of bargaining can also rationalise union wage-rigidity. McDonald and Solow generalise earlier work by Cartter on bargaining outcomes and show that demand fluctuations need not lead to procyclical union wage-changes. Essentially, they begin with a contract curve – a schedule of possible wage-employment outcomes – which has the standard indeterminacy characteristic. The precise outcome depends on bargaining power. If there is indeterminacy in the static case, the problem compounds when demand fluctuations are added to the model.[13]

The McDonald and Solow model is in no way dependent on long-term contracts. Their outcomes and conclusions would apply if unions

[12] Some contracts contain 'most favoured nation' clauses (a phrase borrowed from international trade terminology) in which the terms of the contract can be overridden if one of the parties gives a more favourable agreement to another employer or union.
[13] For a critique of McDonald and Solow, see Chapman and Fisher.

and firms bargained on a daily basis. Moreover, their model is exclusively concerned with bargaining; it does not extend to non-union wage policy in a competitive environment.

(iii) Wage rigidity and strike costs

McDonald and Solow did not take explicit account of the long-term linkage between union and employer in designating preferred wage outcomes. Consideration of the nature of this attachment can provide insights into wage rigidity in the union sector. Both parties to the negotiation know that they will be bargaining again, a fact which should have strategic implications.

Bargaining over a union contract is critically different from bargaining over the price of a used car. In the former case not only will the parties meet again in a future negotiation, but they must in the current negotiation be aware of the potentially high costs of impasse, i.e. a strike. In the latter case failure to make a deal imposes no significant costs and the parties are unlikely to meet again.

Given strike costs, both parties have an incentive to avoid a dispute. Hence strikes should be random events, generated by 'mistakes' by unions and managements about their opponents' true positions. Both parties would be better off arriving at the settlement that would result from a strike, but without having the strike, and somehow splitting the resulting cost savings.

In a variant of rational expectations, it should not be the case that strike frequency could be predicted by the business cycle. If business-cycle fluctuations had a systematic effect on the bargaining strength of one or both parties, both parties ought simply to adjust their demands accordingly so that the systematic influence disappears.

Unfortunately for this theory, the empirical evidence from US data is that strikes are pro-cyclical (Rees; Ashenfelter and Johnson; Kaufman). A common theme in much of the empirical strike literature is that such cyclical strike activity can be traced to an information imperfection problem. Perhaps the union leadership 'understands' management resistance but cannot fully convey its understanding to the rank and file. Or perhaps both parties have trouble determining the other sides' 'true' (as opposed to expressed) bargaining position. In any case it appears that the bargaining demands of both parties are characterised by a rigidity which raises the union's lowest offer relative to management's highest offer during boom periods. There is supportive empirical evidence that during strikes union concession schedules are not much influenced by the unemployment rate (Farber).

Rigidity of bargaining-demands probably reflects the union-management attachment. In a bargaining context both parties must be concerned about credibility. An assertion that a particular demand is critical and that a strike will ensue if it is not met must be followed by consistent behaviour. If a union, after making such an assertion, backs off, management will be less likely to take its position seriously in the next negotiation. The same logic applies to management assertions that a strike will be taken rather than concede to a particular union demand. (It is the function of mediators to help the parties find a plausible excuse for reversing such stances, without damaging future credibility.)

Given the long-term nature of their relationship, both parties should move to a policy of reducing the indefinite *stream* of strike costs. This means behaving consistently in any particular negotiation – even if a strike results – so that loss of credibility in the current negotiation will not lead to 'mistakes' by the opposing party concerning demands made in future negotiations. Both parties might seek to adopt demand 'formulas' which would allow the other party to predict their behaviour in a variety of circumstances.

For example, a union might seek to establish a position that it wanted to achieve a given nominal-wage increase at least partially protected from inflation by an escalator clause. Management might seek to establish a role for prospective profitability as a guide for wage adjustments. These positions would systematically clash at the peak of the business cycle when inflation might be high but the future downturn was beginning to loom.

Thus the bargaining process itself in the union sector could engender wage rigidity because of the long-term nature of the union-management relationship. However, this relationship must be carefully differentiated from the long-term employee-employer attachment on which implicit contract theory is based. Unions and managements can have long-term relationships even in industries – such as construction – where high employee-turnover is endemic. And employees can have long-term relationships with employers without union representation. Insights from union bargaining theory are thus not likely to provide guidance on wage rigidity in the non-union sector.

(iv) Unions and wage rigidity: summary

Flexible wage formulas are absent from union contracts mainly because unions don't want them, not because they can't be written. The existence of long-term contracts undoubtedly makes *some* contribution to union wage rigidity. For example, there might be difficulties in obtaining union and management agreement on an appropriate contingency formula, even if both parties wanted to include such a clause. But the rigidifying effects of a written contract should not be overstated. In any case wage rigidity under union contracts does not carry an obvious theoretical implication for non-union wage rigidity. There are some important historical and institutional connections, however, which will be explored below.

8. *Efficiency wages*

Some recent work proposes that wage rates influence worker effort. The marginal productivity of a given worker is not taken to be a function of personal characteristics and skill (combined with other factors of production and technology), but is seen as a variable. Under such circumstances, employer pay policy must be concerned about incentive effects and must seek to avert employee 'shirking' of responsibility.

Various implications of efficiency wages can be drawn. The approach can be combined with implicit contracting models to determine an optimal wage/tenure profile, i.e. the degree to which earnings rise with seniority over a working life (Lazear). An upward-sloping profile can be viewed as an incentive system; the worker is effectively promised a reward in the future for good behaviour today.

But efficiency wages can also be viewed as an alternative to implicit contracting theory. One possibility is to view loss of employment as a disciplinary device. In a classical auction labour market, a single employer who wished to avoid shirking might pay a wage premium so that a loss of employment would be costly to a worker. Workers at this firm would be afraid that if they were caught shirking they would lose the premium via termination. But if all employers try to use wage premia to forestall shirking, they will raise the market wage above its clearing level. Unemployment will result and the penalty for shirking will become a spell without wage income as terminated workers seek new jobs (Shapiro and Stiglitz).

It is not clear that either of these approaches necessarily results in wage rigidity. Even if wages are too high (above the market clearing level) or if firms find it advantageous to offer working-life wage schedules, the wages or schedules could move up and down in response to labour-market conditions. To produce nominal-wage rigidity, it is necessary to suggest reasons why productivity would fall if nominal wages are cut. It might be suggested, for example, that workers' morale depends on relative wage-standing and that with asynchronous wage-setting nominal-wage cuts are inherently relative wage cuts (Stiglitz). Each individual employer would be reluctant to cut wages despite falling demand because of the adverse productivity effect. Layoffs, rather than wage cuts, might be preferred by employers.

9. *Wage flexibility via gain-sharing?*

If there are rational reasons for rigidity of the wage, perhaps employers and employees (or unions) might be induced to provide for another element of compensation which would be flexible. There are examples of gain-sharing plans in which the economic circumstance of the firm is reflected in a component of pay. The best-known type of gain-sharing is profit-sharing.

Historically, profit-sharing has been viewed by employers as a variant of an incentive plan. The argument is that when workers understand that they will share in firm profits, they will work harder to add to those profits. It is difficult to know precisely how many workers and firms are covered by profit-sharing, since the studies taken tend to be confined to medium- to large-sized employers. A recent study in the US found that 20 per cent of firms surveyed reported having a profit-sharing plan. Another 1–2 per cent had other forms of gain-sharing.[14] But because of perverse incentives in the US tax code and in pension regulatory programs, some so-called 'profit-sharing' plans may be largely unrelated to profits and may be substitutes for formal pension schemes.

Union concessions during the post-1979 economic slump in the US sometimes involved establishment of a profit-sharing plan in exchange

[14] Little difference was found between the practices of large firms (1,000 or more workers) and small firms. The figure in the text omits worker stock-ownership arrangements since – except in the case of complete worker ownership – these plans do not have the desirable properties discussed below. Results of the survey can be found in Bureau of National Affairs, 7–8.

for a wage freeze or cut. This development marked a change in union attitudes toward profit-sharing; less than 2 per cent of private-sector union workers were reported as covered by profit-sharing in the late 1970s.[15] Among the most prominent examples were the plans created by General Motors and Ford with the United Automobile Workers. A survey taken in 1983 indicated that many top company executives expected 'greater emphasis' to be placed on profit-sharing.[16]

Since profit-sharing represents a form of substitute for wage flexibility, the renewed interest by practitioners in profit-sharing would itself justify further exploration of the topic. But in addition there has been an expansion of interest in profit-sharing by academics and policy-makers concerned about macroeconomic performance. Two streams of macroeconomic thought have developed.

(i) The macroeconomics of gain-sharing

Martin L. Weitzman (1983, 1984) has put forward a micro-model of firm behaviour in the labour market with important macro implications. He begins with the standard wage = marginal revenue product condition from the theory of the firm which determines the amount of labour utilised. If the firm operates with a conventional time-based wage, e.g. $10 per hour, and if that wage is – for some reason – relatively rigid, the firm will reduce its labour utilisation (lay off workers) during business downturns. Weitzman argues that the same firm would behave quite differently if it were constrained to offer workers a *share* of revenues or profits rather than a fixed wage.

Suppose, says Weitzman, the firm initially offered a revenue share equivalent in hourly value to the previous wage. Workers and the employer would be no worse off. But employer incentives would be different. As long as the worker share of revenue is less than 100 per cent, the firm would want to hire more workers. In fact it would go on hiring – if it could – until marginal revenue product = zero. The firm would not be able to find workers, however, if its effective hourly payment was too low relative to what other firms were paying. But it would stand ready to hire any qualified worker willing to accept its offer; there would be no 'No Vacancy' signs.

An economy made up of such gain-sharing firms would be

[15] The survey covered only workers under contracts involving 1,000 or more employees. However, there is little reason to suppose that a substantial difference would arise were data for the entire private union sector available. See US Bureau of Labor Statistics, 49.   [16] See William M. Mercer, 7.

composed of labour-seeking vacuum cleaners (an analogy employed by Weitzman (1983) 777) which would suck up any unemployed workers. During business downturns, such firms would tend to remain at full employment (or be willing to do so). The aggregate level of output would thus be much more stable than under the current rigid wage system.

Much of the Weitzman model would remain even if the compensation system at the archetypal employer was a mix of fixed wage and gain sharing (as is the case at most firms with profit-sharing plans). The profit maximising condition for the firm would be to set wage equal to marginal revenue product. But the firm would 'ignore' the gain-sharing element of pay and consider only the fixed wage in the calculation. (The non-effect of gain-sharing on the employment decision is analogous to the non-effect of income taxes on monopolies under the textbook theory of the firm.)

With a wage-plus-gain-sharing system, the effective wage for employment decisions would be lower than the actual payment received by employees. Firms would hire more workers, thus relieving structural unemployment. During business downturns, firms would tend to hang on to their workers, as under pure gain-sharing. However, as the fixed wage-share parameter rises toward 100 per cent of long-run compensation, the beneficial macroeconomic effects are attenuated.

A second strand of macroeconomic argument for increased gain-sharing highlights the interaction between monetary policy and inflation (Mitchell (1982)). Weitzman considers this view to be less important than his micro-based approach, but the former has captured the interest of policy-makers, perhaps because it is easier to understand.[17] Essentially, the argument is that restrictive monetary policy is used primarily to halt 'excessive' inflation and that a rigid wage economy causes such restrictive episodes to be costly in lost real output and unemployment. But if gain-sharing were widespread, the demand restriction would lead to reduced bonus payments. And if these cost reductions were translated into pricing, the monetary authorities would reduce inflation more quickly. They would permit

[17] See, for example, the statements made by Paul Volcker and Henry C. Wallich, chairman and member, respectively, of the Federal Reserve Board in, 'Alternatives to direct pay hikes urged to help moderate inflation', *Daily Labor Report*, 29 December 1983, A8; Henry C. Wallich, 'Why bonuses make sense for unions', *New York Times*, 22 January 1984, Section 3, p. 3.

the economy to resume expanding sooner and the cost in lost output during the restriction would be less.

The two approaches lead to the same policy conclusion, i.e. gain-sharing should be encouraged, although they are not entirely compatible. Under the pure theory of the firm employed by Weitzman, gain-sharing bonuses would not directly affect firm pricing policy. Just as the firm considers the marginal cost of hiring to be the fixed wage (which may be zero) under the Weitzman model, so, too, would it calculate the marginal cost of production without reference to the gain-sharing bonus. Thus price variability arises because supply was constrained by the full-employment labour shortage Weitzman predicts would chronically result. Due to the shortage, demand curves would shift against relatively fixed supply schedules producing price variation. In contrast, the argument involving interaction with monetary policy depends on an (average cost) markup model of pricing.[18]

(ii) The low incidence of gain-sharing

Both of the macro approaches have in common the prediction that gain-sharing will be underutilised in practice because its benefits are external to the firm. All firms would benefit if the economy were more stable, closer to full employment, and less inflationary. But no single firm, by adopting gain-sharing, can make a noticeable contribution to these desirable objectives. Thus employers who adopt such plans do so largely on the basis of their effects on motivation and morale.

At the micro level, then, the explanation of the low incidence of gain-sharing must include reasons why employers do not expect the motivation/morale effects to be large. It must also include reasons why unions have not pushed for gain-sharing until recently, and why policy makers neglected the subject until the 1980s. There are historical and institutional reasons for this lack of interest. They turn out to be much the same reasons that explain the historical loss of wage flexibility.

10. *The Great Depression and its aftermath*

As already noted, modern personnel management practices – includ-

---

[18] Under the Weitzman model, a gain-sharing plan geared to industry (or national) economic conditions would not have the desirable employment stabilising properties he seeks. Under the model featuring interactions with monetary policy, such plans would be useful.

ing those involving wage-setting – became firmly ensconced in American enterprises during the 1930s and in later years. The Great Depression of the 1930s brought together various forces of public policy, economic theory and social expectations. These forces influenced employee attitudes regarding treatment to be expected from employers (Mitchell, 1985a).

One important element was a theory of underconsumption which already existed in the 1920s, but was given credence by the Depression. According to this theory, business depressions resulted from depressed wages. If wages were too low, labour's share of national income would be too low to sustain a full-employment level of consumption.

As might be expected, the underconsumption theory was an important element of labour union ideology (and remains so). But it was also supported by such prominent economists of the day as Paul H. Douglas (67–77) and by political leaders such as President Hoover. Indeed, Hoover urged businesses not to cut wages as the Depression began, an exhortation which seemed to have some effect. Wage cuts did not begin on a wholesale basis until 1931. At least one prominent firm (Ford) *raised* wages in response to the President's statement.[19]

The underconsumption theory seems not to have been carefully analysed by its contemporary proponents. Since the theory is really one of share rather than wage rates, exhortations and policies aimed at propping up wage rates alone seem inappropriate. Labour's share is the product of wage-rate times hours-per-employee times employees. Employers who maintained wage rates but cut hours per employee or who laid off workers were not necessarily maintaining labour's share. Nevertheless progressive employers tended to be seen as those who held up wage rates, avoided layoffs, but cut hours (worksharing) (Jacoby).

Despite these inconsistencies, the underconsumption theory made its way into legislation. Even before the New Deal, laws such as the Davis-Bacon Act of 1931 were adopted to limit downward wage adjustments.[20] But with the coming of the New Deal itself, the underconsumption theory became a basic element of government economic policy.

The centrepiece of the early New Deal was the National Industrial

---

[19] Ford later cut wages as the Depression worsened. See Dickinson, 178.

[20] The Davis-Bacon Act requires that construction contractors who receive funding from the federal government pay 'prevailing' wages as determined by the US Department of Labor. Many states passed similar laws covering state construction contractors.

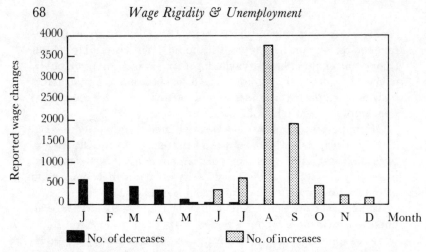

Figure 3. **Manufacturing wage changes, 1933**

Source of data: US Bureau of Labor Statistics, *Employment in Selected Industries,*
various issues. (also known as *Trend in Employment*). See also
Data appendix on pp. 73–74.

Recovery Act of June 1933, legislation premised on the belief that a
boost in wage earners' purchasing power could end the Depression.
(Dearing, 9). Until it was declared unconstitutional in 1935 by the
Supreme Court, the NIRA organised industries into cartel-like
arrangements through the establishment of industry codes. These
government-approved codes included labour provisions which
boosted wage rates and provided guidance for other workplace
practices (Marshall). The codes also provided encouragement to
unions and collective bargaining. Dramatic evidence of the impact of
the codes is shown in Figure 3; despite the depth of the depression, a
spate of wage increases developed as the codes came into force.

Even after the NIRA was abruptly terminated, its spirit lived on in
other legislation and in economic thought (Dickinson, 173–4). The
Wagner Act of 1935 formalised the NIRA's collective-bargaining
provisions and actually contained the underconsumption theory in its
preamble.[21] The Fair Labor Standards Act of 1938 provided for a

[21] Section 1 of the Wagner Act (49 Stat. 449) declares that 'the inequality of
bargaining power between employees who do not possess full freedom of association
. . . and employers . . . tends to aggravate business depressions, by depressing wage rates
and the purchasing power of wage earners . . .'

federal minimum wage. The Social Security Act of 1935 created the state unemployment insurance systems which provide a net subsidy to layoffs rather than wage cuts as a response to falling demand.[22] And, of course, the basic Social Security benefits (and many subsequently established private pension plans) are geared to past earnings. For senior workers unlikely to be laid off, wage cuts during working years could adversely affect retirement income.

The Depression years changed social expectations. 'Good' employers did not cut wages. Wage cutters were seen as harmful to the national economy as well as to their own employees. And wage-cutters were also discouraged by the knowledge that their disgruntled workers might unionise.

Once it became clear that the post-war period would not feature a return to the Great Depression, the business community lost its interest in ability to pay as a criterion for wage setting. Such a criterion could only encourage demands to share in rising profit levels by unions (Slichter, 25–27; Fairchild, 40–46). The idea that ability to pay should not be a matter of special significance in wage setting was also apparently held by neutrals engaged in interest arbitration (Bernstein, 80–90). Pattern bargaining and wage comparisons were seen as much more important.

Profit-sharing was not widely adopted by employers as a substitute for lost wage flexibility. The technique of profit-sharing was well known by the 1930s; a number of prominent employers had experimented with it and studies had been done of the results (Mitchell, 1985a). During the First World War the federal government encouraged works councils in private enterprises to enlist worker cooperation in production. Some of these arrangements also provided for 'collective economy dividend' plans, a form of profit-sharing, and persisted into the 1920s as company unions.

Most employers, however, found profit-sharing difficult to explain to workers and believed that other arrangements were preferable for retaining loyal, non-union workforces. In some cases stock ownership plans were established. These plans were often associated with profit-sharing in the public mind. Thus the dramatic decline in stock prices from 1929 to 1932 undoubtedly harmed the cause of profit-sharing.

Unions had an aversion to profit-sharing which was entrenched by

[22] State unemployment insurance laws typically feature less than full 'experience rating' of employers. Thus employers with high levels of involuntary turnover (and their employees) receive a net subsidy from other sectors.

70 *Wage Rigidity & Unemployment*

the 1930s (National Industrial Conference Board, 15–16). Sometimes paternalistic employers used the name 'profit-sharing' to describe bonuses which were actually unrelated to profits. At Ford, for example, during the First World War period, employees who met company standards of morality – as determined from home visits by Ford investigators – were eligible for bonuses. Employers were also likely to use profit-sharing as part of their union avoidance tactics, a practice which continued into the post-Second World War period (Foulkes, 253; Czarnecki).

But perhaps the greatest handicap for profit-sharing was its variable payments. The essence of the New Deal was stability and security. Firms were to be guaranteed their markets and, in turn, were to provide stable employment and wages to their workers. Unions and collective bargaining were to reinforce their incentives to do so. Even if there were layoffs, stable incomes were to be maintained through employer-financed unemployment insurance. And income in old age was to be guaranteed through Social Security. Although these notions were not fully put into practice, profit-sharing – with its inherent uncertainty and instability – was at odds with the spirit of the times.

The drive for income security continued after the New Deal. In the post-Second World War period, unions began to press for a 'Guaranteed Annual Wage'. Although the precise meaning of this phrase varied, it represented a demand that blue-collar workers should have the same stability of wages and employment that white-collar employees enjoyed.

Employers were unwilling to make such guarantees in the 1950s, but they did negotiate agreements for private supplemental unemployment benefit (SUB) funds. SUB funds paid benefits to laid-off workers above and beyond what they received from state unemployment insurance. They represented, therefore, union acceptance and recognition of the layoff system for adjusting to fluctuations in demand.[23]

---

[23] Before his death, President Roosevelt commissioned a government study of the guaranteed annual wage concept. The resulting study (the 'Lattimer Report') was generally positive about the proposal, although it did not favour government compulsion. Rather it recommended that such plans be considered by the parties to collective bargaining. Included in the report was a study by Paul Samuelson and Alvin Hansen. While indicating that Keynesian fiscal policy was the best way to stabilise the economy, Samuelson and Hansen found that certain types of guaranteed wage plans had desirable, anticyclical macroeconomic policies. These were programs in which funds were set aside in good times to pay supplemental unemployment benefits in bad times. As noted above in the text, such plans were the eventual outcome of the

11. *The past and future of wage rigidity*

Recent theorising about wage rigidity has been healthy for professional economists. It focused attention on a topic which had been neglected and provided new insights. However, there is little reason to expect a unified theory of wage rigidity to emerge from this effort.

Even in a labour market which approached classical theory, there would be *some* costs of mobility to employees – and possibly to employers – due to imperfect information and search costs. Thus there would be some degree of attachment between employee and employer. Wage cuts would not be popular with workers in such a world; if they stayed with their employer, their incomes would be reduced. And if they left, the workers might not immediately find other employment. Even the much-maligned foreman might be reluctant to cut wages, faced with worker resentment. Wage-setting would therefore be less flexible than an auction market. A layoff system would result, thus increasing the costs of labour mobility.

It is not difficult to understand why the focus would be on the nominal wage. First, the availability of reliable, current price statistics did not develop until well after the wage/layoff system was established. Second, the concept of using price indexes to adjust wages – while second nature to economists – is complex for the average person to comprehend. Money is the standard of value, after all. And standards are important for making judgments. Economists do not accuse themselves of irrational 'clock illusion' because they follow official rather than solar time or because they change their waking habits when someone announces a shift from daylight to standard time. The same courtesy should be extended to actors in the labour market.

Finally, a nominal wage cut is *always* a real wage cut, regardless of what prices are doing, in a decentralised wage and price setting system. If prices fall by 10 per cent and your wage falls by 5 per cent, you are still 5 per cent worse off than you would have been if your wage had not been cut at all!

Some of the theories described above, such as Okun's career labour markets, open the door to a strong influence of social concepts of fairness and equity. Thus there is nothing in the institutional and historical analysis of wage rigidity that need fly in the face of economic

---

guaranteed annual wage debate. (US Office of Temporary Controls, especially 10–18 412–73).

theory. If the Great Depression had never occurred, if certain government policies had not been adopted, notions of fairness might be different. Wages might be more flexible. Since history and institutional development vary across countries, there will be differences in national wage setting practices and outcomes.

But what of the future? The significance of the dramatic union wage concession movement in the US which occurred in the early 1980s has been much debated. Does concession bargaining mark a turning point in American wage setting, heralding a new age of wage flexibility? Or is it a temporary phenomenon associated with a deep recession, dollar appreciation and international competition, and de-regulation of certain sectors?

So far the evidence is mixed. The union sector of the workforce shrank in the early 1980s, a factor which might lead to a marginal increase in wage flexibility. Within the union sector, profit-sharing was adopted in some key contracts, notably in autos. Bonuses began to be substituted for guaranteed wage increases. Union leaders showed more concern about the economic conditions of the employers with which they dealt, and even demanded a greater voice in management.

On the other hand, the long duration union contract remained intact. Non-union workers, who account for roughly 8 out of 10 private wage and salary earners in the US, seemed to be much less affected by wage freezes and cuts than their unionised counterparts. There is little evidence (one way or the other) that non-union wage-setting practices have been altered by the experience of the early 1980s. And even though wage freezes and cuts covered an unprecedented proportion of union workers, many union members did not experience concession bargaining.

If increased wage flexibility, either directly or through gain-sharing, is deemed desirable for macroeconomic reasons, the historical evidence indicates that reforms can be made. In the 1930s wage flexibility (at least in a downward direction) was deemed undesirable. Public policies were adopted which shifted wage-setting practices. The concession bargaining movement in the early 1980s suggests that a window of opportunity is open for encouraging a reverse shift, through such devices as tax incentives for gain-sharing.

Data appendix

Data for Figure 1

	Full Period	Except 1974,79,80
CPI	3.32	2.10
CPIA	2.42	1.79
PPI	4.78	3.07
PPIK	5.03	2.47
HEI	1.37	1.18

Data for Figure 2

	Proportion of Wage Decisions in each Bracket	
	1924	1925
− 20% or less	2.4%	1.1%
− 19·9 to − 18%	·1	·1
− 17·9 to − 16%	·3	·1
− 15·9 to − 14%	1·4	·5
− 13·9 to − 12%	2·9	1·0
− 11·9 to − 10%	20·8	10·7
− 9·9 to − 8%	16·2	7·2
− 7·9 to − 6%	5·4	3·5
− 5·9 to − 4%	2·7	2·1
− 3·9 to − 2%	3·0	3·1
− 1·9 to − ·1%	1·4	·3
·1 to 2%	1·5	4·7
2·1 to 4%	2·1	5·9
4·1 to 6%	8·9	13·2
6·1 to 8%	12·1	13·2
8·1 to 10%	12·3	21·9
10·1 to 12%	1·3	2·9
12·1 to 14%	1·5	2·1
14·1 to 16%	·9	2·2
16·1 to 18%	·9	·5
18·1 to 20%	1·3	1·8
Over 20%	·5	1·8

74 *Wage Rigidity & Unemployment*

Data for Figure 3

Month	No of decreases	No of increases
1	595	3
2	552	3
3	467	1
4	370	6
5	129	48
6	58	350
7	38	630
8	2	3776
9	5	1937
10	5	468
11	15	247
12	21	174

References

Abraham, K.G. and Medoff, J.L., 'Length of service and the operation of internal labor markets', in Dennis, B.D. (ed.), *Proceedings of the Thirty-Fifth Annual Meeting*, Industrial Relations Research Association, December 28–30, 1982 (Madison, Wisc.: IRRA, 1983), 308–318.

Ackley, G., *Macroeconomic Theory* (New York: Macmillan, 1961).

Akerlof, G.A., and Main, B.G.M., 'An experience-weighted measure of employment and unemployment durations,' *American Economic Review* 71 (December 1981), 1003–1011.

Ashenfelter, O., and Johnson, G.E., 'Bargaining theory, trade unions and industrial strike activity', *American Economic Review* 59 (March 1969), 35–49.

Bernstein, I., *Arbitration of Wages* (Berkeley and Los Angeles: University of California Press, 1954).

Bureau of National Affairs, Inc., *Productivity Improvement Programs*, PPF Survey No. 138 (Washington: BNA, 1984).

Cartter, A.M., *Theory of Wages and Employment* (Homewood, Ill.: Irwin, 1959).

Chapman, P.G., and Fisher, M.R., 'Union wage policies: comment', *American Economic Review* 74 (September 1984), 755–761.

Czarnecki, E.R., 'Profit-sharing and union organizing', *Monthly Labor Review* 92 (December 1969), 61–62.

Dearing, C.L., et al, *The ABC of the NRA* (Washington: Brookings Institution, 1934).

Dickinson, Z.C., *Compensating Industrial Effort: A Scientific Study of Work and Wages* (New York: Ronald Press, 1937).

Douglas, P.H., *Controlling Depressions* (New York: W.W. Norton, 1935).

Doeringer, P.B., and Piore, M.J., *Internal Labor Markets and Manpower Analysis* (Lexington, Mass.: Heath, 1971).

Fairchild, F.R., *Profits and the Ability to Pay Wages* (Irvington-on-Hudson, N.Y.: Foundation for Economic Education, 1946).

Farber, H.S., 'Bargaining theory, wage outcomes, and the occurrence of strikes: an econometric analysis', *American Economic Review* 68 (June 1978), 262–271.

Foulkes, F.K., *Personnel Policies in Large Non-Union Companies* (Englewood Cliffs, N.J.: Prentice-Hall, 1980).

Freeman, R.B., and Medoff, J.L., *What Do Unions Do?* (New York: Basic Books, 1984).

Gordon, R.J., 'A century of evidence on wage and price stickiness in the United States, the United Kingdom, and Japan', in Tobin, J. (ed.), *Macroeconomics, Prices, and Quantities: Essays in Memory of Arthur M. Okun* (Washington: Brookings Institution, 1983), 85–121.

Grubb, D., Jackman, R., and Layard, R., 'Wage rigidity and unemployment in OECD countries', *European Economic Review* 21 (March/April 1983), 11–39.

Hall, R.E., 'The importance of lifetime jobs in the US economy', *American Economic Review* 72 (September 1982), 716–724.

Haltiwanger, J.C., 'On the relationship between risk aversion and the development of long-term worker-firm attachments', *Southern Economic Journal* 50 (October 1983), 572–577.

Jacoby, S.N., *Employing Bureaucracy: Managers, Unions, and the Transformation of Work in American Industry* (New York: Columbia University Press, 1985).

Jacoby, S.M., and Mitchell, D.J.B., 'Does implicit contracting explain explicit contracting?' in Dennis, B.D. (ed.), *Proceedings of the Thirty-Fifth Annual Meeting*, Industrial Relations Research Association, December 28–30, 1982 (Madison, Wisc.: IRRA, 1983), 319–328.

——, 'Employer preferences for long-term union contracts', *Journal of Labor Research* 5 (Summer 1984), 215–228.

Kaufman, B.E., 'Bargaining theory, inflation, and cyclical strike activity in manufacturing', *Industrial and Labor Relations Review* 34 (April 1981), 333–355.

Keynes, J.M., *The General Theory of Employment, Interest, and Money* (New York: Harcourt, Brace & World, 1936).

Lazear, E.P., 'Agency, earnings profiles, productivity, and hours restrictions', *American Economic Review*, 71 (June 1981), 606–620.

Marshall, L.C., *Hours and Wage Provisions in NRA Codes* (Washington: Brookings Institution, 1935).

McDonald, I.M., and Solow, R.M., 'Wage bargaining and employment', *American Economic Review* 71 (December 1981), 896–908.

Medoff, J.L., 'Layoffs and alternatives under trade unions in US manufacturing, *American Economic Review* 69 (June 1979), 380–295.

Mitchell, D.J.B., 'Gain-sharing: an anti-inflation reform', *Challenge* 25 (July-August 1982), 18–25.

——, 'Union wage determination: policy implications and outlook', *Brookings Papers on Economic Activity* 3 (1978), 537–582.

——, *Unions, Wages, and Inflation* (Washington: Brookings Institution, 1980).

——, 'Wage flexibility in the US: lessons from the past', *American Economic Review*, Papers and Proceedings, 75 (May 1985a), 36–40.

——, 'Wage flexibility: then and now', *Industrial Relations* (1985b).

National Industrial Conference Board, *Profit-sharing and other supplementary-compensation plans covering wage earners*, Studies in Personnel Policy, 2 (New York: NICB, 1937).

Nordhaus, W.D., 'The worldwide wage explosion', *Brookings Papers on Economic Activity* 2 (1972), 431–464.

Okun, A.M., *Prices and Quantities: A Macroeconomic Analysis* (Washington: Brookings Institution, 1981).

Phillips, A.W., 'The relation between unemployment and the rate of change of money wage rates in the United Kingdom, 1861–1957', *Economica* 25 (November 1958), 283–299.

Pigou, A.C., *Employment and Equilibrium: A Theoretical Discussion* (London: Macmillan, 1941).

Rees, A., 'Industrial conflict and business fluctuations', *Journal of Political Economy* 60 (October 1952), 371–382.

Riordan, M.H., and Wachter, M.L., 'What do implicit contracts do?' in Dennis, B.D., (ed.), *Proceedings of the Thirty-Fifth Annual Meeting*, Industrial Relations Research Association, December 28–30, 1982 (Madison, Wisc.: IRRA, 1983), 291–298.

Ross, A.M., 'Do we have a new industrial feudalism?', *American Economic Review* 48 (December 1958), 903–920.

Sachs, J.D., 'Wages, profits, and macroeconomic adjustment: a comparative study', *Brookings Papers on Economic Activity* 2 (1979), 269–319.

Shapiro, C., and Stiglitz, J.E., 'Equilibrium unemployment as a worker discipline device,' *American Economic Review*, 74 (June 1984), 433–444.

Slichter, S.H., *Basic Criteria Used in Wage Negotiations* (Chicago: Chicago Association of Commerce and Industry, 1947).

Solow, R.M., 'Arthur Okun's last work', *The Public Interest* (Fall 1981), 91–102.

Stiglitz, J.E., 'Theories of wage rigidity', Working Paper No. 1442, National Bureau of Economic Research, September 1984.

Taylor, J.B., 'Union wage settlements during a disinflation', *American Economic Review* 73 (December 1983), 981–993.

US Bureau of Labor Statistics, *Characteristics of Major Collective Bargaining Agreements*, 1 January, 1980, bulletin 2095 (Washington: GPO, 1981).

US Office of Temporary Controls, *Guaranteed Wages: Report to the President by the Advisory Board* (Washington: GPO, 1947).

Wachter, M.L., 'Primary and secondary labor markets: a critique of the dual approach', *Brookings Papers on Economic Activity* 3 (1974), 637–680.

Weitzman, M.L., *The Share Economy: Conquering Inflation* (Cambridge, Mass.: Harvard University Press, 1984).

Weitzman, M.L., 'Some macroeconomic implications of alternative compensation systems', *Economic Journal* 93 (December 1983), 763–783.

Welch, F., and Topel, R.H., 'Self-insurance and efficient employment contracts', unpublished working paper presented to Labor Economics Workshop, University of California, Los Angeles, October 25, 1983.

4. Is Wage Rigidity Caused by 'Lay-offs by Seniority'?*

Andrew J. Oswald

1. Introduction

It seems to be rather widely believed that wage rates are 'rigid' or 'sticky'. This view probably stems from two observations about the world. The first is that real wage rates are much less variable than employment and unemployment levels; the second is that there exist workers who claim to be involuntarily unemployed. If one accepts these propositions – it is possible to dispute both – one is then required to explain the inflexibility of the price of labour. That has not proved to be an especially easy task.

This paper attempts to make precise, and to assess, a theory of wage rigidity which was proposed many years ago and which continues to be propounded today. Despite its rather striking appeal, the theory has rarely been written down in a formal way, has apparently never been tested and is only now becoming quite widely known. It is based on the idea that, because lay-offs and redundancies are normally made by inverse seniority within the firm, wage rates will not fall in a recession. Because the theory has been lucidly proposed by others, it may be best to quote directly from their work.[1]

In 'The theory of union wage rigidity', published in the *Quarterly Journal of Economics* in 1943, Joseph Shishter suggested the following argument.

* I am grateful to Daniel Mitchell and others at the symposium for helpful suggestions, and to Peter Turnbull who kindly helped me to compile some of the data used in Figure 4. I am grateful to ESRC for financing this research assistance as part of an award to the Centre for Labour Economics, LSE.

[1] To the best of my knowledge I am not here setting up a straw man with which the cited authors would disagree. But two facts ought to be recorded. First, Gene Grossman's model does not predict that wages will be wholly rigid. Second, Daniel Mitchell took the view at the symposium that it was to be expected that lay-offs by seniority would not cause wage rigidity; but I was not able to understand how this could be compatible with his earlier view in the 1978 *Brookings Papers* article.

If the employed members in a given organisation constitute a majority, it can well happen that the employed will pursue a wage policy which increases their income at the expense of the unemployed in the union (fn.: This assumes, of course, that lay-offs are based on seniority) . . . . Although a wage reduction would increase the employment opportunities of the furloughed workers, as well as increase the income of the membership as a whole, it would definitely reduce the income of those who had been employed all along. It would thus be disadvantageous to the majority to accept a wage reduction under these circumstances.

Some labour economists have recently taken an identical approach:

> Protected by seniority arrangements from lay-offs during moderate cyclical fluctuations, the median union voter recognises a fixed wage policy for what it is – a fixed (nominal) income policy for all but the least senior workers.

> With job security well protected by seniority arrangements, the median union voter has little incentive to accept a compensation scheme that offers a less certain income . . .
>
> Flanagan (1984)

> Unless the median voter's job is threatened, concessions would simply produce income reductions for the majority in exchange for extra employment for the minority . . . Thus unless there are imminent threats of bankruptcy or permanent plant closings – crisis situations that threaten senior workers – it is unlikely that union wage behaviour will be strongly sensitive to recessions.
>
> Mitchell (1982)

Exactly the same idea can be found in a new textbook by Begg, Dornbusch and Fischer (1984), and in a less extreme form in a paper by Grossman (1983).

An obvious way to attack this argument would be by showing that what the Americans call 'lay-offs by seniority', and the British refer to as 'last in, first out', is actually rare. However, some months of work by a joint LSE-Oxford team have recently been put into a study of the principal features of American and British labour contracts, and the results suggest that lay-offs by seniority are dominant in both countries. The evidence for the US is documented in Oswald (1984), for example, and for Great Britain in Oswald and Turnbull (1985). The seniority lay-off system is the most widely used method for deciding who will lose jobs in a down-turn, and it is to be found in the non-union sector and the union sector. The institution of lay-offs by seniority is apparently ubiquitous.[2]

One purpose of this paper is to argue that the seniority explanation of wage rigidity is not wholly convincing. This is done by a formal argument; but it is the intuition which matters, and that can be put quite briefly. If senior workers are risk-averse, they will find it in their own interest to share risk with a risk-averse employer. It will pay them to say to their firm 'We are willing to take wage cuts when times are hard, but in return you must offer us a much higher average income over the trade cycle'. The firm's welfare will then improve, because in a slump the workers are willing to accept less, and in a boom the firm is (reasonably) happy to part with some of its profits. This is why the seniority argument of Shishter, *among others*, is unconvincing. Why is it that the senior employees do not use wage cuts in a downturn as a way of securing an agreement in which there are large wage rises in a boom? No satisfactory answer has been given.

One might think that the assumption that the firm is risk-neutral would rescue the argument. Baily (1974) and Azariadis (1975), for example, produce a model of sticky wages in this way.[3] With lay-offs by seniority, however, this does not work. Even with a linear utility function defined on profits (the requirement for a firm to be risk-neutral), the firm's maximum profit function is in general a non-linear and convex function of the wage. This is irrelevant in conventional contract theory. With lay-offs by seniority, however, the union is indifferent about employment, so that in an efficient bargain the level of jobs will be set unilaterally by the employer. Then profits are non-linear in the variable (the wage rate) over which the bargain is to be struck. That is what destroys the wage rigidity proposition of conventional contract theory.

2. *A look at the stylised facts*

Although there has been much written on the theory of wage rigidity,

<hr/>

[2] The 1982 US contract between General Motors and the UAW, for example, states: 'employees shall be laid off and re-hired in accordance with local seniority agreements.' The British agreement between the London Brick Company and its trade unions, for example, says: 'where selection for redundancy is necessary employees will be selected on the principle of 'last in – first out' within the work groups affected always provided that the Company retains a viable and effective work force.'

[3] They assume that lay-offs are made randomly across the workforce. There is no evidence that any British or American contracts are like this.

Wage Rigidity & Unemployment

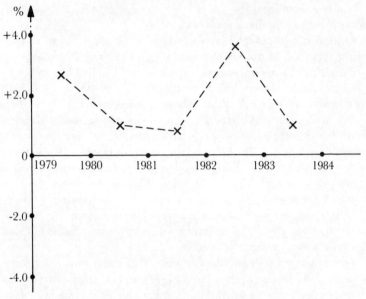

Figures for 'whole economy'. Source: *Economic Trends*

Figure 1. Real earnings changes: Britain 1979–1984

empirical evidence is presented rather less often. There may be some point, therefore, in beginning by a look at the stylised facts. The figures are restricted to those for the British economy. They may not be representative of other economies.[4]

From 1979 to 1984 the level of unemployment in Britain rose from 1.3 million to 3.2 million. By the middle of this decade, one in eight of the workforce were unemployed. Figure 3 plots the data. A natural question to ask is whether there was any comparable fluctuation in real wage rates. In a sense the case of the British economy over this period is akin to a laboratory experiment of extreme economic conditions. Did real wages fall as excess supply[5] in the labour market grew so dramatically?

There are two ways to measure pay levels. Figure 1 depicts changes in real earnings; Figure 2 sets out the equivalent for wage rates. In both

[4] As far as I know, US real wage rates are rather more flexible.
[5] Of course the natural rate of unemployment may have tripled, in which case there would not be excess supply. Yet this seems too extreme.

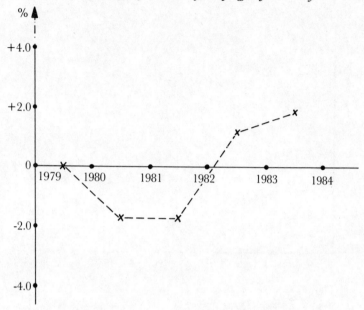

Figures for manual workers, all industries.

Source: *Economic Trends*

Figure 2. Real wage changes: Britain 1979–1984

diagrams the real changes are calculated by subtracting from the nominal changes the percentage rise in the retail price index. There is certainly little indication from these data that real wage rates and earnings are sensitive to large quantities of unemployment. This is not at all rigorous, of course, because the figures are inevitably the product of a complicated world in which many variables changed at once. Nevertheless unemployment over these few years moved so markedly, by historical standards, that the raw data themselves may be instructive. Two particular points seem worth noting. First, the earnings statistics show no falls in real pay, whereas the wage data do. This difference – between wage rates and incomes – may be important. Second, if any hint of wage flexibility is to be found, it seems to occur in the years 1980–1982, which was the time when unemploy-

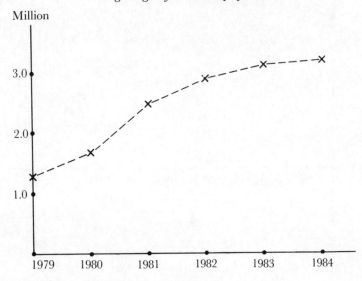

Figures exclude school-leavers.

Source: *Economic Trends*

Figure 3. Unemployment in Britain: 1979–1984

ment *grew* most sharply.[6] By 1984, however, despite an astonishingly large amount of joblessness, real pay was growing noticeably.

There is good reason to be sceptical of inferences drawn from aggregate data. Composition effects, in particular, can bias figures on national wage rates; the reason is that low-paid workers tend to be sacked before the high-paid. Hence it could still be the case, no matter what Figures 1 and 2 apparently reveal, that the real wage in particular establishments and firms was reduced by the British economy's recession.

This is fairly easily to check. The adjoining table summarises real wage changes for a selection of occupations and employers. These microeconomic data, recording actual wage settlements, are drawn from published booklets prepared by a commercial company, *Incomes Data Services*, which sells information to employers. Only a sample can be printed here. Although there was no conscious bias in the choice of

---

[6] It would be interesting to test the hypothesis that it is *rises* in unemployment, not large amounts of unemployment, which reduce real pay.

Some microeconomic data on real wage changes (%)

Occupation	(Employer)	79/80	80/81	81/82	82/83	83/84
Sales						
Assistant	(Woolworths)	0*	+0·3	−2·0	−0·6	+2·8
Clerk	(Albright &					
	Wilson)	−1·0	−4·6	+6·7	+3·1	+0·7
Cleaner	(Boots)	−5·2	+1·1	−1·4	+1·6	+1·8
Cashier	(Burtons)	−4·5	−4·9	−0·7	+3·9	+2·5
Cleaner	(BHS)	−1·3	−2·4	+1·8	+1·7	+2·4
Typist	(BICC)	−2·0	−3·4	−0·4	+2·8	+2·4
Sales						
Assistant	(Littlewoods)	−1·0	−2·5	−1·1	+0·7	+4·0
Cleaner	(Imperial					
	Tobacco)	+2·0	+9·6	+3·4	+4·6	+4·0
Cook	(Imperial					
	Tobacco)	+2·0	+8·6	+2·1	+3·7	n.a.
Labourer	(Scottish &					
	Newcastle					
	Breweries)	−0·1	−4·9	−5·9	+6·8	+18·0
Canteen	(Shulton					
Worker	GB)	−3·5	−2·9	+0·4	+2·5	+2·0

*This is my estimate. There was a 15-month pay deal.
Source: Own calculations from *Incomes Data Services* material
n.a = not available

these figures, it should be remembered that they were not picked in a scientifically objective way.[7]

All the figures are for relatively unskilled, poorly paid jobs. This is because one might expect that wage flexibility would be most obvious in labour markets in which competitive pressures are strongest. When British unemployment exceeds three million,[8] there are presumably many unemployed workers who could act, without training or significant employer expense, as cleaners, sales assistants, canteen workers and the like. Thus it is in this category that excess supply should operate most obviously. Yet, as for the aggregate data, the statistics in the table provide little evidence for the hypothesis that high aggregate unemployment significantly reduces real wage rates.

[7] The figures ignore changes in hours of work. In some cases they were reduced over this period.
[8] Aggregate employment fell by 2 million over the period.

3. *The seniority theory of wage rigidity*

The previous section's microeconomic and macroeconomic data suggest (for Britain) that real wages change rather little in the face of large movements in unemployment. Is this something to do with the fact that senior workers are insulated – by the 'last in, first out' convention – from the threat of redundancy? An obvious way to tackle this problem is to write down a formal model and to test it by normal methods. Only the former will be attempted here.

Imagine a labour market in which a group of employees (it will be convenient to call them a trade union, but the story does not depend on that) face a single firm. Assume that both the firm and the union are risk-averse, that there is uncertainty about the product price at which the firm will be able to sell in the next period, and that a wage 'contract' of some kind must be agreed in the present period. Assume that there is no chance here that the employer will want to sack the majority of its workforce. The interesting question, now, is whether the union and firm will wish to set a wage that is rigid.

The answer is that, except in a very special case, the efficient contract will not be one in which the wage rate is insensitive to demand pressure. The reason is straightforward enough: it pays the firm and the union to share the profits and the risk. If the union is dominated by senior members, who will not lose their jobs (because of 'last in, first out'), we can think of that agent's utility as being simply the utility function of the typical senior worker. The firm, correspondingly, might be thought of as having a utility function defined on profits. Hence we might write something like

$$Eu(w) \qquad \text{Union's expected utility}$$
$$Ev(\pi) \qquad \text{Firm's expected utility}$$

where E denotes expectation, $u(w)$ is a concave utility function defined on the wage, and $v(\pi)$ is a concave utility function defined on profits.[9] It is then possible to show (the details are in Appendix 1) that the efficient bargain, namely an outcome of the kind we would expect two rational parties to fix, takes the form that the employees' pay will vary with how well the firm is doing in its product market. The wage is not rigid. If it were, the firm would get good profits in a boom and large losses in a slump, while the senior workers were left untouched by all

---

[9] In exceptional cases even the dominant senior workers may lose their jobs. In these circumstances we would expect to see the contract renegotiated.

economic fluctuations. Both sides could then become better off by sharing the risk. The firm would be willing to provide the union's workers with higher average wage rates, and higher expected utility, if the union were willing to agree on a contract in which it suffered slightly in bad times. This would be to their mutual advantage.

When both agents are risk-averse, therefore, a model built on the assumption that lay-offs are by seniority does not, in general, predict that wages will be rigid over the cycle. The literature (Shishter (1946), Mitchell (1982), Flanagan (1984) among others), may well be misleading.

This is not quite the end of the matter. Appendix 1 proves that, in the kind of world described above, the optimal wage will be completely inflexible if the following condition holds:

$$\rho = (1-s)\ \varepsilon$$

where

ρ = the firm's relative risk aversion $(-\dfrac{v''}{v'}\pi)$

s = the share of labour costs in the firm's total revenue

ε = the labour demand elasticity.

It is important to stress that this would only occur by chance; there is no mechanism to bring it about. Nevertheless some may see this as a reasonable way to generate wage inflexibility in a model.[10]

What if the firm is risk-neutral? Though it will surprise those familiar with implicit contract theory, the optimal wage is still not rigid. When there are lay-offs by seniority the famous fixed wage result of Baily (1974) and Azariadis (1975) no longer holds. Baily's assertion, at the end of his *Review of Economic Studies* paper, that lay-offs by seniority could only strengthen his theoretical predictions is thus wrong.[11] Remarkably, in fact, in this framework a union and risk-neutral firm will agree on a contract in which the wage declines when product prices increase. The intuitive explanation is that this is what increases the variability of the employer's profit stream most effectively. As prices rise, or as wages fall, profits increase. Because the employer can substitute in and out of labour as it wishes,[12] its average

[10] My own view is that models in which by fluke the wage is rigid are not the most satisfying. In fact McDonald and Solow (1981) is also of this general type.

[11] Introducing 'lay-offs by seniority' into an otherwise conventional implicit contract model actually destroys the famous wage rigidity results. The proof is in Appendix 1.

[12] The maximum profit function is convex, in other words.

profits are highest when prices and wages are varying a great deal. Hence a risk-neutral firm sets wage rates to fall in a boom and to rise in a slump.

4. *A suggestion*

For the reasons outlined above, it is not clear that the institution of lay-offs by seniority is likely to be the cause of the apparently inflexible wage rates in the world. The institution is almost certainly important in other ways, but my own view is that we need to look elsewhere for a theory of wage rigidity.

Psychologists have for decades been doing experiments on the effects of pay on productivity and satisfaction. Argyle (1972) and Ribeaux and Poppleton (1978) give textbook treatments, and Adams and Rosenbaum (1962), Adams (1963), Andrews (1967), Lawler (1968), Pritchard, Dunnette and Jorgensen (1972) and Taylor (1982) describe some of the experiments. Runciman (1966) and Vroom (1964) are also relevant and widely cited. There seem to be two ideas of real importance to the way we construct microeconomic models of the labour market.

1. Utility is thought to depend on the gap between achievements and aspirations, and there is experimental evidence that there is an asymmetry between responses to 'over-pay' and 'under-pay'.
2. The *aspiration wage*, which is the level of pay which is seen as the 'fair' amount or the 'norm', is believed to depend on past achievements and experiences.

The work of psychologists is not often used by economists, but in this case it provides us with a new way to think about the utility function of an individual worker.

Say we imagine w^* to be the wage to which an employee aspires, and take w to be the actual wage. Assume that a single unit of labour is supplied by the worker (this is inessential). If utility functions are smooth, we are not readily going to manage to construct a theory of wage rigidity, because $u(w,w^*)$ can easily be used in otherwise normal contract models. Making w^* a function of past wage rates then just complicates the mathematics. But say the utility function of an employee is like that in Figure 4, where there is a kink at w^*. This is not hopelessly unconventional, it is worth pointing out, because $u(w,w^*)$ is still an increasing, concave function of pay. The implications of this

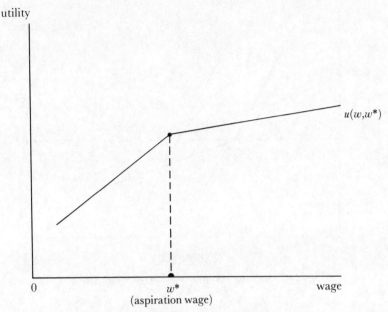

Figure 4. An individual's utility function

form – one apparently favoured by the psychologists – are intriguing. If aspirations have adapted, so that w^* is the same as the current wage (that fixed in the previous period), the equilibrium wage in all sorts of otherwise conventional labour-market models will be rigid. The reason is that the marginal utility of income is discontinuous, and this idea obviously has something in common with Duesenberry (1962) and Hahn (1982).[13]

Two models will be sketched here. One is for unionised markets, the other a version of the efficiency wage hypothesis for non-union markets. Take the McDonald and Solow (1981) model as an example of the first. The union's utility function there, which is defined on both wages and jobs, will have kinks in it at $w = w^*$. It is still quasi-concave, but now the indifference curves take the kinked form represented in Figure 5. The union's indifference curves are I_0, I_1; the firm's initial iso-profit contour is π_0. It follows immediately that the wage will be rigid,

---

[13] Frank Hahn drew my attention privately to this point, and I am grateful. Hahn's model assumes that w^* depends on the wage of other workers and is an attempt to capture Keynes' idea that relativities matter.

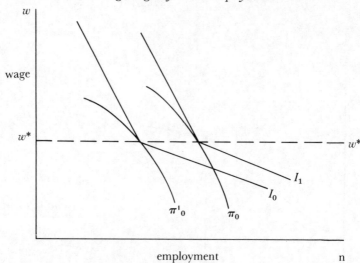

Figure 5. A trade union model with wage rigidity

for small and medium demand shocks, so that a shift from π_0 to π'_0 produces only an employment change. Large shocks, however, will change the wage. Appendix 2 gives more details.

The second model does not require that there be a trade union. Efficiency wage models (Yellen (1984) summarises the literature) postulate that the productivity of a worker will depend upon his wage. Good pay raises morale and hence productivity; poor pay lowers both. This means – applying the asymmetry found in experiments – that the marginal benefit to the firm from increasing their workers' wages is discontinuous at w^*, the level seen as the just reward for the job. The marginal cost is constant throughout (it is unity when measured on the same scale as pay). Hence an equilibrium can be represented as in Figure 6. The firm is assumed to maximise a function

$$\pi = pq(w,w^*) - w,$$

which measures profits at an output price p. Employment is fixed at unity (it is clear that the main idea will go through without this), and $q(w,w^*)$ is a productivity function which is taken to be kinked at $w = w^*$, and increasing in w but decreasing in w^*. Let $B(w,w^*)$ in Figure 6 be the marginal benefit function of the firm, which is given by

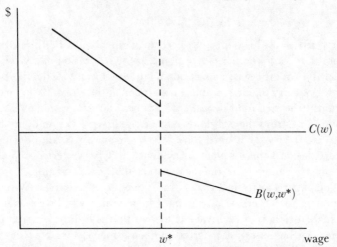

Figure 6. An efficiency wage model with wage rigidity

pq_w wherever the π function is differentiable, and let $C(w)$ be the marginal cost function, which is horizontal in this particular case.

The efficiency wage equilibrium is at $w = w^*$. A small rise (fall) in product price p will raise (reduce) the B schedule but leave the optimal wage unchanged. Wages are rigid unless there is a large demand shock.

The central idea in this section does not have to be written down in equations or diagrams. Ask yourself how you would feel if your real wage was cut, very slightly but unexpectedly, after you had got used to living at the previous standard of living. Would your utility fall only marginally, namely by the amount it would rise if instead you were given a small increase in income (this ignores concavity, but that cannot matter locally)? That does not seem to me likely. Human beings get used to their standard of living.

Wage rigidity exists here for two reasons. First, the aspiration wage adapts to previous experience. This ensures that equilibria are close to the w^* kinks. Second, wage reductions from the aspiration level of pay produce 'large' falls in utility. This non-differentiability of the utility (or individual's productivity) function ensures that small falls in demand do not trigger off small cuts in wage rates. It is this idea that seems to have some potential. Notice, however, that nothing has been said here to explain why it is all right for a firm to sack workers altogether. This presumably lowers their utility a great deal.

5. Conclusion

The purpose of this paper has been to argue against the literature's claim that wage rigidity is a response to the institution of lay-offs by seniority. An otherwise conventional labour contract model has been used. Contrary to, for example, an assertion at the end of Baily's justly famous 1974 *Review of Economic Studies* paper, the assumption of 'last in, first out' destroys the well-known wage rigidity prediction of implicit contract theory. It is hard to see this as a mere wrinkle on an old theory, because there is plenty of evidence that, in Western economies, lay-offs by seniority are the norm rather than the exception.

The paper's analytical result can be explained intuitively. When a slump occurs, there is a way in which senior employees can be persuaded to accept real wage cuts, and that is if they are promised large wage increases – as deferred compensation, as it were – when the boom finally comes. The literature's main and repeated notion, that senior workers have secure jobs and will therefore refuse cuts in pay in bad times, is misleadingly short-run in its thinking.

What is it, then, that explains the apparent inflexibility of real wage rates? This paper has suggested that it may be the fact that utility functions are kinked at the equilibrium (or 'aspiration') wage. This is just a way of saying that if my real wage is cut by one per cent I feel *very* badly treated, whereas if my pay is raised by that amount I do not care much. This idea – for which there is experimental evidence in the psychology literature – has not been tackled in a fully satisfactory way here, but it may be worth pursuing. Perhaps it will even have to be combined with the realistic assumption that workers are sacked in inverse order of seniority.

Appendix 1

Assume that the trade union is made up of many members each of whom has the concave utility function $u(w)$ where w is the wage rate. Workers each supply one unit of labour. Let the firm's utility function be $v(\pi)$, where π is profit. Assume that $v(.)$ is concave (risk neutrality is where that is only true weakly). Let product price be p, and assume that it is an uncertain variable with density function $g(p)$.

It simplifies the mathematics if we concentrate on demand fluctuations (that is, product price changes) which never require that half the labour force be laid off. Then the typical senior worker has expected utility

$$U = \int u(w)g(p)dp, \tag{1}$$

which, because (i) the majority will have exactly these preferences and (ii) we assume majority voting, we can think of as the trade union's utility function. The equivalent function for the firm is

$$V = \int v(\pi)g(p)dp. \tag{2}$$

It is natural to follow implicit contract theory and to assume that there is a single factor input. Then

$$\pi = pf(n) - wn. \tag{3}$$

The problem is now entirely conventional except that the labour group's utility function does not assume unemployment by random draw. An efficient contract solves the problem

Maximise $\int u(w)g(p)dp$ (4)
$w(p),n(p)$

subject to $\int v(pf(\mathrm{n}) - wn)g(p)dp \geq \bar{v},$ (5)

where $\bar{v}$ is a constant. One interpretation of $\bar{v}$ is that it is the going return for entrepreneurs, so that the union knows that the firm will collapse if profits are driven any lower. But the mathematics applies in other cases, because any efficient point will be characterised by the same first-order condition.

We can take a short-cut by noticing that employment does not enter this union's utility function. Hence it will be rational for the firm to be given the power to set employment unilaterally – something which apparently squares with reality. Then, because efficient contracts are necessarily on the labour demand curve, and not above it as normal implicit contract theory suggests, we can use the maximum value function

$$v(w,p) = \max_n v(pf(n) - wn). \tag{6}$$

The maximisation, solving for the optimal contract, then becomes

Maximise $\int u(w)g(p)dp$ (7)
$w(p)$

subject to $\int v(w,p)g(p)dp \geq \bar{v},$ (8)

with a first-order condition (this ignores corners, assumes differentiability, and so on)

$$u'(w) + \lambda v_w(w,p) = 0, \tag{9}$$

where $\lambda \geq 0$ is a multiplier, which is independent of p because the constraint is an isoperimetric one.

Equation (9) shows us that the wage will not normally be independent of product prices. It is quite different from that for conventional implicit contract theory, where $u'(w) - \lambda = 0$. Differentiating in equation (9),

$$[u''(w) + \lambda v_{ww}(w,p)]dw + \lambda v_{wp}(w,p)dp = 0. \tag{10}$$

As long as the second-order condition holds, we can sign the terms in square brackets as negative. But v_{wp} may be positive or negative. A perfectly rigid wage rate requires that $v_{wp}=0$, which is a very special case.

Equation (9) can be rewritten as

$$u'(w) - \lambda v'(\pi)n = 0. \tag{11}$$

Define the elasticity of labour demand as

$$\varepsilon \equiv -n_w(w/n) = -f'(n)/(f''(n)n), \tag{12}$$

labour's share in revenue as

$$s \equiv wn/(pf(n)), \tag{13}$$

and the firm's relative risk aversion as

$$\rho \equiv -\pi v''(\pi)/v'(\pi). \tag{14}$$

Then, by differentiating the first-order condition, we find eventually that

$$\frac{dw}{dp} \gtrless 0 \ as \ \rho \gtrless (1-s)\varepsilon. \tag{15}$$

This establishes that lay-offs by seniority will generate wage rigidity only in one special case.

Appendix 2

A simple way to specify trade union preferences is to write union utility as McDonald and Solow (1981) do:

$$U = \frac{n}{m}u\,(w) + \left(1 - \frac{n}{m}\right)u\,(b),\tag{16}$$

where n is employment, m is membership, $u(w)$ is the utility from working at wage w, and $u(b)$ is the utility from being unemployed on income b (which we might think of as unemployment benefit). The difficulty with this is that it is based on the assumption that lay-offs are by random draw. That does not fit the facts. An alternative form, with the same mathematical properties, is that of utilitarianism (Oswald (1982), for example), which we can represent by the function

$$U = nu(w) + (m-n)u(b),\tag{17}$$

where we need to assume that $m \geq n$. This maximand is also open to objections, but it may be useful as a starting point.

We would like to know what happens in a wage-bargaining model when individuals have utility functions of the kind described in the paper and depicted in Figure 5. The main ideas can be captured by assuming that a worker's utility is given by the function $u(w,w^*)$, where, defining $1 > \sigma > 0$ as a constant,

$$u = w \qquad\qquad \forall w \leq w^*$$
$$u = \sigma(w - w^*) + w^* \qquad\qquad \forall w \geq w^*$$

Put more succinctly, as a single function,

$$u(w,w^*) = \min\,[0,(1-\sigma)(w^*-w)] + w.$$

This imposes both piece-wise linearity and the assumption (or normalisation) that the marginal utility of income for low wage rates is unity. It is meant only as an example.

The utilitarian union now maximises the function

$$U = n\{\min\,[0,(1-\sigma)(w^*-w)] + w\} + (m-n)u(b).\tag{20}$$

Hence the marginal rates of substitution for $w > w^*$ and for $w < w^*$ are constant and different. The function is semi-strictly quasi-concave, and is presumably to be maximised against a convex choice set. In an

94   *Wage Rigidity & Unemployment*

efficient bargain the relevant constraint will be an iso-profit contour, say

$$\hat{\pi} = pf(n) - wn. \qquad (21)$$

When the price of output changes to $p' \equiv p + \delta p$, but $\hat{\pi}$ stays constant, we would like to know what happens to the optimal wage rate. Although it can be done more carefully, the basic point is seen most easily in Figure 6. There exist equilibria in which product price changes leave $w = w^*$. The whole adjustment is made by quantities: employment rises in a boom and falls in a slump.

For sufficiently large alterations in demand for the product there will be a change in the wage rate. However, to analyse this properly we would have to specify more fully the mechanism by which the aspiration wage, w^*, depends on the history of w.

References

Adams, J.S., 'Inequity in social exchange', in Bekowitz, L. (ed.), *Advances in Experimental Social Psychology* 2, (New York: Academic Press, 1965).

Adams, J.S. and Rosenbaum, W.E., 'The relationship of worker productivity to cognitive dissonance about wage inequities', *Journal of Abnormal and Social Psychology* 69 (1964) 19–25.

Andrews, I.R., 'Wage inequity and job performance: an experimental study', *Journal of Applied Psychology* 51 (1967), 39–45.

Argyle, M., *The Social Psychology of Work* (Harmondsworth, Middlesex: Penguin, 1972).

Azariadis, C., 'Implicit contracts and under-employment equilibria', *Journal of Political Economy* 83 (1975), 1183–1202.

Baily, M.N., 'Wages and employment under uncertain demand', *Review of Economic Studies* 41 (1974), 37–50.

Begg, D., Fischer, S. and Dornbusch, R., *Economics* (Maidenhead: McGraw-Hill (UK), 1984).

Duesenberry, J.S., *Income, Saving and the Theory of Consumer Behaviour* (Cambridge, Massachusetts: Harvard University Press, 1962).

Flanagan, R.J., 'Wage concessions and long-term wage flexibility', *Brookings Papers on Economic Activity* 1 (1984), 183–216.

Grossman, G.M., 'Union wages, seniority and unemployment', *American Economic Review* 73 (1983), 277–290.

Hahn, F.H., *Money and Inflation* (Oxford: Basil Blackwell, 1982).

Lawler, E.E., 'Equity theory as a predictor of productivity and work quality', *Psychological Bulletin* 70 (1968), 596–610.

McDonald, I.M. and Solow, R.M., 'Wage bargaining and employment', *American Economic Review* 71 (1981), 896–908.

Mitchell, D.J.B., 'Recent union contract concessions', *Brookings Papers on Economic Activity* 1 (1982), 165–204.

Oswald, A.J., 'The microeconomic theory of the trade union', *Economic Journal* 92 (1982), 576–595.

Oswald, A.J., 'Efficient contracts are on the labour demand curve: theory and facts', Working Paper 178, Industrial Relations Section, Princeton University (1984).

Oswald, A.J. and Turnbull, P.J., 'Pay and employment determination in Britain: what are labour contracts really like?', Discussion Paper, Centre for Labour Economics, LSE (1985).

Pritchard, R.D., Dunnette, M.D. and Jorgensen, D.O., 'Effects of perceptions of equity and inequity on worker performance and satisfaction', *Journal of Applied Psychology* 56 (1972), 75–94.

Ribeaux, P. and Poppleton, S.E., *Psychology and Work* (London: Macmillan, 1978).

Runciman, W.G., *Relative Deprivation and Social Justice* (Berkeley: University of California, 1966).

Shishter, J., 'The theory of union wage rigidity', *Quarterly Journal of Economics* 57 (1943), 522–542.

Taylor, M.C., 'Improved conditions, rising expectations, and dissatisfaction: a test of the past/present relative deprivation hypothesis', *Social Pschology Quarterly* 45 (1982), 24–33.

Vroom, V.H., *Work and Motivation* (New York: Wiley, 1964).

Yellen, J.L., 'Efficiency wage models of unemployment', *American Economic Review*, Papers and Proceedings 74 (1984), 200–205.

5. Wage Rigidity, Union Activity and Unemployment*

Assar Lindbeck & Dennis J. Snower

1. *Introduction*

Economists tend to approach the phenomenon of wage rigidity from two distinct perspectives. The first focuses on the variability of real wages relative to some other economic variable. For example, it has often been noted that real wages fluctuate less than employment over cyclical swings in macroeconomic activity. The second is concerned with the failure of real wages to clear the labour market. Here the underlying presumption is that 'flexible' wages could bring labour demand and supply into equality and thus the presence of involuntary unemployment becomes evidence of wage 'rigidity'.

Clearly the two perspectives bear no logical relation to one another. It is conceivable that real wages may fluctuate widely through time, but that involuntary unemployment nevertheless exists. Conversely there may be full employment while real wages remain constant. Although a number of unemployment theories incorporate both wage non-variability and involuntary unemployment, it is nevertheless important to opt for either one or the other perspective in an analysis of wage rigidity.

This paper concentrates exclusively on the second perspective. We will argue that wage rigidity – of the sort mirrored in the existence of involuntary unemployment – may be rationalised in terms of a conflict of interest between the employed workers (the 'insiders') and the unemployed workers (the 'outsiders'). This approach also enables us to gain some basic insights into the macroeconomic role of labour unions.

Needless to say, our theory of wage rigidity is just one of several current ones. Before presenting it, let us gain a brief overview of its immediate rivals and inquire what desirable features the rivals lack

* The financial support of the ESRC, the Leverhulme Trust and the Bank of Sweden Tercentenary Foundation is gratefully acknowledged.

that our theory attempts to embody. This is done in Section 2. Section 3 tells the intuitive story underlying our insider-outsider analysis. Section 4 describes the macroeconomic equilibrium with wage rigidity when employees bargain individualistically over wages with their employers. Section 5 examines what happens to this macroeconomic equilibrium when insiders form unions and pose strike threats. Finally, Section 6 is the epilogue.

2. *Rival theories of wage rigidity with involuntary unemployment*

Our theory of wage rigidity has four particularly prominent rivals. Each of them associates the failure of wages to clear the labour market with a different phenomenon:

(i)   government wage regulations (such as minimum wage legislation);
(ii) monopoly power of labour unions;
(iii) deficient aggregate demand (as originally conceived by the Keynesian economists and recently reinforced by the macroeconomic literature on increasing returns and imperfect competition); and
(iv) firms' use of wages as a screening device for productivity (in what have come to be known as the 'efficiency wage theories').

There are of course many ways of evaluating these rival theories, but for the purposes of this paper it is convenient to focus on two criteria:

(a) Do the theories explain why unemployed workers are not successful in underbidding their employed counterparts?
(b) Do the theories account for the salient stylised facts concerning wages and employment in free-market economies over this century?

These criteria are of crucial importance, not only for understanding the nature of wage rigidity and involuntary unemployment, but also for suggesting policy remedies.

First, there is the proposition that, although wages in free-market economies *do* move towards levels compatible with full employment, the economies of the UK, US, Germany, Japan, Sweden and other major capitalist countries are not genuinely 'free-market'. In particular, there are *government wage regulations* (e.g. minimum wage laws, public sector remuneration provisions) which keep wages from adjusting sufficiently to eliminate involuntary unemployment. The implied policy is to obviate these obstacles and thereby let the market do its magic.

This diagnosis has a certain simple appeal, but the stylised facts fail to support it. The volatile statistics of wage inflation (from sector to sector and from one year to the next) do not give the impression that there are institutional forces keeping wages steadily and inexorably rigid. Besides, it stretches the imagination to picture the Great Depression as springing from this source. Even in severe recessions there are many people receiving more than their legally mandated minimum pay.

Second, it may be argued that *the monopoly power of labour unions* keeps wages above their full-employment levels. Firms usually accede to unions' wage demands and respond by limiting employment. The implication is that if the unions' power were reduced, involuntary unemployment would be reduced as well. There is a body of prominent economists which believes that the reason why the US recovered so much better than Europe from the 1980–82 recession is to be found here.

This is a powerful argument, but it does not go far enough to convince unbelievers. Why do firms usually accede to unions' wage demands? Why don't they turn to non-unionised labour whenever it is available? What gives unions their clout? Needless to say a number of cogent responses can be given to these questions – unions have various instruments for punishing employers who ignore them. The size of unions' wage demands must depend critically on what these instruments are. Unfortunately economists have devoted little attention to them and thus the underlying causes of union wage setting remain partially unexplored. This (as we shall see) is an area in which it is fruitful to view wage rigidity as the outcome of an insider-outsider conflict.

Third, Keynesian economists generally insist that involuntary unemployment is due to *deficient demand for goods*. The role of wage rigidity in this analysis has been the subject of much dispute. In the Reappraisal of Keynes (e.g. Barro and Grossman (1976), Malinvaud (1977) and Muellbauer and Portes (1978)), nominal wages and prices are assumed fixed for a span long enough for agents to formulate demand and supply decisions which are compatible with the rations they face. Given the fixed wages and prices, firms do not hire the unemployed workers, because they could not sell the goods and services which the workers would produce. Keynes (1936) himself, however, did not rest his analysis of unemployment on this assumption of wage-price fixity. He maintained that even if wages and prices were to respond to excess supplies in their respective markets, the deficient demand for goods – and thus also the involuntary unemployment – would not disappear. Firms would still employ too little labour on account of customers' limited purchasing power; and customers would still have limited purchasing power because of the existing unemployment.

Recently this view has received cogent support from the literature on the macroeconomic implications of increasing returns to scale combined with imperfect competition (see Weitzman (1982)). The increasing returns prevent the unemployed workers from finding individual opportunities for self-employment, while the imperfect competition implies that workers who join forces in order to exploit the increasing returns will glut their product markets. The general policy implications of this analysis are the same as that of its Keynesian precursors: government demand-management policies can break the vicious circle of deficient labour demand and deficient product demand.

The problem with this approach is that it does not explain why the unemployed do not underbid. In the Reappraisal-of-Keynes models we are not told why wages and prices are fixed. The original Keynesian models and their increasing-returns counterparts provide no obstacles for underbidding. Thereby they run foul of an important stylised fact: in practice, unrestricted underbidding – generating precipitate wage deflation in the face of unemployment – hardly, if ever, occurs. We are left with the suspicion that the absence of underbidding – rather than the deficient aggregate demand – may provide the key to understanding wage rigidity with persistent involuntary unemployment.

Fourth and finally, the *efficiency wage theories* address the problem of underbidding explicitly. Here employers are poorly informed about how productive their employees are and thus they use wages to manipulate productivity. When an employer grants a wage increase, he hopes to attract more qualified workers and to induce the incumbents to try harder. Consequently employers may refuse to let wages fall to their full-employment levels: to do so would mean losing more profits through productivity declines than is saved through labour cost.

The policy implications are straightforward. Unemployment is not caused by unions; so nothing is gained by trimming union power. Moreover government demand-management policies may not influence wages, but they do affect employment: the greater the demand for goods the more workers will be hired.

This theory has a strong logical appeal, but it is difficult to believe that firms' imperfect information about their employees' productivity has accounted for a dominating proportion of the unemployment in the Western world over the past five years or, for that matter, over the Great Depression.

3. *The insider-outsider story*

The theory of wage rigidity advanced here offers a radically different rationale for involuntary unemployment and has radically different policy implications. It begins from the premise that firms may find it rather costly to respond to underbidding. The insiders know this and take advantage of it in their wage demands; the outsiders know it, too, and thus do not bother to underbid in the first place.

The reason why it may not be profitable for firms to accept underbidding is that the process of firing an insider and hiring an outsider is costly. This cost may take a variety of forms. For example, in Shaked and Sutton (1984), the cost lies in the value of time involved in wage negotiations; in Lindbeck and Snower (1984c), it takes the form of foregone work effort that comes with higher rates of labour turnover; in Lindbeck and Snower (1985), it arises from the loss of productivity due to the withdrawal of cooperation among employees. In this paper, we concentrate on the explicit costs of hiring, training and firing.

These costs come in many guises. For firms, the hiring and training costs cover the entire sequence of events which firms must follow to find workers, check their skills and make them qualified for the jobs they are to perform. The firing costs may include severance pay, the implementation of legally and socially acceptable firing procedures, the preparation for and possible conduct of litigation, and 'bad will' on the part of the remaining employees (commonly manifested in their productivity).

Another crucial ingredient in our story is the observation that the activities above take time. Whereas screening can often be performed over a rather short time interval, training is frequently a lengthy process. Furthermore the act of firing may be preceded by an extensive process of negotiation or litigation.

Consequently, workers may be classified by the following groups:

(i) 'insiders' (the fully-fledged employees of firms, on whom the full range of hiring and training costs has already been expended and whose dismissal would entail the full range of firing costs);

(ii) 'entrants' (who are in the process of being hired and thus are not associated with the full range of hiring, training, and firing costs); and

(iii) 'outsiders' (the currently unemployed workers).

The hiring, training and firing costs generate economic rent which may be divided between firms and their employees. In particular, the rent from the employment of insiders vis-à-vis entrants arises from the training and some firing costs. It may be measured by the difference between the maximal wage which the firm would be willing to pay its insiders (before finding it worthwhile to replace them with entrants) and the entrant wage. Similarly the rent from the employment of entrants arises from the hiring and some firing costs. We assume that all the turnover costs are firm-specific.

We assume that wages are determined through a bargaining process between each firm and its employees, whereas the employment decisions are made unilaterally by the firms. Each entrant goes through an 'initiation period', whereupon he generates as much rent as an insider *and* his wage contract may be renegotiated. In effect, the entrant *becomes* an insider after this time period.

Moreover, we assume that insiders and entrants are able to capture at least some of their respective rent in the wage-bargaining process. Thus the insiders have an inherent advantage over the entrants. They can raise their wage (W_I) above the entrant wage (W_E); but so long as the $W_I - W_E$ differential does not exceed the rent of insiders vis-à-vis entrants, the firms have no incentive to replace the insiders by entrants. Similarly, the entrants can raise their wage (W_E) above the reservation wage (R) of the outsiders.

However, the $W_E - R$ differential might exceed the rent of entrants vis-à-vis outsiders if workers have limited access to credit. The reason is that, the higher W_I, the lower R; indeed if W_I is high enough, R may be negative. But if entrants are credit-rationed for efficiency-interest reasons, (e.g. Stiglitz and Weiss, 1981), or due to loan repayment risk (Lindbeck, 1964), then the entrants might not be able to borrow enough to achieve R. In this case, W_E will be greater than it would be by reason of economic rent alone.

These circumstances generate a macroeconomic equilibrium characterised by wage rigidity and unemployment. This unemployment is involuntary whenever W_I, W_E and R are such that (a) the wage differentials between insiders and entrants (on the one hand) and outsiders (on the other) are greater than the corresponding productivity differentials and (b) outsiders prefer employment to unemployment. This may occur under credit rationing. It may also occur when the wage differentials above arise from rent due to 'dispensable' labour turnover costs, i.e. those turnover costs (such as severance pay) which are not expended on activities which are intrinsically important to the process of production. The reason is that these turnover costs have no bearing on the productivity differentials above, but they may affect the corresponding wage differentials when workers have the market power to exploit their rent. Thus the outsiders may unsuccessfully seek work at wages which more than compensate for their lower productivity vis-à-vis entrants and insiders. Firms have no incentive to hire the outsiders because the hiring, training and firing costs of doing so would exceed the associated wage saving.

This is where the unions enter the picture. Not only do unions strengthen insiders' bargaining position, not only do they amplify the costs of hiring and firing, but they give the workers a whole potent set of tools – for example the strike and work to rule – which serves to augment the firm's cost of replacing its employees. Thereby the unions enable workers to achieve much higher wages than they could have done in isolation.

But that is not all. Unions' wage demands depend not only on how much damage they are potentially able to inflict on firms ('union punch') but also on the 'credibility' of their threats. A union which threatens to strike must be able to induce its members to observe the strike once it has been called. Union credibility depends on quite different things from union punch. For example, a rise in personal income-tax rates may reduce union credibility by reducing the return to a successful strike but have no effect on union punch. On the other hand, a rise in firms' payroll tax rates may increase the punch by amplifying the wage-cost increase but leave the credibility unchanged.

Although the policy implications of the insider-outsider theory will receive only cursory attention in this paper, they are far-reaching and deserve mention at this point. Since the theory deals with unemployment that arises from a conflict of interests between employed and unemployed workers, policy measures which mitigate this conflict – e.g. reducing legal limitations on firing, reducing severance pay, reducing union power – lead to a fall in unemployment.

Yet the insider-outsider theory certainly does not imply that all government measures which promote job security, would have unemployment as a by-product. Although the measures which operate by hiring and firing costs do have this effect, those which affect the time horizon for wage agreements may work in the opposite direction. The longer the feasible duration of the agreements, the lower the level of unemployment.

Government-run vocational training schemes – even if they were to be able to stimulate labour productivity significantly – can have quite different effects on insider-induced unemployment, depending on the degree to which jobs require skills specific to particular firms, skills that are more generally applicable. If the latter skills are an important constituent of workers' overall productivity, then the vocational training schemes may serve to reduce unemployment.

4. *The behaviour of individualistic agents and the macroeconomic equilibrium*

The economy is composed of firms, households and a government. There are three goods: a consumption good, labour and another factor of production – say, 'capital'. The firms produce the consumption good by means of capital (which they own) and labour. The households buy the consumption good and may provide labour services to the firms. These are the flows of purchases.

The expenditure flows are straightforward. The firms use their revenues to remunerate labour and distribute what is left over to the households. The households use their non-wage incomes and their wage incomes (if they are employed) or their unemployment benefits (if they are unemployed) to make consumption purchases from the firms and pay taxes to the government. The government collects taxes from the households in order to pay unemployment benefits. The reason for giving the government such a limited role in the model is that we are not going to analyse the effects of government policy in this paper (in contrast to Lindbeck and Snower (1984b), where a wide variety of government policy actions are investigated).

As noted, the firms make the hiring and firing decisions, and wages are set through bargaining between each firm and its employees. The time span involved in formulating and implementing the wage and employment decisions is assumed to be exogenously given and identical for all workers and firms. It corresponds to the time period of our analysis.

For simplicity, we consider only the behaviour of economic agents under *stationary Nash equilibrium* conditions. In the context of our analysis, this means that (a) firms' investment outlays are zero, (b) firms' employment decisions are made under the assumption that wages are at optimal levels for the workers, and (c) workers' wage-setting decisions are made under the assumption that employment is optimal for the firms.

(i) The firms

The output of each firm is Q. K is its capital input. Two types of labour are available to the firm: entrant-labour, L_E, and insider-labour, L_I (both measured in terms of numbers of people). There is no retirement from or entry into the labour force during the period of analysis. For simplicity, we make the following assumption about the firm's factor availability and technologies:

A1: The firm's supply of capital is fixed:

$$K = \bar{K},$$

where $\bar{K}$ is a positive constant. The firm's current supply of insiders (L_2) is also fixed; yet it can obtain as many entrants (L_1) as it requires.

The firm does not have a deficient supply of entrants, because (as shown later) wages may be set so as to generate involuntary unemployment.

A2: Insiders and entrants use the same amount of capital per head, but insiders are more productive than entrants:

(1) $$Q = \alpha \cdot L_E + L_I$$

$$L_E + L_I = v \cdot K,$$

where the productivity of insiders is normalised to unity and the productivity of entrants is α;

$$0 < \alpha < 1.$$

(This depiction of technologies is particularly convenient since we aim to show how the behaviour of insiders can give rise to involuntary unemployment quite independently of their influence on entrants' productivity and firm's capital-labour substitution.)

All insiders of the firm receive the same real wage (W_I) (see Proposition 2 below) and all entrants receive the same real wage (W_E) as well. The firm's cost of hiring L'_E entrants is $H(L'_E)$ and its cost of firing L'_I insiders is $F(L'_I)$, where $H(0) = F(0) = 0$ and H', $F' > 0$. The firm seeks to maximise its cash flow, $CF = Q - [W_E \cdot L_E + W_I L_I] - H(L'_E)$ (i.e. its revenue minus its variable costs), where $L_E = L'_E$ (since all workers hired in the current time period remain entrants only during this time period) and $L_I \leq \bar{L}_I$. (Since the firm's capital supply is fixed, this is equivalent to profit maximisation.)

In equilibrium, no firing or hiring takes place and only insiders are employed, since insiders do not find it worthwhile to post wages that are sufficiently high to occasion their dismissal, nor do they retire voluntarily from their jobs. Under these circumstances, the firm's maximisation problem (for a single time period) becomes:

(2) $$\text{Maximise } CF = Q - W_I \cdot L_2$$

$$\text{subject to } L_1 \geq Q, \ v \cdot \bar{K} \geq Q.$$

Whenever $(1 - W_I) > 0$, the firm has a positive cash flow and thus its insider employment will be $L_1 = v \cdot \bar{K} = \bar{L}$. On the other hand, if $(1 - W_I) < 0$, then $L_1 = 0$.

(ii) The workers

Each worker maximises his utility subject to a budget constraint. His utility is a function of his consumption, C, and his labour, ℓ. For simplicity, we make the following assumptions about the worker's decision-making:

A3: For each worker, work (measured in units of time) is an on-off activity. When $\ell = 0$, he is unemployed; when $\ell = 1$, he has a full-time job. There is no part-time employment. No worker can work more than $\ell = 1$.

A4: Each worker's utility function may be expressed as $U = U(C, \ell)$, where $U_C > 0$ and $U_\ell < 0$. Utility is maximised over a single-period time horizon. All workers have identical preferences.

A5: Each worker's non-wage income is A, which is exogenous to his decision-making. An unemployed worker receives an unemployment benefit of B, which is also exogenous. All employed workers face a constant income tax rate of τ.

A6: Insiders capture all the available bilateral monopoly power.

The last-mentioned assumption means that insiders are wage-setters. It is made for expositional simplicity only. The basic argument of this article requires only that insiders capture some of the bilateral monopoly power and that the higher the maximal wage achievable by doing so, the higher the actual wage achieved.

A7: There is perfect competition among the outsiders in the labour market.

This assumption is natural enough in an economy characterised by involuntary unemployment.

In addition, we make a further assumption which will be modified in Sections 3 and 4 (where union activity is introduced):

A8: In setting his wage, each insider behaves individualistically. In particular, his wage demands are not related to the firing or hiring of other workers.

Since the unemployed are perfect competitors, they offer to work at their reservation wage, R. This is defined as the wage at which workers are indifferent between employment $(\ell = 1)$ and unemployment $(\ell = 0)$:

$$(3) \qquad U\{R \cdot (1 - \tau) + A, \; 1\} = U\{B + A, \; 0\}$$

where U is a household's utility and the time horizon covers one period.

We assume that the entrant wage (W_E) is set as a fixed mark-up over R, the size of the mark-up depending on entrants' borrowing constraints and the rent of entrants vis-à-vis outsiders (see Section 3).

Each insider sets his wage so as to maximise his utility. This means that the wage is set as high as possible subject to two constraints.

(i) *the zero-cash-flow constraint*: the wage must not be so high that the firm achieves a negative cash flow (and consequently closes its operations); and

(ii) *the firing-hiring constraint*: the wage must not be so high that it is in the firm's best interest to fire the insider and hire an outsider (at wage R) instead.

Let W_{ZC} and W_{FH} be the wages corresponding to these two constraints, respectively.

From the firm's maximisation problem (2), it is apparent that in equilibrium:

$$(4) \qquad\qquad W_{ZC} = 1.$$

Furthermore, W_{FH} is the wage at which the cash flow generated by an insider $(1 - W_{FH})$ is equal to that generated by firing the insider and hiring an entrant $(\alpha - W_E - F(1) - H(1))$. Consequently:

$$(5) \qquad\qquad W_{FH} = W_E + [(1-\alpha) + F(1) + H(1)].$$

this condition indicates that the 'wage spread' $(W_{FH} - W_E)$ is equal to the 'productivity spread' $(1 - \alpha)$ plus the firing-hiring cost per worker $(F(1) + H(1))$.

Thus, the wage which the insider actually demands is:

$$(6) \qquad\qquad W_I = \min(W_{ZC}, W_{FH}).$$

$W_I = W_{FH}$ is the case with which this paper is primarily concerned. It is interesting to note that here all three determinants of W_{FH} – the reservation wage, the productivity spread, and the firing-hiring costs – may be influenced by the insiders.

First, by being unfriendly and uncooperative to the entrants, the insiders are able to make the entrants' work more unpleasant than it otherwise would have been and thereby raise the wage at which the latter are willing to work. In practice, outsiders are commonly wary of underbidding the insiders. This behaviour pattern is often given an *ad hoc* sociological explanation: 'social mores' keep outsiders from 'stealing' the jobs from their employed comrades. Our line of argument, however, suggests that these mores may be traced to the entrants' anticipation of hostile insider reaction and that this reaction may follow from optimisation behaviour of insiders.

Second, insiders are usually responsible for training the entrants and thereby influence their productivity. Thus insiders may be able to raise their wage demands by threatening to conduct the firm's training programs inefficiently or even to disrupt them.

Observe that if $W_I = W_{FH}$, then not only do insiders generate a non-negative cash flow (i.e. $W_I \leqslant W_{ZC}$), but entrants do so as well: $\alpha - W_E > 0$. This implies a positive lower bound on the productivity of entrants. Unless this lower bound is exceeded, the entrants would be unable to compete with the insiders and the insiders, knowing this, would raise their wage until the firm's profit were reduced to zero.

For this reason, firms have an incentive to supervise the training of entrants and ensure that workers are productive during their training period. In practice, firms may undertake on-the-job training (rather than job-unrelated training), not only because this type of training may be the most effective way of raising an entrants' productivity and because (in the case of firm-specific training) it reduces entrants' incentive to switch to other firms, but also to dampen the wage demands of the insiders.

Third, insiders are commonly able to affect their potential firing and hiring costs. Threatening litigation and insisting on lengthy and expensive firing and hiring procedures are ways of doing this.

In sum, to raise his wage, an insider may find it worthwhile to threaten to become a thoroughly disagreeable creature, as summarised in the following proposition:

Proposition 1: Under the assumptions above, whenever a firm has a positive cash flow, each of its insiders has an atomistic incentive to be maximally uncooperative towards entrants, to provide minimal training, and to make the process of firing and hiring as costly as possible.

Moreover, our model of wage setting suggests an explanation for a commonly observed labour market phenomenon:

Proposition 2: If insiders behave atomistically (Assumption A8) and firms differ with regard to their firing-hiring costs or their insider-entrant productivity differentials, then while there is equal pay for equal work within each firm (with positive cash flow), this is not so across such firms.

An economy populated by the agents above may get stuck in a macroeconomic equilibrium with involuntary unemployment. If firms have positive cash flows, then the insider wage exceeds the entrant wage which, in turn, exceeds the outsider reservation wage. Consequently the outsiders prefer employment to unemployment. Moreover, as indicated in Section 3, the wage differentials $W_I\text{-}W_E$ and $W_I\text{-}R$ may exceed the associated productivity differentials on account of credit rationing or worker market power based on dispensable labour costs. In that event, the unemployment may be classified as involuntary. It is also persistent since, no matter what wage the outsiders offer to work for, they are either unable to gain job offers (for offers in excess of R) or have no incentive to accept these offers (for offers less than R).

Proposition 3: For an economy with agents described above, wages may be set so as to generate persistent involuntary unemployment.

5. *Union activity*

Let 'union activity' refer to any activity which workers perform in unison in order to achieve an outcome which they could not have achieved individually. Within the microeconomic context oulined above, we rationalise this form of cooperative behaviour by showing that insiders, acting together, can each achieve a higher wage than they could have done on their own.

Ways of doing this can be inferred from Section 4. With regard to firms with positive cash flows, unions may be able to stimulate insiders' wages relative to the wage achievable atomistically by (i) raising the entrant wage (through threats of organised harassment of entrants), (ii) diminishing entrant productivity (through organised training disruption), (iii) capturing a greater share of the economic rent (provided that they do not capture it all when bargaining atomistically), and (iv) raising the firms' firing-hiring costs. As the first three rationales are rather obvious, let us concentrate on the last one, which may be pursued by a common union activity: the threat of strike. (The threat of work-to-rule may be analysed in a similar way; see Lindbeck and Snower (1984a).)

This threat makes the productivity of insiders dependent on the firms' hiring-firing decisions and thereby makes the potential process of hiring and firing more expensive for firms than when workers behave individualistically. Clearly this can be done only if employees cooperate with one another and that, in short, is our basic approach to unionisation.

In order for the threat to operate in this manner, two conditions must be fulfilled:

A9: All firms have positive cash flow (i.e. their zero-cash-flow constraints are not binding: $W_I < W_{ZC}$).

(Whenever a firm's zero-cash-flow constraint is binding, changes in firing-hiring costs have no effect on the insider wage.)

A10: The marginal firing and hiring costs (i.e. F' and H') are increasing functions of the number of workers fired and hired (i.e. F'' $H'' > 0$).

Provided that the revenues and costs of different firms are independent of one another, unions issuing strike threats in our model will be firm-specific. Thus we consider union activity within a single firm. Workers have no incentive in our model to form unions covering more than one firm as long as firms act atomistically. Yet this incentive may arise in reaction to the organisation of *employers*, in response to the organisation of employees within individual firms. Indeed, this is commonly the order in which employees and employers have become organized in practice: firm-specific unions have been followed by employers' associations which, in turn, have been followed by industry-wide or even economy-wide unions.

Let the threat of strike be interpreted as the following implicit contract which the union imposes on the firm:

Contract C1: If a firm retains all its union members, then none of them go on strike; yet if any of them are fired, then some (possibly all) of the remaining ones strike.

Incorporating this union activity in the theoretical frame-work of Section 4 broadens our analysis in three ways: (i) it raises the number of control variables in the hands of both the firm and the workers, (ii) it makes the analysis inherently intertemporal, and (iii) it requires an explicit representation of the firm's and its workers' behaviour under uncertainty. These complications are not expendable baggage; they lie at the heart of the strike threat above.

In the model of Section 2, the firm and its workers each have one control variable: the firm decides whether to replace insiders and the insiders set their wages. Under Contract C1, by contrast, the interaction between workers and their firm may be viewed as a sequence of events pictured in Figure 1. First, workers set their wages (Decision W1). We assume that all the members of a union demand the same wage. Second, in response, the firm decides whether to replace (non-striking) insiders (Decision F1). Third, if workers have indeed been replaced, the remaining insiders decide whether to strike

(Decision W2). Fourth, the firm decides whether to replace the strikers (Decision F2). Then, given (F1) and (F2), workers reset their wages and the process begins anew.

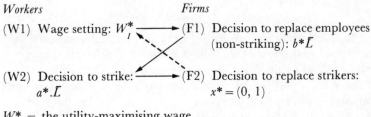

Workers   *Firms*

(W1) Wage setting: W_I^* ────→ (F1) Decision to replace employees (non-striking): $b^*\bar{L}$

(W2) Decision to strike: ────→ (F2) Decision to replace strikers: $a^*.\bar{L}$ $x^* = (0, 1)$

W^* = the utility-maximising wage

a^* = the utility-maximising proportion of a firm's labour force which is on strike (given that the firm has replaced non-strikers)

b^* = the profit-maximising proportion of a firm's labour force which is replaced

x^* = the profit-maximising decision to replace ($x=0$) or retain ($x=1$) the strikers in a firm.

Figure 1. The sequence of wage-setting, strike, and employment decisions

We study the Nash equilibrium of this process. In other words, the firm's employment decisions (with regard to strikers and non-strikers) are exogenously given to the workers, and the workers' wage and strike decisions are exogenously given to the firm. At the equilibrium, the workers take into account employment decisions which maximise the firm's profits, and the firm takes into account wage and strike decisions which maximise the workers' utilities.

A union's strike activity and a firm's response to it are inherently intertemporal. Union members strike now in order to achieve something in the future. A firm's employment decisions are also forward-looking. Once the firm has precipitated a strike by firing some of its employees, there are three possible outcomes (in any given time period): (1) the union members win the strike, in which case all those who have been fired are rehired (at the insider wage); (2) the firm wins, in which case the fired workers irrevocably lose claim to their original jobs, and (3) the strike continues. Since the essence of the labour conflict can be captured in the context of two periods, let us assume that the workers and their firm have a two-period time horizon.

It lies in the nature of strike activity that its outcome is uncertain. A strike occurs only if the affected parties do not know how it will end. Thus, their subjective probabilities with regard to the possible outcomes become relevant to their strategies.

Let us now consider each of the decisions by the workers and their firm in turn. It is convenient to study these decisions in the reverse order from that which appears in Figure 1.

Decision F2

Let δ^F be the firm's rate of time discount, ρ_w^F its perceived probability that the workers will win the strike, and ρ_ℓ^F its perceived probability that they will lose it. Assume that the firm is risk neutral and seeks to maximise the present value of its expected cash flow over two time periods.

If the firm decides to *hold all the strikers' positions vacant* $(F\,2: x = 1)$, then this cash flow may be expressed as follows:[1]

$$(7) \qquad CF_{x=1} = [\alpha - W_E] \cdot \mathrm{b} \cdot \bar{L} - H(b \cdot \bar{L}) - F(b \cdot \bar{L})$$

first-period cash flow generated by the entrants (net of firing-hiring costs)

$$+ (1 - a - b) \cdot \bar{L} \cdot [1 - W_1 \cdot (1 + \delta^F)]$$

cash flow generated by the non-striking insiders

$$+ \delta^F \cdot \rho_w^F \cdot \{(1 - W_I) \cdot (a + b) \cdot \bar{L} - F(b \cdot \bar{L})\}$$

additional second-period cash flow generated if the strikers win

$$+ \delta^F \cdot \rho_\ell^F \cdot \{(1 - W_E) \cdot (a + b) \cdot \bar{L}\}$$

additional second-period cash flow generated if the strikers lose

[1] Regardless of whether a marginal insider is fired or goes on strike, he is replaced by an entrant in the first period (and the associated firing-hiring costs are expended); in the second period, he is rehired if the strikers win, irrevocably loses his job if the strikers lose, and remains on strike if the strike continues.

$$+ \delta^F \cdot (1 - \rho_w^F - \rho_\ell^F) \cdot \{(-W_I) \cdot b \cdot \bar{L}\}$$

$$\underbrace{\phantom{+ \delta^F \cdot (1 - \rho_w^F - \rho_\ell^F) \cdot \{(-W_I) \cdot b \cdot \bar{L}\}}}$$

additional second-period cash flow generated if the strike continues

$$= (\alpha - W_E) \cdot b \cdot \bar{L} - (1 + \delta^F \cdot \rho_w^F) \cdot F(b \cdot \bar{L}) - H(b \cdot \bar{L})$$

$$+ (1 - W_I) \cdot \{\bar{L} \cdot (1 + \delta^F) - b \cdot \bar{L} - \alpha \bar{L} \cdot [1 + \delta^F \cdot (1 - \rho_w^F - \rho_\ell^F)]\}$$

On the other hand, if the firm decides *to replace all the strikers* $(F2: x = 0)$, then $(a + b) \cdot \bar{L}$ workers enter the firm in the first time period and, in the second time period, these workers are fired if the strikers win or turn into insiders otherwise. It can then be shown that the present value of the firm's expected case flow is

$$(8)\ CF_{x=0} = (\alpha - W_E) \cdot (a + b) \cdot \bar{L} - (1 + \delta^F \cdot \rho_w^F) \cdot F[(a + b) \cdot \bar{L}]$$

$$- H[(a + b) \cdot \bar{L}] + (1 - W_I) \cdot \bar{L} \cdot [1 - (a + b) \cdot (1 - \delta^F)]$$

A comparison of Equations (7) and (8) leads to an interesting result: In the Nash equilibrium, the Decision $(F2: x = 0)$ – to replace all strikers – is never effective. The reason is that if the firm decides to replace its strikers, it thereby makes the Contract (C1) ineffective: the workers lose their incentive to strike and the firm has no strikers to replace. (For an explanation see Lindbeck-Snower (1984a).)

Since the strike threat is not used when the firm replaces all the strikers it is not necessary to consider this case further. Instead, we can restrict our attention to the case in which it is in the firm's best interests not to replace all the strikers (i.e. $x = 1$).

Decision F1
Given that the firm decides to retain the strikers $(x = 1)$, there remains only one decision variable for the firm to set: b. The firm decides on how many of its non-striking employees to replace by maximising its cash flow, $CF_{x=1}$, with respect to b (for an exogenously given values of W_I and W_E:

$$(9)\ \frac{\partial CF_{x=1}}{\partial b} = [(W_I - W_I) - (1 - \alpha)] \cdot \bar{L}$$

$$- H'(b^* \cdot \bar{L}) \cdot \bar{L} - (1 + \delta^F \cdot \rho_w^F) \cdot F'(b^* \cdot \bar{L}) \cdot \bar{L} = 0$$

This equation is illustrated by the *firm's reaction function* $b^* = b^*(W_I)$

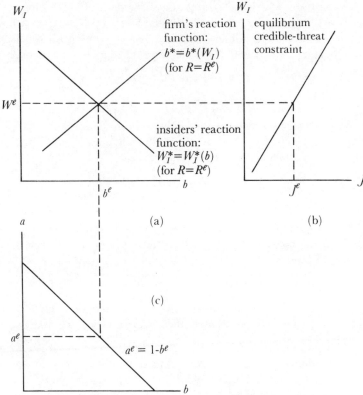

Figure 2. The Nash equilibrium under threat of strike

(which can be shown to have an unambiguously positive slope) in Figure 2a.

The fact that b^* may be positive in the Nash equilibrium does not mean that non-striking insiders will actually be fired. In fact, the insiders set their wage so as to prevent this from happening. All that $b^* > 0$ implies is that *if* the firm were to fire any of its non-striking insiders, it would be most profitable to fire $b^* \cdot \bar{L}$ of them.

Decision W2

The firing-hiring constraint which the workers face is not the same as that of Section 2. The constraint must be redefined to take into account the four instruments of workers and their firm, the two-period time horizon, and the uncertainty involved in posing the strike threat. At this constraint, the wage setting and strike decisions (Decisions W1 and W2, respectively) are such that the firm's two-period cash flow from retaining all its insiders is equal to its two-period cash flow from its employment decisions (F1) and (F2) ($b \cdot \bar{L}$ and $x = 1$, respectively):

$$(10) \qquad [1 - W_I] \cdot (1 + \delta^F) \cdot \bar{L} - CF_{x=1} = 0.$$

From this equation it can be shown that $(dW_I/da) > 0$ (for given b, which is exogenous to the workers). Since the insiders seek to maximise their wage, they set a as high as possible. Recall that $a + b \leq 1$. Thus, the optimal level of a illustrated in Figure 2c, is

$$(11) \qquad a^* = 1 - b^*.$$

This result may be summarised as follows:

Proposition 5: If it is in the firm's best interests to retain all its strikers, then *all* the insiders of the firm have an incentive to issue the strike threat of Contract C1.

In other words, Contract C1 may be reworded as follows:

Contract C1′: If a firm retains *all* its insiders, then none of them go on strike; yet if any of them are fired, then *all* of the remaining ones strike.

The only union that can implement the above contract is a firm-specific union of maximal size. In other words, *insiders have an incentive to join unions each of which cover the entire work force of a firm.*

Once again, a positive value of a^* does not mean that workers actually go on strike. As noted, the insider wage is low enough to discourage firms from firing non-strikers and consequently the workers have no cause to strike (according the Contract C1). A positive a^* simply means that if the firm were to fire $b^* \cdot \bar{L}$ non-strikers (where $0 < b^* < 1$), $a^* \cdot \bar{L}$ of the insiders would have an incentive to strike.

Decision W1

Substituting Equation (11) into (10), we obtain the insiders' wage-setting decision given the firm's employment decisions, $b \cdot \bar{L}$ and $x = 1$:

$$(12) \qquad W_I^* = 1 - \frac{(\alpha - W_I) \cdot b \cdot \bar{L} - [1 + \delta^F \cdot \rho_w^F] \cdot F(b \cdot \bar{L}) - H(b \cdot \bar{L})}{\{b \cdot \bar{L} + (1 - b) \cdot \bar{L} \cdot [1 + \delta^F \cdot (1 - \rho_w^F \cdot \rho_\ell^F)]\}}$$

This equation is illustrated by the *insiders' reaction function* $W_I^* = W_I^*(b)$ in Figure 2a, which can be shown to have an unambiguously negative slope in the neighbourhood of the Nash equilibrium.

The Nash equilibrium

Thus far we have considered the decision-marking of the firm and its insiders. It remains to analyse that of the outsiders and entrants. As noted in Section 4, the outsiders are perfect competitors in the labour market and thus they offer to work at their reservation wage, over which the entrant wage is marked up.

We assume that outsiders, like the insiders, have a two-period time horizon. In that case (unlike the single-period case) the reservation wage comes to depend on the insider wage. The reservation wage relevant to our analysis of strike threat may be defined as the wage at which workers are indifferent between (a) unemployment in both time periods (i.e. $\ell = 0$ and income of $A + B$ in each period) and (b) employment as entrant in the first period (i.e. $\ell = 1$ and income of $R + A$) and, in the second period, unemployment if fired and employment as insider otherwise (i.e. $\ell = 1$ and income of $W + A$). Let δ^H be the workers' rate of time discount and b^H be their perceived probability of being fired in the second period. Then the reservation wage is given by

$$
\begin{aligned}
(13) \quad (1 + \delta^H) \cdot U[B + A, 0] \\
= U[R \cdot (1 - \tau) + A, 1] + \delta^H \cdot b^H \cdot U[B + A, 0] + \\
\delta^H \cdot (1 - b^H) \cdot U[W_I \cdot (1 - \tau) + A, 1],
\end{aligned}
$$

which implies that

$$
(13a) \qquad\qquad R = R(W_I, B)
$$
$$
\qquad\qquad\qquad\quad (-) \ \ (+)
$$

In other words the higher the insider wage which the outsider anticipates in the future, the lower the entrant wage for which he is willing to work at present; the higher the benefit he receives when unemployed, the greater the reservation wage he requires to compensate him for accepting employment.

In the Nash equilibrium firms and their insiders not only take each other's decisions as exogenously given, but also the reservation wage of the outsiders above. Substituting this reservation wage (13a) plus the appropriate entrant mark-up into the firm's and the insiders' reaction functions (Equations (9) and (12) respectively), the Nash equilibrium may be characterised as the intersection of the corresponding reaction functions, as given by point (b^e, W^e_I) in Figure 2a.

Provided that $b^e < 1$, a^e is positive, i.e. *the strike threat is ex ante desirable for each of the union members.* This means that, given the firm's employment decisions (F1) and (F2), each union member can achieve a higher wage by issuing the strike threat of Contract C1′ than by foregoing this threat.

Strike credibility

Yet in order for the strike threat to be effective, it must be credible, i.e. the *strike threat must be ex post desirable for each of the union members.* Once the firm has fired some of the non-striking insiders, the remaining insiders – confronted with this *fait accompli* – must have an incentive to fulfil their strike threat. Clearly, such an incentive exists if and only if their ex-post utility from striking exceeds their ex-post utility from remaining on the job.

Recall that each worker's utility depends positively on consumption (which is purchased with the worker's income) and leisure. For simplicity, let the utility function be additively separable, normalise the utility from maximal leisure (viz. no employment: $\ell = 0$) to zero, and let the utility from minimal leisure (viz. employment: $\ell = 1$) be $-\Gamma$ (where Γ is a positive constant). Let ρ_w^H and ρ_ℓ^H be the worker's (households) perceived probabilities of winning and losing the strike, respectively, and b_1 be his perceived probability of being fired if he loses.

Suppose that if the worker does strike, then his only source of non-profit income is a payment out of a strike fund. Let this payment be J (a positive constant) per time period. (Recall that his profit income is A, also a positive constant.)

Under these circumstances, the worker's ex-post utility from striking (i.e. his utility, given that the firm has engaged in firing activity) can be shown (see Lindbeck and Snower (1984a)) to be

$$(14) \quad U_1 = U[J + A] \cdot \{1 - \delta_w^H \cdot (1 - \rho_w^H - \rho_\ell^H)\}$$
$$+ \{U[W_I \cdot (1 - \tau) + A - \Gamma] \cdot \rho_w^H + \rho_\ell^H \cdot (1 - b_1)\} \cdot \delta^H$$
$$+ U[B + A] \cdot \rho_\ell^H \cdot b_1 \cdot \delta^H.$$

(This expression is derived in the same way, in principle, as Equation (7), viz. as the sum of all the worker's possible utilities, weighted by their respective probabilities.)

Let b_2 be the worker's perceived probability of being fired if he remains on the job. Then his ex-post utility from not striking can, in a parallel fashion, be shown to be

$$(15) \qquad U_2 = \{U[W_I \cdot (1-\tau) + A] - \Gamma\} \cdot \{1 + \delta^H \cdot (1 - b_2)\}$$
$$+ \delta^H \cdot b_2 \cdot U[B + A].$$

As noted, the strike threat is credible if and only if $U_1 \geq U_2$, i.e.

$$(16) -\{U[W_I \cdot (1-\tau) + A] - \Gamma - U[\mathcal{J} + A]\} \cdot \{1 + \delta^H$$
$$\cdot (1 - \rho_w^H - \rho_\ell^H)\}$$
$$-\{U[W_I \cdot (1-\tau) + A] - \Gamma - U[B + A]\} \cdot \delta^H \cdot (\rho_\ell^H \cdot b_1 - b_2] \geq 0.$$

This condition may be called the 'credible-threat constraint'.

It contains only two of the worker's decision variables: W_I and $\mathcal{J}$. For any given value of W_I, there exists a minimal value of $\mathcal{J}$, for which the condition (16) is satisfied as equality. Since the strike fund can be augmented only at the expense of insider income (and therefore also insider consumption), this is indeed the utility-maximising value of $\mathcal{J}$. Condition (16) as equality is illustrated in Figure 2b.

In equilibrium, the strike fund is not in fact changed and thus strike-fund contributions do not enter the insiders' utility maximisation problems. The sole purpose of the strike fund in equilibrium is to establish a credible threat. Consequently, the optimal equilibrium strategy for insiders is to set their wage as high as the firing-hiring constraint (12) will allow and then to set $\mathcal{J}$ high enough so that the credible-threat constraint (16) is just satisfied. In this sense, condition (16) implies the optimal equilibrium size of the strike fund.

Macroeconomic implications

Is the level of involuntary unemployment higher when insiders unionise to issue the strike threat than when they act atomistically? To make a valid comparison, consider two economies which are identical except that one is unionised in the sense above and the other is atomistic.

The firm's reaction function under atomistic wage setting is the same as that under the strike threat (Equation 9), except that the firm's perceived probability of strikers winning their strike (ρ_w^F) is obviously zero in the former case and generally positive in the latter.

Similarly, the insiders' reaction function under atomistic wage setting (Equation (5)) is the same as that under the strike threat (Equation (10)), except that the proportion of strikers (a) and the insiders' perceived probabilities of winning and losing the strike $(\rho_w^H$ and ρ_ℓ^H, respectively) are zero in the former case and generally positive in the latter.

Substituting the expression for the reservation wage (Equation (13)) into the firm's reaction function (Equation (9)), we find that, for any given value of the insider wage, the firm's optimal firing under atomistic insider behaviour $(b_{at} \cdot \bar{L})$ is less than that under the strike threat above $(b^* \cdot \bar{L})$ (*ceteris paribus*).[2] Thus, the firm's reaction function is lower (in $b - W$ space) for a non-unionised work force than for a unionised one, as shown in Figure 3(a).

Furthermore, substituting the expression for the reservation wage (Equation (13)) into the insiders' reaction function (Equation (12)), we find that, for any given value of firm firing $(b \cdot \bar{L})$, the insider wage is lower under atomistic than under union conditions $(W_{at}$ and W^*_i,

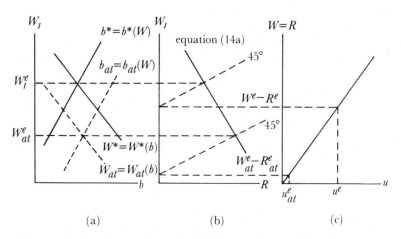

(a) (b) (c)

Figure. 3. Involuntary unemployment under strike threat and atomistic wage setting

[2] For ease of comparison, we assume that, in determining the reservation wage (Equation (13)), the outsiders' perceived probability of being fired in the second period (b^H) is the same under atomistic and unionised wage setting. With regard to the firm's reaction function (Equation (9)), given that $\rho_w^F = 0$ in the atomistic case but $\rho_w^F > 0$ in the unionised case and given that $(\partial^2 CF_{x=1}/\partial b^2) < 0$, it is evident that $b_{at} < b^*$ (*ceteris paribus*).

respectively). Thus, the insiders' reaction function is also lower in the former case than in the latter, as shown in Figure 3a.

Consequently, an economy in which a fixed number of firms face atomistic insiders will display a lower insider wage (W_{at}^e in Figure 3a) than the one (W_I^e) which emerges when all these firms face unions posing the strike threat (C1′).

Recall that the reservation wage (Equation (14)), illustrated in Figure 3b for a given value of b^H is inversely related to the insider wage. Thus, it is evident that the differential between the insider wage and the reservation wage must be larger under unionization ($W_I^e - R^e$) than under atomistic behaviour ($W_{at}^e - R_{at}^e$). Assuming (as in Section 2) that the amount of labour services offered by the outsiders depends positively on this differential (as pictured in Figure 3c), we arrive at the following proposition:

Proposition 6: The level of involuntary unemployment and the level of the insider wage are greater (*ceteris paribus*) when all insiders in the economy unionise to issue the strike threat (C1′) than when they set their wages atomistically.

In Section 4 (Proposition 3), involuntary unemployment was portrayed as a phenomenon which the insiders, setting their wages individually, impose on the outsiders. Now we find that insiders can augment their wage claims by forming unions to pose strike threats and, as by-product, they raise the level of involuntary unemployment.

The macroeconomic implications of our union analysis may be clarified by various comparative static experiments.

Suppose that the productivity of entrants (relative to insiders (α)) rises exogenously. Then (by Equation (9)), the cash-flow-maximising number of non-strikers to be fired ($b^* \cdot \bar{L}$) rises for every given insider wage and reservation wage; thus, the firm's reaction function (b^*) shifts to the right in $b - W$ space. In addition (by Equations (12) and (13)), the utility-maximising insider wage falls for every given value of b (as the reservation wage rises) – thus, the insiders' reaction function (W_I^*) shifts downwards as well. However, the credible-threat constraint remains unchanged. These effects are shown in Figure 4 and may be summarised as follows:

Proposition 7: When unions issue the strike threat (C1′), an *increase in the productivity* of entrants (α) leads to a reduction in the equilibrium levels of the insider wage and the strike fund.

(With regard to the insider wage, this effect of entrant productivity is qualitatively the same as that in the world of atomistic wage setting (see Equation (5)).

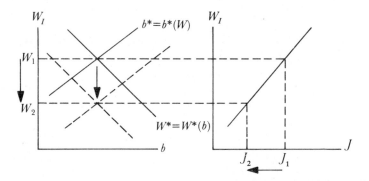

Figure 4. The effect of an increase in entrant productivity

The effect of an increase in the firm's perceived probability that the strike will persist $(1 - \rho_w^F - \rho_\ell^F)$ is pictured in Figure 5. The firm's reaction function (b^*) remains unchanged; that of the insiders (W_I^*) shifts upwards; and the credible-threat constraint shifts to the right.

Proposition 8: When unions issue the strike threat (C1′), an *increase in the firm's perceived probability that the strike will persist* $(1 - \rho_w^F - \rho_\ell^F)$ leads to a rise in the equilibrium levels of the insider wage and the strike fund.

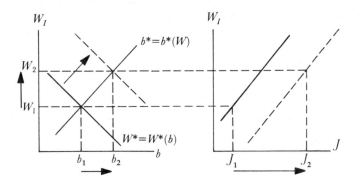

Figure 5. The effect of an increase in the firm's perceived probability that the strike will persist

Figures 6 and 7 are concerned with the effects of an increase in firing or hiring costs, in lump-sum (*F* or *H*) and marginal (*F′* or *H′*) terms, respectively. They illustrate the following comparative statics result:

Proposition 9: When unions issue the strike threat (C1′), both *a lump-sum and a marginal increase in the costs of firing or hiring* leads to a rise in the equilibrium levels of the insider wage and the strike fund.

(In the world of atomistic wage setting, a lump-sum increase in firing-hiring costs also raises the insider wage, but a marginal increase in these costs has no effect.)

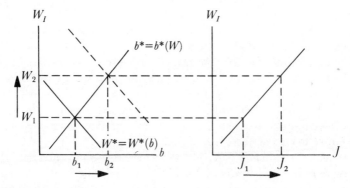

Figure 6. The effect of a lump-sum increase in firing or hiring costs

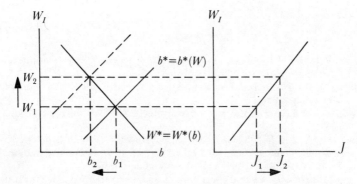

Figure 7. The effect of a marginal increase in firing or hiring costs

It is also obvious that the macroeconomic consequences of a rise in the unemployment benefits (B) may be summarised as follows:

Proposition 10: A rise in unemployment benefits (B) raises the reservation wages and the insider wages. Under atomistic wage-setting, there is no effect on unemployment; under union wage-setting the unemployment effect is ambiguous.

6. *Epilogue*

Wage rigidity is explained in this paper as a consequence of the employed workers (the 'insiders') exploiting the monopoly power that they obtain in wage-setting as a result of the costs of hiring and firing. The unemployed workers (the 'outsiders') are unable to undercut the 'monopoly wages' of the insiders, not only due to conceivably existing 'social mores' against such attempts, but also because the firms would have no incentives to fire the insiders and hire the outsiders. Thus, although the resulting involuntary unemployment is a disequilibrium market phenomenon in the sense that excess supply for labour exists, there is no tendency for the situation to be rectified, as neither the firms nor the employed workers (possibly acting through unions) have an incentive to change their behaviour.

Involuntary unemployment of this type exists even when workers bargain individualistically, although (as shown) unions serve to raise their members' wage levels and thereby the involuntary unemployment is amplified. In this vein, our analysis provides a rationale for the existence of unions and for their use of strike threats, operating in the interests of the insiders and against those of the outsiders.

References

Barro, R.J. and H.I. Grossman, *Money, Employment and Inflation* (Cambridge: Cambridge University Press, 1976).

Keynes, J.M., *The General Theory of Employment, Interest, and Money* (London: Macmillan, 1936).

Lindbeck, A. *A Study in Monetary Analysis* (Stockholm: Almquist and Wiksell, 1963).

Lindbeck, A. and D.J. Snower, 'Involuntary unemployment as an insider-outsider dilemma', Seminar Paper No. 282, Institute for International Economic Studies, University of Stockholm, 1984a.

——, 'Strikes, lock-outs and fiscal policy', Seminar Paper No. 309, Institute for International Economic Studies, University of Stockholm, 1984b.

——, 'Labour turnover, insider morale and involuntary unemployment', Seminar Paper No. 310, Institute for International Economic Studies, University of Stockholm, 1984c.

——, 'Cooperation, harassment, and involuntary unemployment', Seminar Paper No. 321, Institute for International Economic Studies, University of Stockholm, 1985.

——, 'Wage setting, unemployment, and insider-outsider relations', *American Economic Review*, Papers and Proceedings, 76 (2).

Malinvaud, E., *The Theory of Unemployment Reconsidered* (Oxford: Basil Blackwell, 1977).

Muellbauer, J. and R. Portes, 'Macroeconomic models with quantity rationing', *Economic Journal* 88 (1978), 788–821.

Shaked, A. and J. Sutton, 'Involuntary unemployment as a perfect equilibrium in a bargaining model', *Econometrica* 52(6).

Stiglitz, J.E. and A. Weiss, 'Credit rationing in markets with imperfect information' *American Economic Review* (1981).

Weitzman, M.L. (1982), 'Increasing returns and the foundations of unemployment theory', *Economic Journal* 92 (1982), 787–804.

6. Policy Lessons from the Post-war Period*

George L. Perry

The years since the 1960s will be a caution to policy-makers for a long time to come. The abiding message of this period will be that inflation is stubborn; once well-established, it is extremely costly to get rid of. This contrasts with the message that ended the 1950s. At that time real goals were emphasised: stimulating investment and real growth, taming the business cycle and minimising wasteful unemployment. A long post-war cycle in economic performance and policy concerns has come full circle.

Unemployment trended higher in most of Europe and Japan during the 1970s. One explanation offered for this was that the unemployment was 'classical', resulting from real wages and the labour share of income rising to levels that made it unprofitable for firms to expand employment further. Other explanations saw the rise as structural, resulting from disincentives in tax and transfer systems or from shifts in the high employment mix of output and labour demand that the existing labour force could not adjust to.

An alternative explanation is that rising unemployment mainly reflected policy reactions to stubborn inflation. The aims in some countries, such as Germany, shifted away from employment objectives and toward disinflation by the middle of the decade. By the end of the 1970s, severe macroeconomic restraint had emerged as the answer to inflation in the United States and United Kingdom. The historical evidence predicted that such policies of macroeconomic restraint would mainly reduce output and only gradually reduce inflation. And that is what happened, although in varying degrees, among the several major industrial nations. Wage rigidity is commonly taken as the reason for this strong response of unemployment to aggregate demand.

By promising to induce a favourable change in wage and price flexibility, the new classical economics, along with some older monetarist doctrines, provided a special justification for the policies of

* I am grateful to Flor Cardenil and Anita Whitlock for their terrific help.

economic restraint. The variant of these models that I found most plausible anticipated that, once the credibility of a permanent anti-inflationary policy was established, structural change would occur in decision-making and institutions so that price stability would be restored relatively quickly and would thereafter be compatible with higher output levels than before. The important common theme of these models was that conventional stabilisation policies should be abandoned, with wage and price flexibility relied on to keep employment and output at their appropriate levels. The persistence in most industrial countries of very high unemployment in the face of steadily restrictive policies belies the strong predictions of these models. Wage flexibility sufficient to restore high employment has not emerged. Quite apart from this episode, how more flexible wages, somehow achieved, would alter macroeconomic performance raises difficult questions, some of which I take up in a later section.

If the structural or classical explanations for the rising trend in unemployment are not accepted, why was inflation so much higher in the 1970s? Supply shocks, particularly the oil price explosions of OPEC I and II, were one important new feature on the economic landscape and explain part of the higher inflation of the decade. But even allowing for the effects of these supply shocks, only a small part of the inflation of the period can be understood in terms of the short-run Phillips curves that tracked inflation reasonably well in the 1950s and 1960s. The short-run dynamics represented by the Phillips curve must be integrated with an explanation of the average inflation rate around which short-run cyclical movements take place.

I have implemented this idea for developments in the United States by hypothesising the existence at any time of a norm rate of wage increase that is relatively stable in the face of typical cyclical variations in the economy and typical fluctuations in the actual inflation rate (Perry 1980). Wage increases that just match the norm are allocation-ally neutral and maintain a firm's relative wage position. The wage norm shifts in response to unusual and prolonged departures from typical economic developments. Based on US economic experience since the start of this century, Charles Schultze (1981) has provided empirical support for the existence of relatively stable wage norms that shifted only in response to extended departures of the economy from its normal cycle. Whether the wage norm is also susceptible to events such as the OPEC price shocks, to unusual policy innovations or changes in the policy regime, or to direct measures such as income policies remain open questions at this point, though I offer some evidence on them below.

Adaptive expectations models of inflation blur the distinction between cyclical variations in wages and the wage norm by relating current inflation linearly to its own past values as well as to current unemployment relative to its natural rate. As a more drastic alternative, rational expectations-credibility models can be viewed as making inflation norms depend on expected policies. How we understand the past and prescribe for the future depends on which of these models we accept. I find the evidence favours the idea of a wage norm that does not continually adjust in a simple way to past inflation and that cannot be shifted easily by expectations of future policy. Some evidence on these points is presented below.

1. *A broad view of performance*

Table 1 summarises economic performance in seven industrial countries starting in 1965. The table is divided into periods of low, medium and high degrees of economic slack – 1965–73, 1975–79 and 1981–83 – and the two periods dominated by oil price increases – 1973–75 and 1979–81. A few points are worth highlighting.

Normally, pricing behaviour can be approximated as a fixed markup over standard unit labour costs – hourly compensation divided by the trend in labour productivity – though this relation may be altered, especially in the short run, by variations in foreign competition and in capacity utilisation. However, it appears that margins of value added prices over standard unit labour costs altered relative to such normal behaviour for significant periods of time in some countries.

The OPEC I period stands out as special. Wages rose rapidly everywhere and the margin between value added prices (P_v) and standard unit labour costs (C) narrowed sharply in several countries – the United Kingdom, France and Japan, a change that was not reversed in the medium-slack period that followed. Real wages accelerated in several countries despite the rise in oil prices. The 1973–75 period seems to have been a special event in these and other ways. With OPEC II, no wage explosions occurred and margins were not importantly affected. The significant and expected special development in OPEC II was the large difference between increases in consumer prices and value added prices in manufacturing. Real-wage

Table 1. Price and cost changes in manufacturing and aggregate unemployment
(percent change per year except for unemployment)

		Low slack 1965–73	OPEC I 1973–75	Medium slack 1975–79	OPEC II 1979–81	High slack 1981–83	(1983)
United States							
Unemployment rate	(U)	4·5	6·3	7·0	6·8	9·0	9·6
Hourly compensation	(w)	6·0	10·7	8·2	10·1	5·9	3·4
Standard unit labour cost	(c)	3·1	9·6	5·8	8·4	2·7	–0·1
Product price	(p_v)	2·3	10·5	5·4	7·7	3·9	3·2
Consumer price	(p_c)	4·3	9·6	7·5	11·3	4·5	3·2
Margin	$(p_v - c)$	–0·8	0·9	–0·4	–0·7	1·2	3·3
Real wage	$(w - p_c)$	1·7	1·1	0·7	–1·2	1·4	0·2
United Kingdom							
Unemployment rate	(U)	2·3	2·8	4·9	6·8	10·4	11·5
Hourly compensation	(w)	9·8	25·6	15·1	15·1	7·8	7·1
Standard unit labour cost	(c)	5·4	23·0	12·7	13·5	3·9	4·4
Product price	(p_v)	4·9	19·0	13·3	13·2	6·1	4·3
Consumer price	(p_c)	5·9	18·2	12·7	13·9	6·4	4·5
Margin	$(p_v - c)$	–0·5	–4·0	0·6	–0·3	2·2	–0·1
Real wage	$(w - p_c)$	3·9	7·4	2·4	1·2	1·4	2·6
France							
Unemployment rate	(U)	1·3	2·7	4·8	6·7	8·5	9·0
Hourly compensation	(w)	9·9	19·3	13·2	14·1	14·3	12·9
Standard unit labour cost	(c)	3·3	15·2	8·2	10·4	9·9	7·2
Product price	(p_v)	3·0	11·7	8·1	11·1	10·5	8·7
Consumer price	(p_c)	5·0	11·9	9·3	12·7	10·2	9·2
Margin	$(p_v - c)$	–0·3	–3·5	–0·1	0·7	0·6	1·5
Real wage	$(w - p_c)$	4·9	7·4	3·9	1·4	4·1	3·7
Germany							
Unemployment rate	(U)	0·9	2·4	3·9	3·8	6·6	8·4
Hourly compensation	(w)	10·0	11·4	7·7	7·4	4·4	3·6
Standard unit labour cost	(c)	4·5	6·9	4·0	4·6	1·5	0·9
Product price	(p_v)	3·7	5·7	3·3	2·9	4·4	3·2

Table 1 (continued)

		Low slack 1965–73	OPEC I 1973–75	Medium slack 1975–79	OPEC II 1979–81	High slack 1981–83	(1983)
Consumer price	(p_c)	3·6	6·2	3·7	5·7	4·2	(3·3)
Margin	$(p_v - c)$	−0·8	−1·2	−0·7	−1·7	2·9	(2·3)
Real wage	$(w - p_c)$	6·4	5·2	4·0	1·7	0·2	(0·3)
Italy							
Unemployment rate	(U)	5·0	5·0	6·4	8·1	10·4	(11·8)
Hourly compensation	(w)	13·0	23·7	16·3	19·0	17·2	(17·7)
Standard unit labour cost	(c)	6·4	19·5	12·7	14·6	12·7	(12·0)
Product price	(p_v)	4·6	18·3	14·4	14·4	13·9	(11·5)
Consumer price	(p_c)	4·4	16·5	14·1	17·8	14·5	(13·7)
Margin	$(p_v - c)$	−1·8	−1·2	1·7	−0·2	1·2	(−0·5)
Real wage	$(w - p_c)$	8·6	7·2	2·2	1·2	2·7	(4·0)
Sweden							
Unemployment rate	(U)	2·2[a]	2·0	1·9	2·2	3·0	(3·5)
Hourly compensation	(w)	10·2	17·8	11·0	10·5	7·9	(9·0)
Standard unit labour cost	(c)	3·8	16·3	8·0	8·0	5·3	(6·3)
Product price	(p_v)	3·3	15·8	6·6	8·3	9·4	(9·9)
Consumer price	(p_c)	5·2	9·4	9·3	12·2	8·4	(8·6)
Margin	$(p_v - c)$	−0·5	−0·5	−1·4	0·3	4·1	(3·6)
Real wage	$(w - p_c)$	5·0	8·4	1·7	−1·7	−0·5	(0·4)
Japan							
Unemployment rate	(U)	1·2	1·5	2·0	2·1	2·4	(2·7)
Hourly compensation	(w)	15·1	21·4	7·0	7·2	3·9	(2·9)
Standard unit labour cost	(c)	3·9	16·4	0·5	−0·3	−1·1[b]	n.a.
Product price	(p_v)	3·8	8·8	0·9	−0·5	−1·9[b]	n.a.
Consumer price	(p_c)	6·0	16·5	6·0	6·2	2·2	(1·7)
Margin	$(p_v - c)$	−0·1	−7·6	0·4	−0·2	−0·8[b]	n.a.
Real wage	$(w - p_c)$	9·1	4·9	1·0	1·0	1·7	(1·2)

(a) 1968–73.
(b) 1981–82.

growth, which is affected by prices outside domestic manufacturing as well as by productivity trends and margins in manufacturing, slowed noticeably everywhere but Japan.

There is a steady improvement in margin growth going from the low- to medium- to high-slack periods. The relative strength of value-added prices in the last period could be related to depreciating exchange rates, although it happens in the United States as well. It may also reflect upward pressure on prices for given standard unit labour costs that comes from sustained, as opposed to cyclically, low levels of capacity utilisation. Real wages rose fastest in the low-slack period everywhere, but particularly óutside the United States. Between the second and third periods, however, there is no uniformity to real-wage behaviour.

2. *Structural unemployment issues*

The secular rise in unemployment in most countries since 1973 raised the question of whether an increasing amount of unemployment was structural. If structural is defined broadly enough, that idea can include growing skill mismatches between workers and available jobs, work disincentives that make unemployment more attractive, changing demographics that increase the relative weight in the labour force of groups with relative high average unemployment rates and related ideas. Changing demographics have accounted for some drift in unemployment in the United States, but not very much. Using an unemployment rate weighted by the mid-1960s relative importance of different demographic groups as an indicator of labour market tightness shows the official unemployment rate has drifted up by at most 2 percentage points relative to labour market tightness between the mid-1960s and mid-1980s. There may have been similar effects in Europe, but they could not account for much of the unemployment rise of the 1970s or of the high inflation experienced at late 1970s unemployment rates.

Work disincentives are a legitimate concern in the design of tax and transfer schemes and may be especially important in the design of income-support programmes for the unemployed. But they are a diversion in analysing the stagnation of the 1970s because such programs did not change appreciably during the decade.

Growing skill mismatches between workers and available jobs are hard to verify. But we know that change is continual and readily adapted to in expanding economies. When new jobs are less available, it disrupts this adaptation and makes cyclical unemployment into quasi-structural unemployment. Thus the stagnation in European employment is likely to be a cause rather than effect of mismatches between workers and jobs.

The rise in capacity utilisation relative to unemployment that has occurred in many industrial countries is also cited as evidence that much of unemployment is structural. But this argument ignores the fact that investment is endogenous and firms will restrain their capacity expansion at a time of weak or declining output growth. If employment were weak as a result purely of insufficient demand, capacity would gradually shrink to conform to actual output and capacity utilisation would rise relative to high or growing unemployment.

Some might interpret the observed shift up in both inflation and unemployment as itself evidence of a shift up in the structural unemployment rate. But that observation is consistent with any explanation for the higher inflation that occurred. Without corroborating evidence that markets are in fact tight, there is no reason to believe rising structural unemployment is an explanation for the rise in actual unemployment.

3. *Real wages and classical unemployment*

The idea that excessively high real wages caused high unemployment has been offered as another explanation of experience in the 1970s. On a strict interpretation, this 'classical' unemployment would be unresponsive to a demand expansion. On a more pragmatic interpretation, unemployment might respond, but only at an exceptionally high cost in added inflation. This weaker version is not incompatible with the main alternative – that inflation eventually became the prime concern of policy in each country and that output was restrained in the process of slowing inflation. But if valid it would constitute an additional complication for policy, now and in the future.

The main attempts to investigate this issue empirically have been made by Jeffrey Sachs (1979, 1983) and Jacques R. Artus (1984), and less directly in work by Michael Bruno (1981). In the model as developed by Sachs, an adjusted labour share (S_{LA}) is calculated using current real product wages (W/P_v) and the productivity levels (Q/H) that would exist if output were at its potential level $(Q/H)^*$:

$$S_{LA} = \frac{W}{P_v}\left(\frac{H}{Q}\right)^*;$$

where P_v is the value added deflator and W is compensation per hour. A wage gap is then defined as the difference between S_{LA} in any year and the value of S_{LA} in the late 1960s. The adjusted labour share can alternatively be thought of as the ratio of standard unit labour costs (hourly compensation divided by trend productivity) to value-added prices, and so simply reflects deviations in price margins. Sachs and others maintain that a large wage gap indicates unemployment is classical.

The wage-gap story is invariably identified with manufacturing sectors where strong unions and import competition are most important. The evidence offered by Sachs and others clearly shows that wage gaps, as they define them, rose in the 1970s in most industrial countries; but the significance of this for understanding economic developments and policy options is not established. Shafiqul Islam (1983) has written an interesting sceptical paper on this point, which raises some of the same issues that I discuss here.

At the level of the firm, the macroeconomic idea that unemployment will not be reduced by a shift out in demand corresponds to the proposition that firms will not welcome more sales at existing price and wage levels. This is a pretty extreme condition to believe, at least as an explanation for high levels of unemployment and excess capacity when marginal cost would be expected to lie well below price for the typical firm. But it is conceivable that developments such as an explosive wage push or a sharp rise in real exchange rates could put firms in such a position.

Figure 1 shows labour shares in manufacturing from the 1950s to 1983 for several industrial countries. Two points are worth noting at the outset. First, in most countries, there is a clear trend in the share. France and Japan have one large change rather than a trend. In Germany, the United Kingdom and Sweden, the trend rises about as much between the 1950s and 1960s as between the 1960s and 1970s. To the extent that the changes in shares between the late 1960s and late 1970s that have attracted attention are mainly extensions of a trend, their significance is greatly diminished.

Second, the countries fall into three pretty distinct tiers in the level of

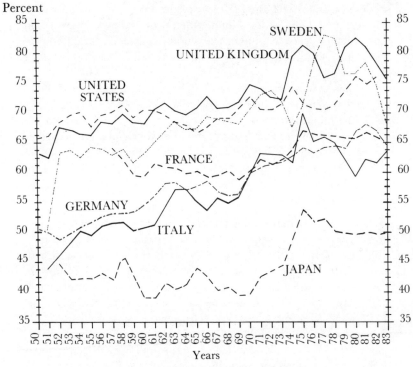

Figure 1. Labour share in manufacturing

the labour share in the 1970s: the United States, United Kingdom and Sweden in a high tier, France, Germany and Italy in a middle tier, and Japan by itself at the bottom. These differences do not go away when shares are adjusted to a trend productivity basis. If we are willing to take seriously changes in the labour share within a country over time, we should probably be interested also in these cross-country differences since technology is mobile across countries. Yet these cross-country differences have no apparent explanatory power for events of the 1960s. Of the three countries usually identifed from their time series as having the largest wage gaps in the 1970s – Germany, Japan and the United Kingdom – one is in each of the three tiers in cross-country comparisons. In the upper tier, United States employment expanded strongly during the 1970s. Of course, even if we think of the manufacturing sectors of all these countries as characterised by a single production function by the 1970s, we might think of reasons why their equilibrium labour share would differ. Low labour shares could represent a protected capital market, for instance. Still, the differences cast doubt on the importance of variations through time in a country's share.

But there is more than just trend in the labour shares. Especially in the United Kingdom, Sweden and Japan, there were episodic bursts up in the labour share in the 1970s which may have had special importance. In order to investigate this and other issues, I turn to some regressions, though with trepidation. There are not many observations and the data are far from perfect.

Shares and unemployment

Sachs (1983) has offered one direct test of the importance of wage gaps by showing product wages (W/P_v) adjusted for productivity trends (the equivalent of the adjusted labour share) explain subsequent movements in unemployment. The first regression for each country in Table 2 duplicates his test, though for a slightly longer sample period. The wage gap coefficient has the right sign everywhere and some significance in some countries. The second regressions test the alternative, or additional, hypothesis that unemployment reflects policy reactions to inflation. There is no simple way to characterise policy itself, particularly monetary policy. Instead I introduce the lagged inflation rate into the Sachs regressions. If policy is reacting to higher inflation by restraining output and employment, lagged inflation should have a significant positive coefficient. In the Table 2 regressions, that hypothesis comes through everywhere but Italy and the importance of the wage gap diminishes greatly or vanishes.

The Table 2 regressions deliberately followed Sachs' specification. Because the time trends and serial correlation corrections that they employ make the interpretation of the other variables uncertain, Table 3 presents alternative regressions along lines suggested by Andrew Oswald (above, Chapter Four). In the first regression for each country, the importance of the product wage is greatly diminished compared with its role in Table 2. When the lagged inflation rate, representing the hypothesis of policy reaction to inflation is introduced, it is often significant and always correctly signed. And the wage gap variable loses all importance.

Table 2. Aggregate unemployment rate equations, 1961–83

	Constant	Lagged unemployment rate	Time trend	1974 trend break	Log of lagged product wage	Lagged inflation rate (CPI)	$\bar{R}^2$	S.E.	Rho
United States	−106·02	0·54	−0·83	0·36	26·65		0·698	0·973	0·119
		(2·75)	(−1·58)	(1·81)	(1·65)				
	−80·64	0·74	−0·75	0·25	20·14	29·66	0·788	0·815	−0·150
		(5·04)	(−1·87)	(1·75)	(1·61)	(3·04)			
United Kingdom	−21·43	0·49	−0·25	0·60	5·84		0·952	0·644	0·366
		(2·33)	(−0·86)	(2·95)	(1·05)				
	−5·66	0·52	−0·15	0·62	1·68	13·65	0·969	0·518	0·709
		(2·89)	(−0·64)	(2·89)	(0·36)	(3·54)			
France	0·26	−0·14	0·16	0·72	−0·01		0·987	0·325	0·543
		(−0·51)	(0·62)	(3·12)	(0·00)				
	−0·42	0·20	0·07	0·48	0·05	14·36	0·993	0·235	−0·021
		(0·98)	(0·50)	(3·32)	(0·02)	(4·74)			
Germany	−3·23	0·59	0·00	0·28	0·94		0·903	0·682	0·496
		(2·37)	(0·00)	(1·13)	(0·10)				
	30·16	0·83	0·50	0·10	−8·88	46·99	0·953	0·477	−0·021
		(5·98)	(1·52)	(0·80)	(−1·70)	(5·35)			
Italy	−13·11	0·71	−0·37	0·52	4·42		0·970	0·338	0·275
		(4·19)	(−1·55)	(2·98)	(1·52)				
	−12·53	0·71	−0·36	0·51	4·24	0·42	0·968	0·349	0·290
		(3·97)	(−1·30)	(2·37)	(1·25)	(0·13)			
Sweden[b]	−3·35	0·56	−0·14	0·20	1·36		0·440	0·427	0·307
		(1·83)	(−0·51)	(0·99)	(0·36)				
	−3·39	1·14	−0·38	0·36	1·52	18·24	0·583	0·368	−0·252
		(4·48)	(−1·89)	(2·67)	(0·58)	(2·56)			
Japan[c]	−6·86	0·27	−0·30	0·14	2·89		0·938	0·108	−0·080
		(1·61)	(−3·66)	(3·53)	(3·93)				
	−3·43	0·44	−0·15	0·11	1·48	1·91	0·955	0·092	−0·100
		(2·85)	(−1·74)	(2·85)	(1·82)	(2·64)			

(a) Dependent variable is the aggregate unemployment rate. The product wage, compensation per hour divided by value added price, refers to manufacturing. Lags are one period. Numbers in parentheses are t-statistics.
(b) 1969–83.
(c) 1961–82.

Table 3. Alternative aggregate unemployment rate equations, 1961–83

	Constant	Unemployment rate (t−1)	Unemployment rate (t−2)	Log of lagged product wage	Lagged inflation rate (CPI)	R^2	S.E.	D-W
					Independent variables[a]			
United States	−14·64	0·79 (4·0)	−0·25 (−1·2)	3·91 (3·1)		0·754	0·897	2·06
	3·22	0·74 (4·1)	−0·03 (−0·1)	−0·64 (−0·3)	26·4 (2·3)	0·802	0·804	1·96
United Kingdom	−5·94	1·31 (5·9)	−0·40 (−1·4)	1·50 (1·5)		0·931	0·774	1·56
	3·88	1·23 (5·7)	−0·14 (−0·5)	−1·08 (−0·6)	11·03 (1·7)	0·938	0·734	1·27
France	−3·34	0·89 (3·5)	0·08 (0·3)	0·91 (2·0)		0·981	0·389	1·98
	−0·72	0·63 (3·0)	0·32 (1·4)	0·07 (0·2)	15·00 (3·6)	0·989	0·300	1·89
Germany	−5·27	1·35 (6·3)	−0·59 (−2·4)	1·41 (1·9)		0·902	0·686	1·76
	0·816	1·17 (5·9)	−0·09 (−0·3)	−0·50 (−0·5)	37·7 (2·6)	0·926	0·601	1·57
Italy	−3·25	1·34 (6·0)	−0·28 (−1·1)	0·73 (2·3)		0·957	0·412	1·65
	−1·11	1·38 (6·4)	−0·37 (−1·5)	0·19 (0·4)	4·49 (1·6)	0·961	0·394	1·68
Sweden[b]	1·01	1·02 (3·4)	−0·55 (−1·5)	0·50 (0·7)		0·481	0·421	1·82
	2·22	1·13 (3·6)	−0·48 (−1·3)	−0·45 (−0·4)	7·76 (1·0)	0·482	0·420	1·78
Japan[c]	0·55	0·82 (3·3)	−0·05 (−0·2)	0·24 (2·8)		0·911	0·148	1·84
	−0·58	0·87 (3·9)	0·02 (0·1)	0·17 (2·1)	1·81 (2·3)	0·928	0·133	1·69

(a) Dependent variable is the aggregate unemployment rate. The product wage, compensation per hour divided by value added price, refers to manufacturing. Lags are one period except where shown otherwise. Numbers in parentheses are t-statistics.
(b) 1969–83.
(c) 1961–82.

Shares and investment

Another implication of the classical unemployment idea is that business investment will be curtailed when real wages are too high. Table 4 reports results of adding the adjusted labour share, current and lagged, to an accelerator explanation of business fixed investment. Here and in the remainder of the paper, the results for France are not reported because principal coefficients always had the wrong signs – in this case the accelerator coefficients. The results lend a little support to the wage gap thesis in some of our countries, though not to anyone insisting on significant coefficients. The sum of the shares' coefficients are positive in three countries, including the United Kingdom which has a large wage gap in Sachs' study, indicating investment is enhanced by a permanent increase in the labour share.

Shares and inflation

Finally, the wage gap thesis implies that inflation will be intensified, other things being equal, in the presence of excessive wage gaps. When the lagged labour share was added to the wage inflation equations reported below, this hypothesis received no support. The coefficients, with t-statistics in parentheses, were as follows:

United States	-0.25	(-0.4)
United Kingdom	-0.54	(-1.2)
Germany	-0.71	(-2.8)
Italy	-0.21	(-0.5)
Sweden	-0.40	(-2.3)
Japan	-0.40	(-0.9)

Labour shares do not appear to be precursors of inflation anywhere. Together with the findings on unemployment and investment, these results suggest that adjusted labour shares have no consistent predictive power in any country or for any of the three variables it may be expected to predict under the classical unemployment hypothesis.

4. Inflation and policy reaction

If structural or classical explanations of unemployment in the late 1970s are not important, that leaves policy reaction. Regarding unemployment since the mid-1970s as a consequence of policies to slow

Table 4. Investment equations, 1968–82

Independent variables[a]

	Constant	Change in log output	Lagged change in log output	Lagged dependent variable	Adjusted labour share	Lagged adjusted labour share	Sum of share	$\bar{R}^2$	S.E.	D.W.
United States	−10·10	12·67 (2·5)	19·95 (4·1)	1·12 (4·8)	−3·56 (−0·4)	13·97 (1·3)	10·41	0·731	0·277	2·43
United Kingdom	0·97	13·38 (3·2)	13·30 (3·1)	0·80 (5·0)	6·47 (1·6)	−4·61 (−1·2)	1·86	0·827	0·337	2·65
Germany	9·72	6·56 (0·6)	19·64 (2·2)	0·56 (3·6)	20·40 (0·9)	−26·43 (−1·2)	−6·03	0·764	0·717	1·22
Italy	−3·46	14·09 (1·7)	11·65 (1·7)	0·49 (1·1)	21·38 (1·5)	−5·20 (−0·5)	16·18	0·471	0·608	1·91
Sweden	8·61	−2·06 (−0·2)	14·08 (1·1)	0·65 (2·8)	2·25 (0·2)	−6·91 (−0·6)	−4·66	0·593	0·679	2·27
Japan[b]	10·83	18·37 (1·1)	23·51 (1·8)	0·48 (1·4)	29·47 (1·1)	−30·21 (−1·4)	−0·74	0·823	0·687	1·62

(a) Dependent variable is the ratio of non-residential construction plus machinery and equipment to GDP. Lags are one period. Numbers in parentheses are *t*-statistics.
(b) 1971–82.

inflation brings us to the hard questions of why inflation got so high and why it remained so stubborn.

As suggested above, I find the most useful way to characterise what goes on at the macroeconomic level is to view the short-run response of wage (and price) inflation to cyclical fluctuations in output as operating around a relatively stable norm for wage increases that only changes in response to extreme or prolonged departures of the economy from what is typical. On this view, a major shift up in the wage norm would have occurred as a result of the historic expansion of the 1960s and the sustained low unemployment rates that the expansion had produced in most countries during the last half of that decade. In the absence of successful incomes policies or other direct measures, a shift down in the wage norm would only occur after a similarly historic period of recession and high unemployment. In between we would observe the relatively modest cyclical fluctuations in inflation that are associated with the short-run Phillips curve.

In Table 5, I present a set of equations for manufacturing wage inflation for each of our six countries. These equations could easily be improved by careful students of the individual countries. Their main purpose here is to see whether unemployment and lagged dependent variables help explain wage inflation in the conventional way and to examine the wage norm thesis against the alternatives I outlined earlier – adaptive expectations and rational expectations-credibility. The equations explain changes in the log of compensation per hour in manufacturing. The OPEC I years, 1974–75, are omitted in each case because that period appears exceptional, as Table 1 showed, even for explaining wage or price indexes that do not directly contain oil prices. The period of estimation ends in 1979 to permit out-of-sample forecasts of the disinflation years that followed.

The three equations for each country compare the basic equation without norm shifts with an equation that allows for a norm shift starting in 1970 and another that allows for a second norm shift after 1975, following the OPEC shock. A more elaborate characterisation of norm shifts could be made to fit the data better. In particular, different starting dates would fit best for different countries. However, it is hard not to overmine the data once one starts down this road.

The simple norm shift starting in 1970 is significant and substantial in all cases. It is consistent with the idea that the sustained and prolonged era of very low unemployment rates experienced during the last half of the 1960s were sufficiently unusual to raise wage norms. The

Table 5. Wage inflation equations, compensation per hour, 1961–79, and dynamic forecast errors, 1980–84

		Independent variables[a]								Dynamic forecast errors[c]
	Constant	Lagged dependent[b]	Unemployment[b]	Lagged Unemployment[b]	Post-1969 norm-shift dummy	Post-1975 norm-shift dummy	R^2	S.E.	D.W.	(actual-predicted) × 100
United States	−0·008	0·774 (4·54)	0·185 (1·30)	−0·083 (−0·67)	—	—	0·676	0·015	2·54	1980 2·9 / 1981 1·1 / 1982 1·3 / 1983 −3·6 / 1984 −3·8
	−0·017	0·451 (2·38)	0·293 (2·33)	−0·113 (−1·08)	0·025 (2·58)	—	0·776	0·012	2·15	
	−0·020	0·046 (0·22)	0·213 (2·03)	0·061 (0·58)	0·026 (3·29)	0·031 (2·76)	0·856	0·010	2·29	
United Kingdom	0·108	0·370 (2·67)	0·052 (0·81)	−0·154 (−2·65)	—	—	0·861	0·024	1·65	1980 2·6 / 1981 −1·5 / 1982 −5·8 / 1983 −6·6 / 1984 −6·0
	0·060	0·195 (1·47)	0·075 (1·40)	−0·085 (−1·55)	0·055 (2·64)	—	0·905	0·020	1·74	
	0·042	0·114 (0·71)	0·088 (1·58)	−0·058 (−0·94)	0·064 (2·77)	0·020 (0·93)	0·904	0·020	1·78	
Germany	0·050	0·321 (1·22)	−0·026 (1·37)	−0·014 (−0·73)	—	—	0·298	0·026	2·11	1980 0·1 / 1981 −0·6 / 1982 −2·3 / 1983 −3·5 / 1984 −4·1
	0·034	−0·083 (−0·34)	0·049 (2·93)	−0·005 (−0·36)	0·044 (2·97)	—	0·428	0·021	1·71	
	0·064	−0·079 (−0·33)	0·039 (2·17)	−0·020 (−1·04)	0·048 (3·28)	−0·033 (−1·38)	0·468	0·020	1·93	
Italy	0·023	0·727 (2·89)	1·386 (1·66)	−1·296 (−1·52)	—	—	0·434	0·043	1·92	1980 2·1 / 1981 3·4 / 1982 2·3 / 1983 −2·5 / 1984 1·4
	0·024	0·416 (2·15)	2·253 (3·61)	−2·147 (−3·38)	0·077 (3·83)	—	0·724	0·039	2·88	
	−0·010	0·697 (6·12)	2·550 (6·48)	−2·551 (−7·01)	0·073 (6·31)	−0·013 (−0·76)	0·837	0·023	1·93	

Table 5 (continued)

			Independent variables[a]							Dynamic forecast errors[c] (actual-predicted) × 100	
	Constant	Lagged dependent	Unemployment[b]	Lagged Unemployment[b]	Post-1969 norm-shift dummy	Post-1975 norm-shift dummy	R^2	S.E.	D.W.		
Sweden	0·073	0·269 (1·73)	0·149 (0·86)	0·166 (0·90)	—	—	0·688	0·018	2·72	1980 1981 1982 1983 1984	1·1 1·2 −0·8 0·7 1·8
	0·081	0·125 (0·70)	0·203 (1·19)	0·197 (1·11)	0·015 (1·47)	—	0·712	0·017	2·73		
	0·078	0·160 (0·70)	0·184 (0·96)	0·182 (0·93)	0·015 (1·43)	−0·004 (−0·26)	0·690	0·017	2·81		
Japan	0·071	0·551 (2·55)	1·123 (3·20)	−0·444 (−1·20)	—	—	0·767	0·025	1·99	1980 1981 1982 1983 1984	−1·0 −1·0 −2·2 −2·5 −4·5
	0·106	0·189 (1·05)	1·345 (5·29)	0·039 (0·13)	0·054 (3·77)	—	0·884	0·018	2·33		
	0·113	0·134 (0·68)	1·174 (3·48)	−0·073 (−0·22)	0·053 (3·67)	−0·025 (−0·79)	0·881	0·018	2·24		

(a) The dependent variable is the rate of change in hourly compensation measured as difference in logs. Dummies for 1974 and 1975 are not shown. Lags are one period. Numbers in parentheses are t-statistics.

(b) The unemployment measure is the inverse of the unemployment rate. For Sweden and Japan, the log of output gaps were used in place of unemployment rates. Gaps are defined as the ratio of actual to potential output in manufacturing for Sweden and in the aggregate economy for Japan.

(c) From equations with both norm-shift dummies.

alternative explanation that adaptive expectations shifted up the inflation rate is not supported by a comparison of the first and second equations. In all cases, allowing for a norm shift substantially reduces the estimated coefficient in the lagged dependent variable. The same result is found in reduced form inflation equations, not reported here, explaining either the CPI or GNP deflators.

Results are mixed with the post-1975 dummy that tests for whether a further norm shift occurred following the inflation explosion of OPEC I. There appears to have been such a further ratchet-up in the United States and United Kingdom. But price and wage controls in the United States during 1972–73 may have masked the size of the post-1969 norm shift and the post-1975 shift may be making up for that. The evidence for an adaptive expectations model is further weakened by allowing for the post-OPEC shift, as the lagged dependent variable falls to insignificance everywhere but Italy.

Disinflation and credibility

The new classical credibility thesis is more elusive and to examine it I turn to recent developments. The hope, in both credibility models and perhaps the minds of some policy-makers, was that determined restrictive policies would bring disinflation more promptly and with less cost in output and unemployment than past cyclical experience would have produced. The more general idea of stubborn inflation norms anticipates a shift down in the inflation equation – or overpredictions in an equation that does not allow for a shift – only after experienced hard times.

I have examined US behaviour in the period since 1979 in some detail (Perry 1983) and concluded that the disinflation was about as expected in the general wage norm model. Wage inflation slowed only gradually and about as predicted from the cyclical response to unemployment until late 1982. At that point, with unemployment approaching 11 per cent and the length and depth of the recession both much greater than in any downturn since the 1930s, a shift down in the inflation norm finally appears and wage inflation begins to slow substantially further. What is more, the exceptional weakness in wages, including wage concessions, is concentrated in particularly hard-hit industries. The new stance of monetary policy in the United States got no apparent bonus or quick response in disinflation for credibility. The norm only shifted after a historic amount of real slack had been imposed on the economy.

The dynamic forecast errors in Table 5 reinforce these results for the United States and find parallel results for several other countries. Actual US wage inflation finally falls below predicted only in 1983, but then does so by a substantial amount. In Germany and the United Kingdom, a shift down in the norm occurs by 1982 and in Japan by 1984. By 1982, conservative policies had been in place in Germany and the United Kingdom for several years, with unemployment rising steadily. These outcomes are consistent with the idea of norm shifts in response to unusually deep and extended hard times. They lend no support to the idea that a credible restrictive policy can provide a short cut to disinflation by producing prompt downward flexibility of wages.

None of these results casts much light on the possible importance of policy credibility as a general matter. In particular, if establishing credibility required that policy create the extended and deep recessions that occurred, one cannot distinguish credibility from the idea that inflation norms would come down only after extended and deep recessions. Furthermore, the ratcheting-down of wage norms that has finally occurred promises nothing about the flexibility of wages in the future. I turn next to some issues concerning flexibility, including whether less wage rigidity would be desirable in all circumstances.

5. *The flexibility issue*

Even if disinflation is finally succeeding, the tremendous inertia that inflation has exhibited has made disinflation very costly in lost output and employment. The increasing awareness of this fact has focused attention on the flexibility of prices and wages and on whether the economy might 'work better' if that flexibility could be enhanced. The question seems to me difficult to pose and the answer unclear, particularly if we recognise that policy-makers care about inflation.

The relevant case to consider is a parallel increase in the flexibility of wages and product prices. A greater flexibility of wages but not of prices would appear to stabilise employment demand of firms; but, abstracting from inventories, a corresponding flexibility of prices would be needed to match product demand with the more stable levels of production. The optimising behaviour of firms will closely match any change in wage flexibility with a corresponding change in price flexibility.

Greater flexibility of average nominal wages and prices in response to variations in output and unemployment – a steepening of the short-run Phillips curve in the way this is often discussed – is unambiguously favoured in natural rate or NAIRU (non-acclerating inflation rate of unemployment) models of inflation dynamics. Whatever produces observed unemployment in these models, inflation will accelerate (or decelerate) if unemployment is above (or below) the natural rate. In response to any real or nominal disturbance, greater flexibility raises or lowers wages and prices more promptly thus returning unemployment to its natural rate more quickly, at least under a policy that stabilises nominal GNP. On this natural rate view, greater flexibility works favourably all the time. But this natural rate model seems a poor description of the world. If the short-run dynamics of inflation are not reflections of a natural rate model, greater flexibility may be either a good thing or a bad thing for stabilisation.

Other views of inflation dynamics predict that wages and prices will rise faster as unemployment is reduced cyclically and will do so before any efficient level of unemployment is achieved. Tobin (1972) outlined such a model centred on transitory excess demands in individual markets. I sketched out a model (Perry 1980) in which firms or sectors respond to shifts out in the demand for their output with positively correlated increases in wages and employment, leading again to inflation before full employment. And Okun (1981) developed a comprehensive model of the macroeconomy and its wage and price-setting behaviour in which 'premature' inflation is one characteristic of the optimal arrangements in labour and product markets.

In an economy with that cyclical characteristic, greater wage flexibility could mean that average wages accelerate more and do so more promptly in the expansion phase as firms respond to their own expanding demand. Steepening the short-run Phillips curve is a mixed blessing if inflation worsens cyclically before high employment is achieved. We alternatively like flexibility and rigidity in average wages depending on whether we are in a phase in which policy is trying to reduce unemployment or is raising it in the process of slowing inflation. The original wage-price guideposts in the United States were conceived as a way to avoid the upward flexibility of wages and prices that might interfere with achieving high employment levels. To extend that idea to the obvious point, if we could have perfectly rigid average wages and value-added prices (with enough relative flexibility to move resources around as needed within the macroeconomy) stabilisation would be no problem since holding nominal GNP at the appropriate level would offset all real shocks and maintain real GNP at the appropriate level. Specifying that appropriate level would be another matter.

One can conceive of increases in relative wage flexibility that provided apparent allocational gains without affecting the behaviour of aggregate wages. But even here there are cautions. The inflexibility that is observed is not simply a symptom of inefficiency in the system. Many product and labour markets have evolved sticky pricing and wage-setting arrangements as an optimal way to conduct business and minimise important transactions costs. As Charles Schultze (1985) has pointed out, these arrangements must work both for relative shocks and aggregate shocks and for permanent and transitory shocks, all of which are hard to distinguish from one another when they occur. Any enforced change in flexibility would have to justify changing those transactionally efficient arrangements.

The case for seeking flexibility is no doubt strongest if what is meant is simply putting more symmetry into the response to positive and negative disturbances. Downward wage inflexibility seems to characterise many parts of modern economies, imparting an upward bias to average wages in the face of even random shocks. Apart from the possible objections to altering optimal wage-setting arrangements, increasing flexibility in this one direction would doubtless improve stabilisation.

Some of the interest in flexibility arises because of the recent history of supply shocks that pushed up price levels. Considering their effects requires going beyond the response of wages to demand and asking whether supply shocks might have long-lasting effects on inflation by raising inflation norms. Certainly policy-makers feared that they would, and the wage explosions that greeted OPEC I in several countries support that fear. In these cases, greater flexibility with respect to demand would minimise the unemployment needed to head off a ratchet-up in the norm. Of course, less flexibility in response to the supply shock in the first place would have precluded the need for much demand restraint anyhow.

Thus, even in this case, the verdict on flexibility is clear only if we choose when we want flexibility and when rigidity. The supply shock case might be viewed as an argument against indexing rather than flexibility. But if the distinction between norm shifts and 'normal' responses is accepted, OPEC I becomes a historic event capable of shifting norms rather than simply a typical disturbance in consumer prices. It is the kind of event for which an incomes policy is hypothetically useful. Exogenous wage push by unions is another such event. That is a form of supply shock that may be responsive to how unions expect the government to respond, including whether stabilisation policy will be accommodative.

6. *Improving the long cycle*

I turn now to what lessons there may be in the long cycle of the past twenty-five years that took most of the industrial world from great prosperity through high inflation rates and finally to prolonged and deep recessions. The fact that this was the first experience of this kind for the major industrial economies suggests that the historic prosperity that ended with OPEC I and the special economic power of unions in this period may have been important in what happened.

Whether unions have special blame for the inflation that came out of this period of great prosperity is hard to say. I could not get data to compare properly union or manufacturing wage gains with economy-wide wage gains. But based on data for compensation per employee, it appears that manufacturing compensation clearly outpaced the economy-wide average mainly in Germany, which had the best overall inflation record of all the countries reviewed here. That is a puzzle in light of much that we know about periods in which unions were a major force for large wage increases. It may be that all they did was catch up with inflation generated elsewhere. More likely, in many countries unions probably set the standard for wages throughout the economy.

I believe a good analytic case can be made for incomes policies to moderate inflation. But the political case for them and their political design never seems to work right. They are more likely to be a last resort when inflation has become a serious problem already. And they are likely to be shaped by political necessity rather than economic logic. Tax-based incomes policies that are institutionalised before inflation becomes a problem could make a difference. But nobody wants to talk about them when inflation is not an issue.

It was generally agreed that excess-demand inflation had become a problem in the United States in the last half of the 1960s. Europe was in a similar situation, with even lower official unemployment rates but perhaps a similar degree of market tightness. Concern over the problems posed by sustained tight markets was not intense, in part because real gains in output and employment were being achieved and in part because the effect it would have on the inflation norm was not appreciated. It is clear now that policy should have worried more about inflation in this period. If inflation had never become deeply imbedded in wage-setting in the 1960s, substantially ratcheting-up the wage norm, the 1970s would have looked very different.

But the problems of the 1970s should not be taken to mean that the long prosperity of the 1960s was a great mistake. For one thing, the inflation of the 1970s was exacerbated by the OPEC I supply shocks to which stabilisation policy had no appropriate answer. Policy everywhere eventually responded with demand-restraint and recession. That whole episode was not a legacy of the 1960s.

The main lesson of the 1960s is that stabilisation policy must be cautious in the neighbourhood of full employment, not that it should avoid employment goals. The disastrous unemployment levels in Europe today are so far from the overtight markets of the 1960s that one experience has no relevance for the other. If inflation norms are finally coming down, as they appear to be, expansion can proceed for many years before inflation again becomes a caution.

For the near term, a change in the policy mix toward more expansionary budgets in Europe, as part of a more expansionary overall policy, and tighter budgets in the United States makes sense. If this helped depreciate the dollar, which is inevitable in any case, it would put downward pressure on European prices as their expansions proceed. The policies of the recent past in Europe, which appeared to fear demand generated domestically but favoured demand generated by weak currencies, were perverse in this regard.

The recent interest in steady policies does not really address the major problems that arose in either of the past two decades. In the United States at least, the variability of money growth or nominal GNP growth was remarkably low in the 1960s and much lower than in either the preceding or following decade. Variability of neither policy nor performance was the culprit. Furthermore, steady policies are generally inappropriate in the face of supply shocks such as those that upset economies in the 1970s. A policy of gearing stabilisation to inflation alone, without concern for output and employment, also gets little support from the record of the past. That record reaffirms that real activity simply does not adjust to near an optimal level over an acceptable period of time. There seems to be no substitute for policy-makers feeling their way toward the appropriate level of unemployment, taking account of inflation risks as they go.

Fine-tuning is a straw man that has received a lot of criticism from advocates of rules over discretion. Although discretion inevitably seems to be needed in policy, the straw man should not become a reality. Downturns are costly but relatively easy to nip in the bud if policy is not inhibited by inflation. Upturns in wage inflation are probably harder to put down because they upset relative wage levels and set in motion tendencies to bring other wages up into line. Unless incomes policies are in place and prove highly effective, an insurance policy against any softening of markets probably risks more inflation than it is worth when the economy is in the neighbourhood of full employment. Refusing to provide such an insurance policy, particularly in the event of extravagant wage demands where unions are especially important, is one way in which the credibility of an anti-inflation commitment may be usefully established and at little cost.

What policy probably should strive for is a balance somewhere between the conservative extreme of reacting to any sign of inflation and the policy of accommodating any wage push that occurs, which at times has characterised policy-making in the United Kingdom. If this middle road cannot improve on the past, maybe we will have thought of something else before inflation norms start ratcheting-up again.

References

Artus, J.R., 'An empirical evaluation of the disequilibrium real wage rate hypothesis, DM/84/27 (Washington, D.C.: International Monetary Fund, 1984).

Bruno, M. and Sachs, J.D., 'Supply versus demand approaches to the problem of stagflation', in Giersch, H. (ed.), *Macroeconomic Policies for Growth and Stability: A European Perspective* (Kiel: Institut für Weltwirtschaft, 1981), 15–60.

Islam, S., 'Unemployment in major industrial countries: structural, classical or keynesian?' (New York City: Federal Reserve Bank of New York, 1983).

Muller, P. and Price, R.W.R., 'Structural budget deficits and fiscal stance', Working Paper No. 15 (OECD, 1984).

Okun, A.M., *Prices and Quantities: A Macroeconomic Analysis* (Washington, D.C.: Brookings Institution, 1981).

Perry, G.L., 'What have we learned about disinflation', *Brookings Papers on Economic Activity* 2 (1983), 587–602.

————, 'Inflation in theory and practice', *Brookings Papers on Economic Activity* 1 (1980), 207–41.

Sachs, J.D. 'Wages, profits and macroeconomic adjustment: a comparative study', *Brookings Papers on Economic Activity* 2 (1979), 269–319.

————, 'Real wages and unemployment in the OECD countries', *Brookings Papers on Economic Activity* 1 (1983), 255–304.

Schultze, C. L., 'Some macro foundations for micro theory', *Brookings Papers on Economic Activity* 2 (1981), 521–76.

————, 'Microeconomic efficiency and nominal wage stickiness', *American Economic Review* 75 (March 1985), 1–15.

Tobin, J., 'Inflation and unemployment', *American Economic Review* 62 (March 1972), 1–18.

7. A Wage-Tax, Worker-Subsidy Policy for Reducing the 'Natural' Rate of Unemployment

R. Jackman & R. Layard

Introduction

The main reason why governments today do not attempt to tackle unemployment by traditional Keynesian expansionary policies is the fear that a stimulus to demand will simply lead to higher inflation with no gain in output or employment. While in some countries that fear may be exaggerated, there is no doubt in our minds that an expansion of demand in current circumstances, and in the absence of other policy measures, will lead to a resurgence of inflation long before adequate levels of employment are reached. That is, we believe that there exists in the economy a rate of unemployment, which (following established usage) we will term the 'natural rate', below which inflation will accelerate. We also believe that the level of the natural rate has increased considerably in recent years. We appreciate that these claims may be contentious, but we believe them to be supported by the bulk of econometric evidence.[1]

It follows that a permanent reduction in unemployment below the level at which inflation starts to accelerate can only be brought about by policies which reduce the natural rate. To investigate such policies it is necessary to start from a model of the determinants of the natural rate. The starting point is that wages are set not in a competitive market but by firms or by trade unions or by collective bargaining. Wages are thus determined in accordance with the self-interest of those who set them rather than at the level which clears the market. The outcome of this process determines the level of aggregate unemployment. In this paper we examine how taxes and subsidies, by changing the incentives perceived by individual wage-setters, can alter wage-setting behaviour, and with it the natural rate of unemployment.

[1] See, for example, Grubb, Jackman and Layard (1983) and Layard and Nickell (1985).

We consider two main types of models. In the first, firms set wages but they may have an incentive to set wages above the market-clearing rate because they can thereby raise the productivity of their workforce. In the second, wages are set by trade unions, who again attempt to set wages above market-clearing levels for the benefit of their members.

The tax-subsidy schemes we consider have two types of effect. First, if one envisages a world of homogeneous labour, taxes and subsidies can alter the trade-off between wages and employment as perceived by wage-setters. Appropriately designed taxes and subsidies can raise the level of employment, and hence reduce the level of unemployment consistent with non-accelerating inflation. Second, if labour is not homogeneous, taxes and subsidies can be used to shift demand from one group of workers to another. Low-wage markets are particularly affected by externally imposed rigidities (such as minimum wage laws) and by fiscal 'distortions' (such as unemployment benefit), with the consequence of higher unemployment rates. Increasing the demand for labour in low-wage markets, at the expense of the demand for labour in high-wage markets, can then reduce aggregate unemployment.

It turns out that a tax on wages offset by a subsidy on employment, in a balanced budget package, operates in the right direction in both these cases: i.e. when there is only one type of labour and when there is more than one. The paper is in three sections. The first demonstrates the impact of a wage tax on employment and unemployment in a model with homogeneous labour. The second analyses the workings of a wage tax with heterogeneous labour. The third summarises our conclusions.

The analysis assumes imperfect competition throughout. We have demonstrated elsewhere that the policies considered work under perfect competition (Jackman, Layard and Pissarides (1986)). But imperfect competition may often be a more realistic assumption, and it is important to be sure that the policies are also effective in that situation.

1. *Aggregate effect of a wage tax plus per-worker subsidy*

In this part of the paper we assume homogeneous labour and analyse the effect of a tax-subsidy scheme, in which each firm pays a tax proportional to its wage bill and receives a subsidy equal to a fixed amount per worker. Each firm takes the tax rate (t) and subsidy rate

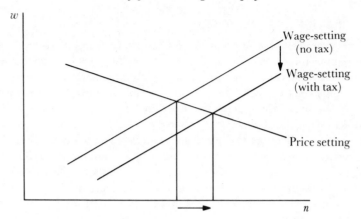

Figure 1. How the wage-tax subsidy works

(s) as exogenous. However, the government sets them so that ex-post the scheme is self-financing. Thus for the representative firm ex-post (*but not ex-ante*) $tw_i = s$, where w_i is the wage. We analyse the effect first assuming that firms set wages and then that unions set wages.

In each case the key to understanding how the level of employment is determined in the long run is to note that when wages are determined the markup of wages over prices must be consistent with the markup of prices over wages when prices are set. If wage targets are excessive this will cause spiralling inflation. Since we have assumed that ex-post the tax-subsidy scheme has no effect on the marginal cost of the representative firm, employment can only be increased by devices which reduce the target real wage that is sought at a given level of employment.

This is illustrated in Figure 1. If employment is higher the target real wage will be higher, but under our scheme the target at a given level of employment will be reduced. By reducing wage pressure, this makes possible a rise in employment.[2]

We show this first for a world where firms set wages and then for one where unions set wages.

---

[2] This assumes that the price relationship slopes up less than the wage relationship. So long as the marginal product of labour is constant or falling, the price relationship will not slope up, unless the elasticity of demand falls when output rises. In the models of this paper the price relationship does not rise.

(i) *Model with firms' wage-setting*

When firms set wages their concern is to maximise their profits but they recognise that their ability to retain or hire workers, and the productive efficiency or morale of their workers, is affected by the wage they offer relative to expected income outside the firm. In our earlier paper we show (using perfect competition) how a wage tax-subsidy works when each of these motives is taken to be the prime influence on the firm. In the present paper (using imperfect competition) we shall concentrate on the case where quitting is the prime concern.[3] It is easy to check that the results go through in the other cases,[4] and we are most anxious that the model we present should not be narrowly interpreted.

Let firm i offer a real wage w_i. Let the general real wage level be w and the unemployment rate be u. Assume that unemployed workers receive a real unemployment benefit, b. Then the expected income[5] of a worker not employed in firm i is $(1-u)w + ub$. The worker's evaluation of the worth of a job in firm i is held to depend postively on the ratio

$$\frac{w_i}{(1-u)w + ub} = \frac{w_i/w}{1-u(1-\rho)} = r_i x$$

where $r_i = w_i/w$ (the firm's relative wage), ρ is the benefit replacement ratio (b/w), which is taken as exogenously determined by the government, and $x = 1/(1 - u(1-\rho))$ and varies directly with unemployment. The firm's quit rate decreases as its wage relative to expected outside income increases, but at a decreasing rate:

$$q_i = q(r_i x) \qquad (q' < 0;\ q'' > 0).$$

The firm chooses the relative wage (r_i) and the relative price (p_i) to maximise its real profits (π_i) which are

(1) $$\pi_i = p_i y_i - n_i(r_i w + \phi q(r_i x))$$

---

[3] The quit model is due to Salop (1979), and see also Calvo (1979).

[4] For example suppose there were no costs of quitting but the production function (2) were $y_i = n_i e(w_i/((1/u)w + ub)) - f$, where e is efficiency and the other variables are as shown below. The implications are exactly as for our quit model.

[5] This formula assumes that the probability of a worker not employed in firm i being unemployed is equal to the proportion of all workers who are unemployed. A rigorous dynamic formulation of the worker's expected income if unemployed, allowing for transition probabilities between employment and unemployment, reduces to the expression in the text as the discount rate approaches zero.

where y_i is output, n_i employment and ϕ the cost associated with each worker quitting the firm – all of this subject to the firm's production function and its demand curve.

Throughout the paper we assume for simplicity that the marginal product of labour is constant.[6] Falling marginal product would, if anything, reinforce (but complicate) our results. So we simply assume in this section that the marginal product of labour is (by choice of units) equal to unity and the firm's employment needed to produce output is a fixed amount (f) plus y_i:

(2) $$n_i = f + y_i$$

The firm faces a demand for its product given by

(3) $$y_i = \frac{Y}{m} p_i^{-\eta}$$

where Y is total real aggregate demand in the economy, and m is the number of firms. The firm chooses its price to maximise profits given that it will meet the resulting demand for output.

The first order condition for wages implies

$$w + \phi q'(r_i x)x = 0$$

and that for prices implies that real marginal revenue equals real marginal cost, i.e.

$$p_i\left(1 - \frac{1}{\eta}\right) = r_i w + \phi q(r_i x)$$

If all firms are identical, equilibrium requires that $r_i = p_i = 1$. Hence the aggregate wage equation is

(4) $$w = -\phi q'(x)x$$

and the aggregate price equation gives

(5) $$w = 1 - \frac{1}{\eta} - \phi q(x)$$

This is a system of the kind portrayed in Figure 1.[7] From it we can determine $u(1 - \rho)$. Thus if the replacement rate (ρ) is one half, a 1 per cent rise in it will produce a 1 per cent rise in unemployment.

---

[6] Our basic imperfect model is essentially that of Weitzman (1982).
[7] We cannot assume that the wage function slopes up – only that it slopes down less than the price function.

We now introduce our tax-subsidy scheme, so profit becomes

$$\pi_i = p_i y_i - n_i \left[r_i w (1 + t) - s + \phi q(r_i x) \right]$$

In consequence the aggregate wage equation becomes

(6) $$w(1 + t) = - \phi q'(x) x$$

while the price equation remains unchanged due to the self-financing character of the scheme. Thus the wage-setting relationship has been shifted down and employment has increased.

To check this we can combine equations (5) and (6) and check that $\delta x / \delta t < 0$.[8] One can also check that if there was no subsidy but only a tax wages would fall by the full amount of the tax with no change in employment. It is the subsidy which makes possible the increase in employment in most models where firms are setting wages.

Corresponding to the natural level of employment (N^*) is a natural level of output (Y^*). To determine this we can in the medium run take the number of firms as given, in which case the natural level of output is

$$Y^* = N^* - mf.$$

But in the long run we assume free entry in which case the number of firms becomes endogenous and is solved for by imposing the zero profit condition.[9] When the tax/subsidy is imposed, the size of firms is unaffected but their number grows, increasing output and employment in the economy as a whole.

(ii) *Wages set by trade unions*

We now examine what would happen if wages were set by trade unions rather than by firms. In particular, we imagine that for each firm there is one trade union which sets the wage, while the employer determines the level of employment taking the wage as given.

The union is assumed to maximise the expected income of its members. If the union in firm i has ℓ_i members its objective function is written

$$v_i = n_i w_i + (\ell_i - n_i) \left[(1 - u)w + ub \right]$$

$$= n_i \left[w_i - w(1 - u(1 - \rho)) \right] + \text{constant}$$

---

[8] $\delta x / \delta t = w / (tq'xq'')\phi.$

[9] $0 = \pi_i = y_i - n_i (w + \phi q) = y_i - n_i \left(1 - \dfrac{1}{\eta} \right).$ Since $y_i = n_i - f$, $n_i = \eta f$ and $m = N/\eta f.$

Thus the union gains by raising wages except in so far as this reduces employment.

The union maximises its objective function subject to the demand for its labour, and its first-order condition is

$$\frac{\partial v_i}{\partial w_i} = [w_i - w(1 - u(1 - \rho))] \frac{\partial n_i}{\partial w_i} + n_i = 0$$

where $\partial n_i / \partial w_i$ comes from the firm's labour demand curve. In equilibrium we set $w_i = w$, so that

$$u = -\frac{1}{\dfrac{\partial n_i}{\partial w_i} \dfrac{w_i}{n_i} (1 - \rho)}$$

The equilibrium unemployment rate is higher the less elastic the demand curve facing the union, i.e. the higher the degree of union monopoly power. It is also higher the higher the replacement ratio.

To find the elasticity facing the union we turn back to the objective of the firm, which chooses employment taking the wage as given so as to maximise profits ($\pi_i = p_i y_i - w_i n_i$) subject to its production function (equation 2) and output demand curve (equation 3). Equating marginal revenue to marginal cost gives

$$p_i \left(1 - \frac{1}{\eta} \right) = w_i$$

so that the firm's demand for labour is given by

$$n_i = f + y_i = f + \frac{Y}{m} (p_i)^{-\eta} = f + \frac{Y}{m} \left[\frac{\eta w_i}{\eta - 1} \right]^{-\eta}$$

Hence

$$\frac{\partial n_i}{\partial w_i} \frac{w_i}{n_i} = \left[-\frac{\eta}{w_i} y_i \right] \frac{w_i}{n_i} = -\eta \frac{1}{1 + f/y_i} = -\eta \frac{1}{1 + mf/Y}$$

Thus unemployment is given by

(7)
$$u = \frac{1 + mf/Y}{\eta(1 - \rho)}$$

If the number of firms (m) is fixed, the equilibrium unemployment rate is determined by (7) together with the aggregate production function

$$Y = N - mf = L(1-u) - mf$$

where L is the labour force. The resulting expression is non-linear, and somewhat complex. If, however, we assume free entry in the long run we get an additional equation (the zero profit condition) which enables us also to determine the number of firms (m). The zero profit condition with $w_i = w$ and $p_i = 1$ is

$$y_i = w \, n_i$$

or

$$\frac{n_i}{y_i} = 1 + \frac{f}{y_i} = \frac{1}{w} = \frac{1}{\left(1 - \frac{1}{\eta}\right)}$$

Hence

$$\frac{f}{y_i} = \frac{mf}{Y} = \frac{1}{\eta - 1}$$

Then (7) implies

(8)
$$u = \frac{1}{(\eta - 1)\,(1 - \rho)}$$

Once again a 1 per cent rise in ρ (at $\rho = 0.5$) will produce a 1 per cent rise in u.

Equation (8) determines the rate of unemployment at which unions are content with the real wage the economy can provide. If unemployment is lower than this, each union will attempt to raise its wage. Their attempts to increase their real wage will in the outcome be unsuccessful and will only result in spiralling inflation. (Unions realise that there is markup pricing and hence they cannot improve their wage relative to their own firm's output price. But what concerns them is their wage relative to the general price level and if any one union can raise its money wage relative to that in other firms, and hence relative to the general price level, it can raise its real wage.)

We now introduce a wage tax. The firm's profit function becomes

$$\pi_i = p_i y_i - (1 + t) w_i n_i + s n_i$$

For any given wage set by the union, the firm maximises profits by setting

$$p_i = \frac{\eta}{\eta - 1} \, (w_i(1 + t) - s),$$

whence, using equation 3,

$$n_i = f + \left(\frac{Y}{m}\right)\left[\frac{\eta}{\eta - 1} \, (w_i(1 + t) - s)\right]^{-\eta}$$

The firm, and union, take s and t as given. Thus in setting the optimal wage the union maximises its utility subject to the above relationship between wages and employment. Following the same procedure as before and allowing the number of firms to be variable, yields

(8′) $$u = \frac{1}{(\eta - 1)\,(1 - \rho)\,(1 + t)}$$

The operation of the tax is depicted in Figure 2. Given the symmetry of the system, the feasible level of real wages is given by the horizontal line marked

$$w = 1 - \frac{1}{\eta}.$$

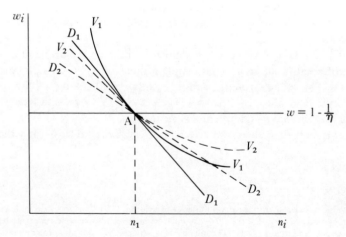

Figure 2. The wage tax in the union model

However, each union, acting independently, perceives itself to be facing a downward-sloping demand curve due to product substitution. Thus, in the figure, D_1D_1 is the demand curve originally perceived by any individual union. Its utility function is represented by a set of indifference curves and its chosen position is A with employment n_1. If a wage tax is introduced, the perceived demand curve will flatten (because a rise in wages relative to wages elsewhere will incur a tax cost which firms will pass on in higher prices thus reducing product, and hence labour, demand). At existing employment levels each union will wish to reduce its relative wage (since its perceived demand curve will tilt from D_1D_1 to D_2D_2).

However, the unions cannot all succeed in reducing their relative wages, and the only way in which equilibrium can be restored is by an increase in demand and a fall in unemployment. A reduction in the unemployment rate flattens the union's indifference curves between real wages and employment,[10] so that one becomes tangential to the new demand curve. The output of the individual firm remains as before, since $y_i = f(\eta - 1)$, but the number of firms grows with the level of national output.

2. *Sectoral effects of wage tax/subsidy*

We now proceed to look at the effects of our policy when there is more than one type of labour. The policy now acquires an additional kick. It not only operates via the mechanisms already described but also by its differential effect upon replacement ratios for the different types of labour.[11]

In what follows we shall first show how different replacement ratios in different occupations could explain their different unemployment rates. This follows from the simple point we shall again establish that what is determined in these models is $u(1 - \rho)$. Thus occupations with high ρs will have high unemployment rates.

We shall then show the effects of a wage tax/subsidy upon these

---

[10] The slope is given by

$$\frac{\partial w_i}{\partial n_i} = -\frac{w_i - w + wu(1 - \rho)}{n_i}$$

which decreases in absolute magnitude if u is reduced.

[11] We have investigated the effect via replacement rates in a market-clearing model in Jackman and Layard (1980). The purpose here is to confirm that result in non market-clearing models and to link it explicitly to the models of Section 1.

replacement rates. We shall assume that, as a matter of social policy, all groups get the same levels of benefit (b) and that these are not altered when a change occurs in the relative wages of different groups (the average remaining constant). To motivate this discussion consider the following simple experiment in which there are two types of labour with equal initial levels of employment. The more skilled type of labour (type 2) has a higher wage than the less-skilled (type 1): $w_2 > w_1$. We now operate a self-financing tax/subsidy scheme such that there is a net tax on skilled labour and a net subsidy to unskilled. As a result w_2 falls by 1 unit and w_1 rises by 1 unit. For each type of labour j we have

$$u_j(1 - \rho_j) = u_j\left(1 - \frac{b}{w_j}\right) = \text{constant}$$

If w_2 changes by 1 unit, the proportional effect on w_2 and thus on ρ_2 is less than if w_1 changes by 1 unit. Thus if w_2 falls and w_1 rises the rise in u_2 is less than the fall in u_1. Total unemployment falls.

Enough by way of introduction. The first step is to show how w_1 and w_2 change when the tax/subsidy scheme is introduced.

Let us assume the two types of worker in the economy are distinguished by their productivity. Group 1 workers have low productivity (a_1) and group 2 high (a_2). We therefore replace the firm's employment function (equation 2) by

(9) $$a_1 n_{1i} + a_2 n_{2i} = f + y_i$$

where n_{1i} are the number of type 1 and n_{2i} type 2 workers employed by the firm. It follows that, in this formulation, the two types of workers, measured in efficiency units, are perfect substitutes. Profit maximisation by firms will thus ensure that, in the absence of taxation or quitting costs,

(10) $$\frac{w_1}{a_1} = \frac{w_2}{a_2} = 1 - \frac{1}{n}$$

The wages of each type of worker are proportional to their productivity, so that unit labour costs are the same whichever type of labour is employed.

If we now impose a wage tax, we have, in place of condition (10),

(10′) $$\frac{1}{a_1}(w_1(1 + t) - s) = \frac{1}{a_2}(w_2(1 + t) - s) = 1 - \frac{1}{\eta}$$

Hence if t changes w_1 and w_2 change in proportion but if s increases w_2 rises less proportionately than w_1 (since $w_2 > w_1$).

To see precisely how a balanced tax/subsidy scheme affects each wage level, let the proportion of skilled workers in total employment be θ. Then the balanced budget condition can be written

$$s = t((1-\theta)w_1 + \theta w_2)$$

Making use of this condition to substitute for s in $(10')$ and re-solving for w_1 and w_2 yields

$$w_1 = \left(1 - \frac{1}{\eta}\right)\left(a_1 + (a_2 - a_1)\theta\,\frac{t}{1+t}\right)$$

and

$$w_2 = \left(1 - \frac{1}{\eta}\right)\left(a_2 - (a_2 - a_1)\,(1-\theta)\,\frac{t}{1+t}\right)$$

For t close to zero, the change in the two wage levels as t changes is therefore given by:

(11)
$$\frac{\partial w_1}{\partial t} = \left(1 - \frac{1}{\eta}\right)(a_2 - a_1)\theta$$

$$\frac{\partial w_2}{\partial t} = -\left(1 - \frac{1}{\eta}\right)(a_2 - a_1)\,(1-\theta)$$

(i) *Model where firms set wages*

We again consider first a model where firms set wages in order to discourage quitting. However, now there are two types of workers, the quit function of each type must depend on the expected outside income of each type of worker. We assume complete market segmentation. The expected outside income of an unskilled worker, for example, will then depend on the wage of unskilled workers elsewhere (w_1), the unemployment benefit (b) and the unemployment rate of unskilled workers (u_1). The quit function facing the firm for unskilled workers is thus

$$q_{1i} = q(r_{1i}x_1) \qquad\qquad (q' < 0;\ q'' > 0).$$

where

$$r_{1i} = w_{1i}/w_1 \text{ and}$$

$$x_1 = \frac{1}{1 - u_1 \, (1 - b/w_1)}$$

w_{1i} being the wage paid to unskilled workers in firm i. There is an exactly corresponding quit function for skilled workers.

The firm then maximises profits subject to its production function (equation 9), demand curve (equation 3) and the two quit functions q_1 and q_2. We assume the costs associated with a quit (i.e. the training of the replacement worker) are a multiple ϕ of the worker's productivity. Then profits are

$$\pi_i = p_i y_i - n_{1i}(r_{1i} w_1 + a_1 \phi q(r_{1i} x_1)) - n_{2i}(r_{2i} w_2 + a_2 \phi q(r_{2i} x_2))$$

Following the same procedure as in Section 1 yields two sets of first-order conditions, the first for r_{1i}, n_{1i} and the second for r_{2i}, n_{2i}. These are exactly analogous to Equations (4) and (5) and read

(12)
$$w_1 = -a_1 \phi q'(x_1) x_1$$
$$w_1 = a_1 \left(1 - \frac{1}{\eta} - \phi q \, (x_1) \right)$$

and

(13)
$$w_2 = -a_2 \phi q'(x_2) x_2$$
$$w_2 = a_2 \left(1 - \frac{1}{\eta} - \phi q \, (x_2) \right)$$

As before the value of x is determined in these equations, and it is immediately apparent that equilibrium requires

$$x_1 = x_2.$$

If follows that the group with the higher replacement rate will also have the higher unemployment rate.

Following the reasoning of Section 1, imposition of a proportional wage tax will simply add a multiplicative term in $(1 + t)$ to the left hand side of the first order condition for wages in Conditions (12) and (13). Thus equilibrium will still require $x_1 = x_2$, though at a lower level of x than in the absence of the tax, as shown in Section 1. Let us use x to denote the common equilibrium value for both types of labour. Thus

$$\frac{1}{1 - u_1 \, (1 - b/w_1)} = \frac{1}{1 - u_2 \, (1 - b/w_2)} = x$$

or, for each sector,

$$u_j = \frac{1 - 1/x}{1 - b/w_j} \qquad (j = 1, 2)$$

The aggregate unemployment rate, $\bar{u}$, is defined by

(14) $$\bar{u} = (1 - \theta)u_1 + \theta u_2$$

To see how this changes when we change t we have to include first the effect via changes in x (already discussed in Section 1) and then the effect via the replacement ratio. The effect upon unemployment via x is equiproportionate on the unemployment rates in both sectors. In addition there is an effect via replacement rates equal to

$$\frac{d\bar{u}}{dt} = (1 - \theta)\frac{\partial u_1}{\partial w_1}\frac{\partial w_1}{\partial t} + \theta\frac{\partial u_2}{\partial w_2}\frac{\partial w_2}{\partial t}$$

Making use of the above expression for the sectoral unemployment rates and equation (11), adjusted for quitting costs,[12] gives

$$\frac{d\bar{u}}{dt} = \theta(1 - \theta)\,(a_2 - a_1)\,b\left(1 - \frac{1}{\eta} - \phi q\right)\left(1 - \frac{1}{x}\right)\left\{\frac{1}{(w_2 - b)^2} - \frac{1}{(w_1 - b)^2}\right\}$$

which is negative given that $w_2 > w_1 > b$.

(ii) *Model where unions set wages*

We turn now to the model of union wage-setting. We continue to assume one union in each firm, and, to avoid complications about union objectives with regard to different groups of workers within the firm, we assume the labour force in each firm is homogeneous, so that some firms in the economy have a labour force consisting only of skilled workers and other firms a labour force consisting only of unskilled workers.[13] With free entry, however, the zero profit condition will

---

[12] Quitting costs entail the replacement of the term $1 - \frac{1}{\eta}$ by $1 - \frac{1}{\eta} - \phi q$ in Equations 10, 10′, and 11.

[13] We could of course introduce substitution between types of workers and different unions for each type of worker. But for the sake of consistency we have not done this.

ensure that Equation (10) holds, that is that unit labour costs in the two types of firm must be equal.

The union in each firm maximises the expected income of its members, again assuming complete segmentation of the labour markets for the two types of labour. Thus, if firm i employs labour of type j the relevant utility function is

$$V_{ij} = n_{ij}w_{ij} + (\ell_{ij} - n_{ij})\,((1 - u_j)w_j + u_j b)$$

The analysis proceeds exactly as before so that, in the presence of the wage tax, we have equilibrium unemployment rates in each sector given by

$$u_j = \frac{1}{(\eta - 1)\,(1 + t)\,(1 - b/w_j)}$$

Thus again the tax directly reduces unemployment equiproportionately for each type of worker, but it also has a secondary effect via replacement ratios. Using (11) and (14) the latter effect is

$$\frac{d\bar{u}}{dt} = \frac{\theta(1 - \theta)\,(a_2 - a_1)\,b}{\eta\,(1 + t)}\left\{ \frac{1}{(w_2 - b)^2} - \frac{1}{(w_1 - b)^2} \right\}$$

which again is negative.

It is interesting to check whether unemployment of skilled workers falls as well as of unskilled.

$$d \log u_2 = -\frac{1}{1 + t}\,\partial t + \frac{\rho_2}{1 - \rho_2}\frac{1}{w_2}\frac{\partial w_2}{\partial t}$$

Using (11)

$$d \log u_2 = \partial t \left(-\frac{1}{1 + t} + \frac{\rho_2}{1 - \rho_2}\left(1 - \frac{a_1}{a_2}\right)\theta \right)$$

For t close to zero and $\rho_2 < \frac{1}{2}$, this has to be negative. Hence the tax/subsidy lowers both unskilled and skilled unemployment.

3. *Conclusion*

We have examined a self-financing tax/subsidy scheme in which firms pay a wage-bill tax and receive a fixed per-worker subsidy. If wages are set by firms, this discourages firms from bidding up wages against each other in order to attract or retain workers or to motivate their staff. In consequence firms are willing to pay the going wage at a higher level of employment.

If wages are set by unions, the tax alters the trade off between wages and employment available to the union. For if a union pushes up wages, it now imposes additional tax on the employer and this adds to the employer's loss of competitive power. Thus the unions will be less inclined to push on wages at a given level of employment. Since in our model the economy real wage is determined by the pricing policy of firms, the natural rate of unemployment is determined at that level at which unions are willing to accept the real wage that business will collectively provide. If unions are less inclined to push for higher real wages at a given level of employment, the level of employment can be allowed to rise. At the equilibrium level unions are willing to settle for the prevailing wage.

The preceding arguments are based on a model in which there is only one type of labour. But there is in fact more than one type of labour. Given this, the policies gain additional force under regimes where the unemployed receive a flat-rate unemployment benefit related to average earnings and not to their individual earnings. For the tax/subsidy scheme involves a net subsidy to low-wage earners and a net tax on high-wage earners. A redistribution of wages from rich to poor lowers the benefit/income replacement ratio of the poor proportionately more than it raises the replacement ratio of the rich. This raises total employment, given the way in which occupational replacement rates affect occupational unemployment rates in our model.

These are the main effects which we identify in this paper. However it is interesting to relate them to the effects of a closely related policy – tax-based incomes policy. This is a tax not on the level of wages but on the growth rate of wages. The simplest tax-based incomes policy would be one in which the permitted growth in money wages equalled the rise in prices, so that the tax was in fact a tax on real wage growth. Again to be self-financing, it would be accompanied by a per-worker subsidy. The net real tax facing the ith firm would be $n_i(T(w_i - w_{i,-1}) - s)$, as compared with the net tax discussed in this paper which is $n_i(tw_i - s)$. It is easy to show that with homogeneous labour and no economic growth the effects of the policies are identical if t equals δT where δ is the relevant discount rate.[14] (This is shown for the case of perfect

[14] There are however no effects via changes in the wage structure since with no economic growth, $s = 0$.

competition in Jackman, Layard and Pissarides (1985)). One possible advantage of the wage inflation tax is that it need not involve changes in wage structure.

So what is the administrative feasibility of each of these two types of tax? We believe they are both feasible. The tax on wage levels plus a per-worker subsidy can easily be introduced by taking existing social security taxes on employers and making them more progressive. A small move in this direction was taken in the 1985 Budget in the UK. A tax on wage growth is also administratively feasible, using the same social security records.[15] It should of course relate to the *average* wage growth in the firm, and not the wage growth of particular individuals. We would favour using both types of tax – both on wage levels and wage growth.

References

Calvo, G., 'Quasi-Walrasian theories of unemployment', *American Economic Review* 69 (May 1979), 102–107.

Grubb, D., Jackman, R.A. and Layard, R., 'Wage rigidity and unemployment in OECD countries', *European Economic Review* 21 (1983), 11–39.

Jackman, R.A. and Layard, R., 'The efficiency case for long-run labour market policies', *Economica* 47 (August 1980), 331–349.

——, 'An inflation tax', *Fiscal Studies* 3 (1982), 47–59.

Jackman, R.A., Layard, R. and Pissarides, C., 'Policies for reducing the natural rate of unemployment', in Butkiewicz, J.L., Koford, K.J. and Miller, J.B. (eds.), *Keynes' Economic Legacy* (New York: Praeger, 1986).

Layard, R. and Nickell, S.J., 'Unemployment, real wages and aggregate demand in Europe, Japan and the U.S.', in Brunner, K. and Meltzer, A. (eds.), *Carnegie-Rochester Conference Series on Public Policy* no. 23 (Autumn 1985).

Salop, S.C., 'A model of the natural rate of unemployment', *American Economic Review* 69 (March 1979), 117–125.

Weitzman, M.L., 'Increasing returns and the foundations of unemployment theory', *Economic Journal* 92 (December 1982), 787–804.

---

[15] Jackman and Layard (1982).

8. The Simple Macroeconomics of Profit-Sharing*

Martin L. Weitzman

This paper is in the spirit of the 'temporary equilibrium' approach to macroeconomics. It basically extends that framework to cover a profit-sharing system and then compares the macroeconomic characteristics with those of the more familiar wage system. A first, preliminary step is to demonstrate how a microeconomic model of monopolistic competition can be built up into a junior member of the Keynesian macro family. The methodology is to create from first principles – including a careful formulation of a monopolistically competitive product market structure – a natural underpinning for the standard aggregate demand specification.[1]

The primary goal of the paper is to apply the integrated monopolistic-competition-Keynesian type apparatus described above to investigate the macroeconomic properties of a profit-sharing economy. The existence of a consistent general framework covering both cases invites meaningful comparisons that indicate clearly why an economy based on profit-sharing principles possesses natural immunity to stagflation. By contrast, the wage economy – a system we have largely accepted

* I am especially indebted to Robert Solow for his detailed, useful comments on an earlier draft, and also to James Meade and Hal Varian for their helpful suggestions. I would also like to thank an anonymous referee for his critical comments. They should not be saddled with opinions or errors of the paper. The research was supported by a grant from the National Science Foundation.

[1] This may be a useful exercise by itself because, in my opinion, any macroeconomic framework is misleading without an underlying model of the firm based upon imperfect competition. For an elaboration of this view, see Weitzman (1982 and 1985), Solow (1985) or Meade (1984). While some contributors to the important market-disequilibrium school have attempted to cope with imperfect competition in the product market, I think it is fair to say that the issue has not been addressed directly and developed from first principles in the spirit of the present paper – using the 'actual', rather than 'perceived' or 'conjectural', demand curves. For an admirable survey of the temporary fixed price approach, see Benassy (1982) and the references cited there. Aside from the emphasis on dealing with monopolistic competition from first principles, the rest of this paper's framework is similar to what is adopted in much of the fixed-price literature, although that approach, so far as I know, has never been used to analyse profit-sharing.

without critically examining its macroeconomic consequences – is more prone to suffer from unemployment and inflation. The policy implications for aggregate demand management in wage and share systems are analysed and contrasted.

In writing this paper, my philosophy has been not to shirk from using those reasonable parameterisations and functional forms which yield nice crisp results and permit me to focus sharply on the essential logic of basic issues. It is certainly possible to present the main results in a somewhat more general formulation (as the astute reader will appreciate), but, I fear, only at some cost of distracting attention from those central features I wish to highlight.

1. *The demand side*

The stylised economy under consideration consists of three types of representative agent. The first type of agent is a producer or firm. There are n firms, each of which produces a different good, indexed $i = 1, 2 \ldots, n$, where n is taken to be a given large number.[2] A second class of agents is the households, of which there are a gigantic number, indexed $h = 1, 2, \ldots, H$, where $H \gg n \gg 0$. An autonomous government sector, the third agent, makes purchases, taxes households, and has an exclusive franchise on the creation of money.

There are three categories of commodities in the prototype economy. The first category consists of the n goods produced by the n firms. Goods are considered to be highly perishable, so that inventories are negligible and sales are always very nearly equal to production. Labour, the second category, is a homogeneous commodity inelastically supplied by the households. Money, the third kind of commodity, is storable, not producible by private agents, and can be costlessly created by the government. Money serves as the exclusive unit of account, medium of exchange, and store of value in the economy.

The production of good i, denoted Y_i, and its price, P_i, are of course chosen by firm i. The eventual analysis of that choice will constitute an ultimate aim of the paper. But, for the time being, suppose that prices are viewed parametrically by buyers, who act as if they can purchase

---

[2] Behind the fixed number of firms are suppressed or suspended some interesting and important issues regarding barriers to entry or exit, economies of scale, sunk costs, irreversible investments and the like. Some hint of what might be appropriate to a longer-run analysis is contained in the already cited articles by Martin Weitzman (1982) and Robert Solow.

as much as they want of any good at the prevailing prices $\{P_i\}$. As might be expected under monopolistic competition, it turns out that prices will always be chosen by firms so customers can buy as much as they want, and in that sense the product market always clears.[3]

Households obtain utility from consuming goods and holding money balances. The utility of money is indirect; it serves as a proxy for the value of future consumption goods that can be purchased when money is carried over into later periods. For simplicity, each household is postulated to have the *same* utility function. When a household consumes goods $\{C_i\}$ and holds money balances M, it obtains utility according to the expression:[4]

$$(1) \qquad U\left(\{C_i\}, \frac{M}{P}\right) = ([\Sigma C_i^{\frac{E-1}{E}}]^{\frac{E}{E-1}})^\theta \left(\frac{M}{P}\right)^{1-\theta}$$

The aggregate price level P in the above expression is defined by the formula:

$$(2) \qquad P \equiv \left(\frac{\Sigma P_i^{1-E}}{n}\right)^{\frac{1}{1-E}}$$

which is the appropriate goods price index, from duality theory, to use for the postulated utility function (1).[5]

Formula (1) is a compound Cobb-Douglas utility function (with parameter θ, $0 < \theta < 1$), whose two arguments are money and a *CES* composite sub-utility function of goods. The elasticity of substitution between money and the composite good is unity, whereas the elasticity of substitution among the n goods is $E > 1$.

With a current budget of B^h, household h confronts the problem

maximise:

$$(3) \qquad U\left(\{C_i\}, \frac{M}{P}\right)$$

[3] Indeed I consider it a deep-seated characteristic of capitalism that the product market is practically always in a state of excess supply. See Weitzman (1984), ch. 3.

[4] Money in the utility function (1) serves as a link between the present and an uncertain future, with θ parameterising the desire to consume now. There is an implicit presumption that the future can be collapsed into a dynamic-programming state-evaluation function like (1). On this point see Benassy (1982), 87–8, or Grandmont (1983), 17–32.

[5] See, e.g., Varian (1984), or Dixit and Stiglitz (1977).

subject to:

$$(4) \qquad \Sigma P_i C_i + 1 \cdot \tilde{M} = B^h$$

For a modified Cobb-Douglas utility function of the form (1), the solution to the above problem is:

$$(5) \qquad M = (1-\theta)B^h$$

$$(6) \qquad C_i^h = \left(\frac{P_i}{P}\right)^{-E} \frac{\theta B^h}{nP}$$

The total amount of good i consumed in the economy is

$$(7) \qquad C_i \equiv \sum_h C_i^h$$

and aggregate consumption C may be consistently defined as

$$(8) \qquad C \equiv \frac{\Sigma P_i C_i}{P}$$

The following relations then hold:

$$(9) \qquad C = \frac{\theta B}{P}$$

$$(10) \qquad M = (1-\theta)B$$

$$(11) \qquad M + PC = B$$

$$(12) \qquad C_i = \left(\frac{P_i}{P}\right)^{-E} \frac{C}{n}$$

where

$$(13) \qquad B = \Sigma B^h$$

$$(14) \qquad M \equiv \Sigma M^h$$

Total government real spending on goods, denoted A, is treated as autonomously determined. The government's trade-off among goods is considered, for convenience, to be the same as the household's, given by the utility function:

$$(15) \qquad V(\{A_i\}) = \left(\Sigma A_i^{\frac{E-1}{E}}\right)^{\frac{E}{E-1}}$$

The government maximises (15) subject to the budget constraint

(16) $$\Sigma P_i A_i = PA$$

which yields the solution

(17) $$A_i = \left(\frac{P_i}{P}\right)^{-E} \frac{A}{n}$$

Aggregate demand for good i by the consumers and the government is

(18) $$Y_i \equiv C_i + A_i.$$

With aggregate real output defined as

(19) $$Y \equiv \frac{\Sigma P_i Y_i}{P},$$

definition (18) yields

(20) $$Y = C + A$$

(from combining with (8) and (16)), and

(21) $$Y_i = \left(\frac{P_i}{P}\right)^{-E} \frac{Y}{n}$$

(from combining with (12) and (17)).

The government collects the fraction s of each household's current income as taxes. National income is PY, all of which is distributed to households as wages plus profits. Aggregate disposable income is therefore

(22) $$PY_d = (1-s) PY$$

and the total budget of all households is

(23) $$B = (1-s)PY + M$$

where M represents the aggregate stock of money initially held by all households at the beginning of the period under consideration.

It follows directly from (23), (11), and (20) that

(24) $$PA - sPY = M - M,$$

i.e., the government finances its deficits by inducing households to hold more money.

Using (9) and (23) to eliminate B gives

$$(25) \qquad C = \theta(1-s)Y + \theta\left(\frac{M}{P}\right)$$

which is the relevant aggregate consumption function for the economy, with $\theta(1-s)$ the marginal propensity to spend out of income.

Combining (20) with (25) yields

$$(26) \qquad Y = \alpha A + \beta\left(\frac{M}{P}\right)$$

where

$$(27) \qquad \alpha \equiv \frac{1}{1 - \theta(1-s)}$$

$$(28) \qquad \beta \equiv \frac{\theta}{1 - \theta(1-s)}$$

are the relevant fiscal and monetary multipliers.

Formula (26) can be interpreted as a reduced form Keynesian-type macroeconomic relation. Strictly speaking, monetary policy (as that term is usually understood) does not have an independent role to play in the current formulation because no distinction is being made between monetary and other financial assets or operations. But I feel that a simplistic association of M with the 'stock of money' (and of open market operations with 'money rain'), conveys the spirit of what a more sophisticated analysis might prove rigorously. Although I have found it valuable to think in terms of an integrated micro-macro framework developed from what I view as first principles, it is possible to treat (26) simply as a behavioural relationship having the traditional IS-LM interpretation.

Condition (26) is the fundamental macroeconomic equation of the paper, summarising all relevant information about aggregate demand given only that buyers are able to purchase whatever goods they want at prevailing prices.

2. *Prices and production*

It is important to realise that the Keynesian demand specification (26) typically forms an underdetermined system. Given A and M (and the parameters α and β), Equation (26) describes a relation that must hold between two macroeconomic variables: Y and P. The traditional procedure for making the system determinate is to postulate a fixed price level

$$(29) \qquad\qquad P = \bar{P}$$

for the short run.[6] In this paper I want to *derive* (29) as the profit-maximising response of a large number of monopolistically competitive firms constrained to pay fixed money wages. The same methodology will then be applied to the case where the fixed contract is of a profit-sharing form, which will yield quite different solution properties and macroeconomic implications from (29).

Suppose that each of the n different goods is produced by the same production technology. Firm i $(1 \leqslant i \leqslant n)$ produces Y_i units of good i from L_i employees according to the formula

$$(30) \qquad\qquad Y_i(L_i) = \gamma(L_i - f),$$

where γ is the marginal productivity of an extra worker and f represents a fixed amount of overhead labour which must be employed to produce any output at all. The production function (30) can be viewed as a first order approximation in the relevant operating range.[7]

The total amount of labour employed is then

$$(31) \qquad\qquad L \equiv \Sigma L_i$$

If L^* represents the total available labour, assumed to be inelastically supplied by households, then the condition

$$(32) \qquad\qquad L \leqslant L^*$$

must be obeyed in the aggregate.[8]

---

[6] An alternative is to postulate an 'aggregate supply function' which is, I feel, a dubious macroeconomic concept at best, especially for a world where firms are price-makers in imperfectly competitive product markets.

[7] That unit variable costs are roughly constant over some range is, I think, a decent enough stylised fact to be used as a point of departure for the purposes of this paper.

[8] The reader who wants to should be able to re-do the analysis of this paper for the case where labour supply is not perfectly inelastic. Nothing of substance changes. In long-run equilibrium, wage and profit-sharing systems will continue to be identical. In the short run, when pay parameters are sticky, a profit-sharing economy effectively banishes involuntary unemployment, while a wage economy may have it, even in the presence of elastically supplied labour. The message is essentially the same as when labour is perfectly inelastic.

In any symmetric situation, aggregate output must be given by the formula

$$(33) \qquad\qquad Y = \gamma(L - F),$$

where

$$(34) \qquad\qquad F \equiv nf.$$

From (30), then,

$$(35) \qquad\qquad Y \leqslant Y*$$

where

$$(36) \qquad\qquad Y* \equiv \gamma(L* - F)$$

represents potential aggregate output.

What follows in this section is an overview of the methodology to be followed in analysing the short-run price and production decisions of the firms. Suppose the cost per worker of hiring L_i workers is $W(L_i)$, where the average pay function $W(\cdot)$ is exogenously given in the short run and is identical for each firm. The relevant equilibrium concept is taken to be a symmetric Nash equilibrium in prices. Each firm charges an identical price, which is the profit-maximising price for it given that all other firms are charging that same price. The corresponding output and employment decisions are those needed to support the profit-maximising Nash equilibrium behaviour.

A short-run macroeconomic equilibrium is a price P, aggregate output level Y, and total employment L simultaneously satisfying (26), (32), (35), and the conditions

$$(37) \qquad P\frac{Y}{n} - W\left(\frac{L}{n}\right) \cdot \frac{L}{n} = \operatorname*{maximum}_{P_i, Y_i, L_i} \{P_i Y_i - W(L_i) \cdot L_i\}$$

subject to:

$$(38) \qquad\qquad L_i \leqslant L* - (n-1)\frac{L}{n}$$

$$(39) \qquad\qquad Y_i \leqslant \gamma(L_i - f)$$

$$(40) \qquad\qquad Y_i \leqslant \left(\frac{P_i}{P}\right)^{-E}\frac{Y}{n}$$

It is easy to verify that any solution of the constrained optimisation problem (37)–(40) will satisfy (39), (40) with strict equality. Since (40) is ultimately derived from consumer-demand conditions, when it holds with full equality buyers are able to purchase whatever they want at prevailing prices and, hence, in the aggregate (26) must be satisfied.

So long as n is a large number, each firm i is justified in regarding its demand Y_i, given by (21), as a true function of only its own price P_i, with aggregate variables P and Y parametrically fixed beyond its control.[9]

3. Short-run equilibrium in a wage economy with a parametrically given wage

In the short run suppose each firm i pays labour an exogenously fixed money wage

$$(41) \qquad W(L_i) = w$$

where w is treated as autonomously given.

The state of the macroeconomy is described by the basic aggregate demand equation (26). The extra degree of freedom in (26) between the variables Y and P is determined by firms' profit-maximising Nash equilibrium behaviour (37)–(40) given the rigid wage (41).

Let

$$(42) \qquad \mu \equiv \frac{E}{E-1}$$

be the markup coefficient for each firm. The coefficient μ represents the ratio of average revenue (price) to marginal revenue.

With the production function (30) and the labour payment schedule (41), the marginal cost of an extra unit of output to firm i is w/γ. For the demand function (21), marginal revenue at a price of P_i is P_i/μ Hence, if availability of labour were not a binding constraint, each firm would choose to set a price

$$(43) \qquad P_i = \frac{\mu w}{\gamma}$$

and the desired or target output of the wage system, denoted Υ, would then be, from the aggregate demand condition (26):

$$(44) \qquad \Upsilon \equiv \alpha A + \frac{\beta M \gamma}{\mu w}$$

[9] This statement can be rigorously defended.

Define the tautness or tension of the wage system as

$$(45) \qquad\qquad \tau \equiv \varUpsilon - \varUpsilon *$$

The variable τ measures the difference between desired output (what firms would like to produce in the aggregate on the given wage contract if there were no overall labour constraint) and potential output (what the system is physically capable of producing). $[\tau > 0]$ is a region of positive excess demand for labour, whereas $[\tau < 0]$ is a region of negative excess demand for labour.

The unique symmetric Nash equilibrium with each firm playing its own price as a profit-maximising strategy given the fixed wage (41) depends on the underlying configuration of parameters. Equilibrium values of the major macroeconomic variables are shown in Table 1.

Table 1. Short-run behaviour of major macroeconomic variables in a wage system

Variable	$\tau < 0$	$\tau > 0$
$\varUpsilon$	$\alpha A + \dfrac{\beta M \gamma}{\mu w}$	$\varUpsilon *$
P	$\dfrac{\mu w}{\gamma}$	$\dfrac{\beta M}{\varUpsilon * - \alpha A}$
$\dfrac{W}{P}$	$\dfrac{\gamma}{\mu}$	$\dfrac{w(\varUpsilon * - \alpha A)}{\beta M}$

That Table 1 describes the unique symmetric Nash equilibrium of a fixed-wage economy should be fairly clear. Condition (43) has already been explained for the case where the firm can buy as much labour as it wants at the fixed wage (41). The corresponding value of $\varUpsilon$ in region $[\tau < 0]$ follows immediately from (26).

In the excess demand for labour region $[\tau > 0]$, aggregate output must be at its maximum feasible amount $\varUpsilon *$, with the corresponding value of P determined from (26). That such a configuration represents a Nash equilibrium in prices is easily verified. Since the marginal revenue product of labour exceeds the marginal cost of labour when $\tau > 0$, the firm would like to reduce its price and to produce more output, if only it could find more labour to hire. With each firm's output level effectively constrained (by (38), (39)) to be no more than $\varUpsilon */n$ in the case $\tau > 0$, it is unprofitable for a firm to lower price unilaterally, and it certainly is not profitable to restrain output further by raising price. (Of course firms could also increase the money wage to attract more workers, and will do so in the long run, but this has been ruled out as short-run behaviour by assumption.)

From Table 1, the macroeconomic properties of a fixed-wage economy depend essentially on whether the system is in a state of positive or negative tension. It is important to understand fully the meaning and significance of this dichotomy, because the same logic will carry over – albeit with an important and unexpected twist – to analysing the short-run behaviour of a profit-sharing economy.

The profit-maximising response to demand changes of a monopolistically competitive firm facing an isoelastic demand curve and constant marginal cost is to charge the same price and vary production accordingly. A Nash equilibrium of such firms with fixed money wages satisfying the condition $\tau < 0$ yields the familiar fixed-price world of Keynesian 'underemployment equilibrium'.

In such a world, prices are basically set by producers as a direct markup over wages independent of the state of aggregate demand. From Formula (43), the coefficient of proportionality between P and w is μ/γ. So it is a fair approximation to treat prices as proportional to unit labour costs in under-employment states of a fixed wage economy – provided there is no systematic tendency for the markup coefficient divided by the marginal productivity of labour to vary significantly over the business cycle.[10]

A fixed-wage economy in region $[\tau < 0]$ exhibits textbook Keynesian behaviour in the short run. P cannot be directly affected by government policy, but Y and L respond via the standard Keynesian multipliers to changes in A, M, or s.

By contrast, a fixed-wage economy in the region $[\tau > 0]$ displays classical or monetarist characteristics. Government aggregate demand management has no influence on real output, already at full employment, but directly and powerfully influences the price level. Monetary policy is strictly neutral, with prices proportional to M. Expansionary fiscal policy has only an inflationary impact, since it crowds out private spending.

---

[10] Note that the main conclusions come from the near constancy of the ratio μ/γ, not from the separate constancies of μ and γ. The model and its basic implications would not be significantly altered if elasticities and marginal costs were allowed to vary systematically in such a way that the ratio μ/γ remained unchanged. Sidney Weintraub long ago drew attention to the important empirical regularity of a near-constant average markup of prices over unit labour costs. See, e.g., Weintraub (1981), and references to other works there cited.

Summing up, then, there is a kind of abstract symmetry in the short-run behaviour of a fixed-wage economy. With $\tau < 0$, government policy is effective at altering real economic activity, but ineffective at changing prices. When $\tau > 0$, government policy is effective in determining the price level, but ineffective at influencing real aggregate variables. While the demarcation between the two regimes is unlikely to be nearly as clear cut in practice as in theory (partly because wages are more flexible upward than downward), I neverthe-less feel the distinction is conceptually useful.

4. *Long-run equilibrium in a wage economy with a competitively determined wage*

Consider a longer-run situation where everything is as described in the previous section only now the wage is endogenously determined by thorough-going competition in the labour market. Under competi-tion, each firm is free to set its own wage rate, and will do so to maximise profits taking as given the prevailing level of pay throughout the economy. The limiting Nash equilibrium behaviour (as each firm becomes a negligible buyer of labour) yields the full employment wage at which the marginal revenue product of labour is everywhere equal to the uniform rate of pay and the sum of labour demands just equals the supply of labour. Each firm is then offering an identical wage, which is the profit-maximising wage for it to offer given that all other firms are offering that same wage.

I should point out that I view the hypothesis of a competitive equilibrium wage not as a literal description of the state of the labour market, but more as an approximation or norm which is never actually attained yet forms a useful basis for talking about possible departures from normalcy. The 'competitive wage' represents a long-term tendency which, on the one hand, cannot be indefinitely thwarted with impunity but, on the other hand, is unlikely to hold fully at any particular time or place because 'other' variables are changing too rapidly and unpredictably.

The long-run competitive equilibrium wage, taking all else about the wage system as given by last section's description, is

$$(46) \qquad\qquad w^* = \frac{\beta M \gamma}{\mu(Y^* - \alpha A)}$$

When $w = w^*$, there is no unemployment, and the demand for labour just equals the supply. Under competitive forces in the labour market, then, the wage system gravitates toward the region $[\tau = 0]$ of zero tautness which just divides the 'Keynesian' $[\tau < 0]$ and 'classical' $[\tau > 0]$ regions.

It follows that an economy whose long term wage tendencies are described by (46) will display all of the neutrality and policy-ineffectiveness results of classical macroeconomics – in the long run. For example, changes in M will 'eventually' generate equiproportionate changes in w, and hence in P, so that nothing real is altered in the economy.

While some long run competitive forces are pushing a wage economy toward $[\tau = 0]$, they are unlikely to be decisive at any given time since the whole system is precariously balanced on the output side. The boundary region $[\tau = 0]$ is a very thin set, a razor's edge of measure zero, so it is extremely improbable that a capitalist wage economy should remain there for long. In fact the *real-politik* of wage capitalism, with its less-than-perfect labour markets and downward-inflexible wages, has the system residing in region $[\tau < 0]$ most of the time, hopefully not too far from the full employment boundary $[\tau = 0]$. It seems a fair empirical generalisation to say that the relevant region for most short-term policy analysis is the Keynesian region $[\tau < 0]$ where

$$(47) \qquad\qquad w > w^*.$$

5. *Short-run equilibrium in a profit-sharing economy with given pay parameters*

In the short run, suppose each firm i pays its workers by the profit-sharing formula

$$(48) \qquad W(L_i) = \omega + \lambda\left(\frac{R_i(L_i) - \omega L_i}{L_i}\right)$$

where $R_i(L_i)$ stands for total revenue as a function of labour, given the demand function (21) and the production function (30). The pay parameters ω, representing the base wage, and $\lambda > 0$, representing the profit-sharing coefficient, are both treated in the short run as exogenously fixed.[11]

---

[11] The above formulation omits intermediate materials, mostly for the sake of simplicity. While there may be some practical problems with profit-sharing due to the

The methodology for determining a short-run equilibrium in a profit-sharing economy is exactly the same as in a wage economy. The profit-sharing firm makes its short-run pricing, output and employment decisions to maximise profits given the rigid labour payment formula (48) and given the prices that all of the other firms are charging. The economy's short-run behaviour is modelled as the Nash equilibrium outcome, (37)–(40), of this individualistic profit-maximising process which simultaneously satisfies the basic macroeconomic condition (26).

The wage bill if L_i workers are hired by firm i is, from (48),

$$(49) \qquad W(L_i) \cdot L_i = (1 - \lambda)\omega L_i + \lambda R_i(L_i)$$

and net profits are

$$(50) \qquad \pi_i(L_i) \equiv R_i(L_i) - W(L_i) \cdot L_i$$

Combining (49) with (50), the net profits of firm i can be rewritten in the form

$$(51) \qquad \pi_i(L_i) = (1 - \lambda) \ (R_i(L_i) - \omega L_i)$$

If unlimited amounts of labour are available to be hired on the share contract (48), from (51), the firm will choose to hire workers to the point where

$$(52) \qquad R'_i = \omega$$

But the marginal revenue product of labour with demand curve (21) and production function (30) is related to price charged, P_i, by the formula

$$(53) \qquad R'_i(L_i) = \frac{\gamma P_i}{\mu}.$$

Combining (52) and (53), with unlimited supplies of labour available on the pay schedule (48), each firm i would choose to set its price at the level

$$(54) \qquad P_i = \frac{\mu \omega}{\gamma}.$$

---

fact that, in the real world, 'profits' is a somewhat elastic concept, I do not see insurmountable difficulties arising here. In any event, treatment of such considerations (and also bankruptcy, legal issues, leverage effects, etc.) is well beyond the scope of the present paper.

The corresponding desired or target aggregate output level of the profit-sharing system with fixed pay parameters (ω, λ), denoted Y', would then be, from (26),

$$(55) \qquad Y' = \alpha A + \frac{\beta M \gamma}{\mu \omega}.$$

The hypothetical variable Y' measures what firms would like to produce in the aggregate on the given pay contract if there were no overall labour constraint.

The tautness of the profit-sharing system is then

$$(56) \qquad \tau' \equiv Y' - Y^*$$

$$\equiv \alpha A + \frac{\beta M \gamma}{\mu \omega} - Y^*$$

Note that the degree of tautness varies inversely with ω, and that a 'pure' sharing system not having any base wage would possess an infinite demand for labour.

The unique symmetric Nash equilibrium with each firm setting its own price at a profit-maximising value given all other firms' prices and given the fixed profit-sharing pay formula (49), depends on the underlying configuration of parameters as shown in Table 2.

The reasoning to explain why Table 2 describes the unique symmetric Nash equilibrium of a profit-sharing economy closely parallels the reasoning behind Table 1 and is omitted here for the sake of brevity. In both cases the key insight is that actual aggregate output must be the smaller of a demand-determined target and a supply-determined capacity. The rest follows directly.

Table 2. Short-run behaviour of major macroeconomic variables in a profit-sharing system

Variable	$\tau' < 0$	$\tau' > 0$
Y	$\dfrac{\beta M \gamma}{\mu \omega}$	Y^*
P	$\dfrac{\mu \omega}{\gamma}$	$\dfrac{\beta M}{Y^* - \alpha A}$
$\dfrac{W}{P}$	$(1-\lambda)\dfrac{\gamma}{\mu} + \lambda\dfrac{Y}{L}$	$(1-\lambda)\dfrac{\omega(Y^* - \alpha A)}{\beta M} + \lambda\dfrac{Y^*}{L^*}$

The most immediately striking thing about Table 2 is that the first two rows are exactly the same as in Table 1 except for ω replacing w. The share parameter λ does not affect real national product or the price level.

When firms are maximising a function of the form (51), their reactions are not influenced by λ. So long as spending behaviour is postulated to depend only on the level of aggregate income, and not its distribution, the pricing and output decisions of firms in any short-run equilibrium of the system must be independent of λ. The particular case $\lambda = 0$ is just the wage economy, which accounts for the near-identity between the first two rows of Tables 1 and 2. While values of λ affect the distribution of national income, they do not influence its determination. Only the value of ω, representing to a firm the 'hard' money cost of taking on an extra worker (as opposed to the 'soft' cost of a share of incremental gross profits), influences the overall level of national income. If workers in a wage economy agree to receive 80 per cent of their pay in the form of base wages and 20 per cent in the form of a profit-sharing bonus, the effect on national product, employment, and prices is 'as if' wages had been cut by 20 per cent while aggregate demand was being maintained at the same level.

When a wage economy suffering from unemployment converts to a profit-sharing formula whose parameters are initially set so that each employed worker is at first paid the same amount, the change will make all workers better off after adjustment. From (48), the real pay in a profit-sharing system is

$$(57) \qquad \frac{W}{P} = (1 - \lambda)\frac{\omega}{P} + \lambda\frac{Y}{L}$$

After conversion from a wage system to an 'equivalent' profit-sharing system initially yielding the same pay, the share economy expands output and employment while lowering price. (Compare Tables 1 and 2 when $\omega < w$.) If labour productivity does not behave counter-cyclically $(F \geqslant 0)$, from (57) real pay must increase.[12] In addition, new jobs have been created, so there are more employed workers, each of whom is receiving higher real pay. In this sense a move towards profit-sharing represents an unambiguous improvement for the working class.

Note that the argument applies only when all (or almost all) firms of

[12] Actually, all that is needed is that $\lambda Y/L$ not decrease faster than $(1 - \lambda)\omega/P$ increases.

a wage economy simultaneously convert to profit-sharing plans. If one firm alone converts, it will hire new workers, but at the expense of driving down the pay of its original workers. So coordination may be required to induce people to convert to a share system; one possibility is to have the government reward profit-sharing workers, by preferential tax treatment of share income, for their part in creating the positive externality of a tight labour market.[13]

Comparing the first two rows of Table 2 with Table 1, the short-run aggregative properties of wage and share systems appear to be very analogous, the only essential difference being in the values of the variables w and ω. That interpretation is true, but it is deceptive, as will be shown presently.

6. *Long-run equilibrium in a profit-sharing economy with competitively determined pay parameters*

Consider next a longer-run situation where the set-up is the same as in the last section, except that pay parameters are endogenously determined by thoroughgoing competition in the labour market. The basic concept of competitive equilibrium in the labour market is essentially the same for a share system as for a wage system. Given the pay parameters every other firm is selecting, each firm is free to choose its own pay parameters but must live with the consequences of labour shortage if it selects too-low values. The underlying solution concept is

[13] I do not currently have a precise formulation of the 'positive externality of a tight labour market' that could serve as an operational framework for analysis. Nevertheless, it seems intuitively clear to me that there may be a basic problem of institutional instability in a profit-sharing economy because high-λ behaviour that is socially rational may not be individually rational. Some preliminary thoughts on this point are expressed in Weitzman (1984), ch. 9. I believe the relevant externality has to do with the idea that high stable pay for 'insider' workers of the existing labour force (at the expense of 'outsider' unemployed workers and the young) suits the interest both of the high-seniority employed workers and of their satisfying employers (who are doing well enough to want to continue enjoying the benefits of a quiet life). Converting outsider non-tenured workers into permanent insiders may require institutional changes in the incentive structure going far beyond anything in current official thinking. Strong material incentives, such as favourable tax treatment of the profit-sharing component of a worker's pay will probably be needed to convince senior workers to acquiesce in a profit-sharing scheme with no restrictions on new hiring. (For a more extensive discussion of the problem of new hires, see Weitzman (1984), 108–9 and 132–4.) A formal development of such ideas is properly the subject of future research, the current paper being limited to describing the macroeconomic implications of wage and profit-sharing systems without yet attempting the grand historical synthesis of explaining how or why they actually come into being.

a symmetric Nash equilibrium in pay parameters, which means that if all firms are selecting (ω, λ) as parameter values, it is not profitable for any one firm to deviate from that pattern. This equilibrium value will be used primarily as a reference point to indicate the approximate region in pay-parameter space where a profit-sharing system is likely over time to end up.

A basic theoretical result to be proved below is that any pair $(\omega, \lambda) > 0$ constitutes a long-run competitive equilibrium in pay parameters if and only if it delivers to each worker the same pay as an equilibrium wage system $(w^*, 0)$ operating under otherwise identical circumstances. From (48), such an equivalence can be written as

$$(58) \qquad w^* = \omega + \lambda\left(\frac{P^* \varUpsilon^* - \omega L^*}{L^*}\right)$$

where w^* is defined by (46) and

$$(59) \qquad P^* = \frac{\beta M}{\varUpsilon^* - \alpha A}$$

There is thus an inverse relationship between long-run equilibrium values of λ and ω and, hence, one extra degree of freedom in determining the pay parameters of a profit-sharing system.

I do not have a formal theory that would explain: (a) why a society chooses a particular (ω, λ) configuration, or, (b) why pay parameters are sticky in the short run. I only have consistent stories about viable long-term combinations of ω with λ, and about the short-term consequences of pay parameters being temporarily frozen at various values. This partly intuitionist, partly formalistic approach strikes me as the best feasible way of addressing the important issues involved. (And, presumably, the present analysis would be needed anyway as a preliminary step toward any more ambitious formulation directly attempting to tackle (a) and (b) above.) In my story, it is perhaps conceptually useful to think of λ as a policy variable chosen by the government automatically to 'stabilise' the macroeconomy at full employment.[14] Then, over a longer term, ω can be envisioned as

[14] The fact that we generally observe $(\omega, \lambda) = (w^*, 0)$ – that is, no profit-sharing might be because $(w^*, 0)$ represents some sort of institutional Nash equilibrium, with other combinations of (ω, λ) not sustainable in the face of possible externality/free-rider problems. (On this, see the suggestive discussion of Weitzman (1984), ch. 9.) Although intuitively plausible, this interpretation remains speculative. If true, it might justify public policy to induce high values of λ. Note, however, that most private companies in

adjusting to satisfy (58). Throughout the short run, in my scenario, ω and λ are both thought of as being quasi-fixed parameters.

The explanation of (58) is roughly as follows. In long-run competitive equilibrium, due to migration pressure, each worker must end up with the same pay no matter what is the ostensible form of the payment (how it is split between straight money wages and shares of profit). Given the fact that every firm must end up paying the prevailing pay whatever parameter values it selects, the profit-sharing firm can do no better in the long run than to hire labour to the point where the marginal revenue product of an extra worker is equal to the prevailing pay, then setting its pay parameters accommodatingly during contract time to yield that going compensation for its workers.

Solely to preserve neatness and to save on space, (58) will be proved here only for the case $\omega = 0$ (pure revenue-sharing). The proof for the more general case is essentially identical, although made considerably messier due to the additional notation which is required.[15]

Let $L(\lambda; \lambda^*)$ stand for the amount of labour any firm is able to attract if it pays a share λ when all other firms are paying equilibrium shares λ^*. If every other firm is paying a share λ^*, and there are a large number of firms, the prevailing level of pay must be $\lambda^* P^* Y^* / L^*$ where, because any long-run equilibrium is at full employment, P^* is given by (59). It follows that $L(\lambda; \lambda^*)$ must satisfy the condition

$$(60) \qquad \frac{\lambda R(L(\lambda;\lambda^*))}{L(\lambda;\lambda^*)} = \frac{\lambda^* P^* Y^*}{L^*}$$

where $R(L)$ stands for a firm's revenue as a function of the labour

---

the immensely successful economies of Japan, Korea, and Taiwan pay a very significant fraction of worker remuneration as a bonus which is, or so it seems in many instances, at least indirectly linked to profits per worker; and in USA, profit-sharing is not an exotic innovation but a current reality for many tens of millions of self-employed workers, professional partners and people who work on commission or tips (see Weitzman (1984), ch. 7).

[15] An alternative approach to proving such propositions in a slightly different context is contained in Weitzman (1983). It is straightforward to generalise the present formulation to include capital, and relatively easy to verify that long-run properties are unaltered when the capital stock is treated as a choice variable. In long-run equilibrium, identical-twin wage and profit-sharing systems stimulate equal investment – to the point where the long-run marginal-revenue product of capital equals the prevailing interest rate. What happens to capital formation out of long-run equilibrium can only be conjectured; but a fair guess might be that the relatively stable environment of a share economy – whose output is permanently maintained at the full capacity level – leads to an increased, steadier volume of investment over the business cycle.

working for it. Since (60) must hold for all λ, differentiating with respect to λ and collecting terms yields

$$(61) \qquad \frac{\partial L}{\partial \lambda} = \frac{R}{\dfrac{\lambda * P * \Upsilon *}{L*} - \lambda R'}$$

The long-run equilibrium problem of the firm, given $\lambda*$, is to select λ to maximise $(1 - \lambda)R(L(\lambda; \lambda*))$, which yields the first-order condition

$$(62) \qquad (1 - \lambda)R'\frac{\partial L}{\partial \lambda} = R.$$

Combining (61) with (62),

$$(63) \qquad R' = \frac{\lambda * P * \Upsilon *}{L*}$$

But from (53), the marginal revenue product of labour for a firm equals γ/μ times its optimally chosen price. Hence there will be system-wide equilibrium if and only if

$$(64) \qquad \frac{\gamma}{\mu}P* = \frac{\lambda * P * \Upsilon *}{L*}$$

or if and only if (from (46) and (59))

$$(65) \qquad w* = \frac{\lambda * P * \Upsilon *}{L*}$$

which is exactly the condition (58) to be proved for the case $\omega = 0$.

There are two major implications of what has been derived in this section. The first is that wage and profit-sharing systems are isomorphic in a long-run stationary equilibrium with competitive labour markets. I take this to mean that both systems have some long-run tendency toward similar resource-allocation patterns.

But, and this is the more important implication, the short-run properties of the two systems (when pay parameters are quasi-fixed) are quite strikingly different in the neighbourhood of a long-run equilibrium position. From (58), (46), and (56), a profit-sharing system with a good-sized share component will be operating well inside the full-employment region $[\tau' > 0]$. (In long-run equilibrium, τ' is bounded below by 0, becoming ever larger as λ is bigger and as ω

becomes smaller, approaching infinity as the pure wage component ω goes to zero and as λ approaches $w*L*/P*\Upsilon*$.) Even allowing for real world disturbances and *realpolitik* non-competitive labour markets, a serious profit-sharing economy should remain at full employment. So it seems a fair generalisation to say that in the real world a genuine profit-sharing system will be operating in the region $[\tau' > 0]$ whereas a wage system will be largely confined to the region $[\tau < 0]$. The wage variant of capitalism, unlike its profit-sharing cousin, cannot long be situated in a state of positive tautness because self-interested wage-economy firms will voluntarily bid up pay parameters.

There is then a marked difference in the degree of tension of the labour markets of wage and profit-sharing systems. A wage firm wants to hire as much labour as it is hiring under its current wage contract. But a profit-sharing firm wants to hire more labour than it is actually able to hire on the profit-maximising contract parameters that it has itself selected.[16] The resolution of the seeming paradox is that while the profit-sharing firm desires more labour on the *old* contract, it will be made worse off if it tries to issue a *new* contract with higher pay parameters. (Indeed, this statement was demonstrated in the course of proving (58).)

It is important to note that it is not disequilibrium *per se* which causes unemployment, but rather a particular method of labour compensation (the wage system) in combination with disequilibrium. A profit-sharing system does *not* eliminate unemployment in a contractionary state by having such a high degree of pay flexibility that, in effect, wages are lowered to the point where long run equilibrium is automatically maintained.[17] To see this point clearly, imagine a pair of 'identical twin' wage and profit-sharing economies, both in long-run stationary equilibrium with competitive labour markets, so that in both systems worker pay equals the marginal revenue product of labour. Then subject the two systems to a contractionary shock and observe what happens in the short run.

In a profit-sharing economy, the marginal revenue product of labour, from (53) and (59), is:

$$(66) \qquad\qquad R' = \frac{\gamma\beta M}{\mu(\Upsilon* - \alpha A)}$$

---

[16] This aspect is elaborated in Weitzman (1984).
[17] See Weitzman (1983) for a more rigorous discussion.

while money pay (from Table 2) is:

$$(67) \qquad W = \frac{\beta M}{\Upsilon^* - \alpha A}\left[(1 - \lambda)\ \frac{\omega(\Upsilon^* - \alpha A)}{\beta M} + \lambda\ \frac{\Upsilon^*}{L^*} \right]$$

Now whenever a profit-sharing economy is in long-run equilibrium, with $(\omega,\ \lambda)$ satisfying (58), then (66) and (67) must be equal, or $R' = W$. After a contractionary shock (say a decrease in A or M), it is straightforward to verify that money pay (67) declines by less than the marginal revenue product of labour (66) (provided $\omega > 0$). The marginal revenue product of labour will then be lower than pay, $R' < W$; yet all workers are retained by the firms. Thus, profit-sharing does more than simply introduce some flexibility of wages. It builds in a permanent incentive for firms to want to retain their employees, not because of low pay, but because the marginal cost of an extra worker is less than the marginal revenue product created by that worker. In a wage system, on the other hand, firms always act to equate the marginal revenue product of labour with pay, and workers are consequently laid off after a contractionary shock.

Incidentally, it is straightforward to use the same 'identical twin' thought experiment to verify that not only is aggregate output and employment higher in a profit-sharing economy than a wage economy immediately after a contractionary shock to a long-run equilibrium state, but so is each employed worker's real pay. The conclusion about comparatively higher real pay in a share system holds as well for inflationary disturbances to a long-run equilibrium position, because there is at least some protection against higher prices.

Summing up, then, it seems a fair generalisation to say that a serious profit-sharing economy will possess basically classical or monetarist macro-economic properties very different from the short-run Keynesian underemployment characteristics of a wage economy. In a share economy, money is neutral and directly affects the price level, while having no effect on real aggregate economic variables. Resources are always fully utilised in a share system. The implication would appear to be that the central bank can directly and relatively easily control prices in a profit-sharing economy by regulating the supply of money, without having to worry about possibly adverse effects on employment and output.

7. *Wage and profit-sharing economies compared*

It has been noted that a wage economy can plausibly be expected to function primarily in a regime where $\tau < 0$, whereas a profit-sharing economy should operate within the region $[\tau' > 0]$. The relevant conditions, I have argued, are:

$$(68) \qquad \alpha A + \frac{\beta M \gamma}{\mu w} < \Upsilon^* < \alpha A + \frac{\beta M \gamma}{\mu \omega}$$

Throughout this section it is assumed that (68) describes the appropriate configuration of parameters, both initially and after unexpected displacements of the system.[18]

Table 3 compares the short-run macroeconomic properties of wage and profit-sharing systems in the regions where each is likely to be operating.

Table 3. Macroeconomic variables compared in the two systems

Variable	Wage Economy	Profit-Sharing Economy
Υ	$\alpha A + \dfrac{\beta M \gamma}{\mu w}$	Υ^*
P	$\dfrac{\mu w}{\gamma}$	$\dfrac{\beta M}{\Upsilon^* - \alpha A}$
$\dfrac{W}{P}$	$\dfrac{\gamma}{\mu}$	$\lambda \dfrac{\Upsilon^*}{L^*} + (1-\lambda)\omega \dfrac{\Upsilon^* - \alpha A}{\beta M}$

In order to be able to make meaningful comparisons between real pay, W/P, in both systems, some assumption of 'comparability' must be made between pay parameters of wage and profit-sharing economies. The assumption made here is that real pay in the profit-sharing system should be the same as in the wage system – under the prices prevailing in the wage system, i.e.,

$$(69) \qquad \frac{\gamma}{\mu} = (1-\lambda)\frac{\omega \gamma}{w \mu} + \lambda \frac{\Upsilon^*}{L^*}$$

---

[18] The interested reader should be able to provide, from Tables 1 and 2, the correct analysis for those situations where (68) might not hold.

(It is not difficult to verify that (69) is merely a rewriting of the long-run competitive labour market condition (58), which allows the fictional interpretation that both systems once upon a time started from the same initial equilibrium condition before being hit by the identical contractionary shock.)

Under conditions (68) and (69), from Table 3, output Y and real pay W/P are lower, while prices P are higher in a wage economy than in a comparable profit-sharing economy. This is the sense, then, in which conversion from a wage system to an equivalent-looking profit-sharing system yields unambiguously superior macroeconomic characteristics.

The basic short-run difference between sticky-pay-parameter wage and profit-sharing systems is no doubt exaggerated in my presentation, but it would, I feel, remain in modified form even after introducing additional real-world frictions, inertias and imperfections. Perhaps the contrast can be summed up as follows. In a wage system, prices are relatively rigid while quantities are relatively flexible and able to be influenced by demand-management policies. In a share system, output prices are relatively flexible and under the control of monetary and fiscal policies, while quantities are relatively rigid at the full-employment level. Without relying on any fictitious 'aggregate supply curve', which has little meaning in an imperfectly competitive environment where firms *set* prices so that there is always an excess supply of their products, the central theoretical result can nevertheless be conveniently stated in the 'as if' language of aggregate supply familiar to conventional macroeconomics.

A wage economy behaves in the short run 'as if' aggregate supply were elastic at fixed prevailing prices (the 'as if' Keynesian case). A profit-sharing economy behaves in the short run 'as if' aggregate supply were inelastic at the full employment level (the 'as if' classical case).

Note that these statements describe the profit-maximising Nash-equilibrium behaviour of a monopolistically competitive economy in the short run, when labour-payment contract parameters are fixed. The conclusions are not limited to the long run, or restricted to a perfectly competitive world. The share system thus behaves essentially like a classical macroeconomy, even while the classical preconditions are not being met. And the wage system, of course, behaves in the short run like the Keynesian macroeconomy that it is.

There is an interesting contrast, from Table 3, between the government's ability to influence prices and quantities in the two systems. Output in a profit-sharing economy automatically self-regulates at the full employment level, independent of government policy or lack of policy. The world of Keynesian 'underemployment equilibrium' on the other hand, with its possibility of, indeed its need for, using demand management to improve the level of aggregate output in the short run, with its attendant entourage of fiscal and monetary multipliers, rests crucially on the institutional assumption of a wage-payment system. Change that particular labour payment feature to a profit-sharing arrangement and macroeconomic properties are dramatically altered for the better.

Compare the price equation of Table 3 for the two systems. In a wage economy, government policy has no *direct* effect on prices, which are determined strictly as a markup on costs. But in a share economy, the short-run price level is a direct function of aggregate fiscal and monetary variables and it does not depend upon short-run cost considerations. Government spending in a profit-sharing system crowds out private spending, and the aggregate effects show up only on the price level. Money is neutral in a share economy – monetary policy can be used powerfully and directly to determine the price level without affecting real economic activity. If there is an inflationary shock, say due to an increase in autonomous spending, the monetary authorities can hold the price level stable – without causing unemployment – merely by contracting the money supply. The share economy is a monetarist's dream – not just in long-run equilibrium, but in the short run with rigid labour contracts and monopolistic product markets.

A good litmus test for any market system is to observe how it reacts to changes in capacity. What happens if potential output, Y^*, is suddenly made larger, say because labour supply has unexpectedly increased?

A profit-sharing economy immediately raises its output level to the new capacity ceiling. Fresh labour is immediately absorbed and put to work producing additional goods and services, without having to wait for any long-run adjustment of pay parameters. From Table 3, the short-run effect of increased capacity on a profit-sharing economy is greater output, lower prices and higher real pay. The opposite conclusions hold when there is diminished potential to produce.

By contrast, in the wage system a firm is not interested in hiring additional workers on the existing labour contract. From Table 3, an increase in Y^* has no immediate effect on output, prices, or real pay for a wage system. Only if A, M, α, or β are increased, say through government policy, or if w is lowered, does a wage system absorb new entrants into the labour market.

The parameter μ is a measure of the degree of competitiveness of an economy. Higher values of μ mean that industry is less competitive. From Table 3, changes in μ have no short-term macroeconomic effects on a profit-sharing system, although there will be predictable long-term effects. By contrast, in a wage economy any industrial policy changing the degree of concentration will immediately move aggregate output, prices and real pay in the expected direction, with macroeconomic performance being improved by increased competitiveness.

In the model of this paper, the coefficient γ stands for the marginal product of labour; its inverse, $1/\gamma$, measures the additional labour requirement per unit increment of output. If raw materials are employed in fixed proportions with output, an exogenous hike in the relative cost of materials could be given an interpretation within the model by appropriately increasing $1/\gamma$. Generally speaking, an adverse supply shock can be captured in the present framework by an autonomous deterioration of the marginal productivity parameter γ.[19]

From Table 3, changes in γ have no short-term macroeconomic effects on a profit-sharing system. But a decline in the marginal productivity of labour has an immediate detrimental impact on output, prices and real pay in a wage economy. The long-run effects of declining marginal productivity of labour are identical in both systems, involving basic adjustments in compensation parameters and real pay. But a share system allows such changes to come about gradually, through the competitive pressures of the market, without ever interrupting the smooth flow of full-employment output. A wage system, by contrast, responds to an adverse supply shock by an abrupt increase in unemployment and inflation that can be very unsettling to society.

Wage capitalism is fundamentally a precariously balanced system. The slightest change – a momentary lowering of the desire to spend money on goods, say – can move it away from the razor-thin $[\tau = 0]$

[19] This is a standard trick, if somewhat heuristic. For some more details, see Dornbusch and Fischer (1984), 410. Changes in sales taxes, employment subsidies, and the like can be given a similar interpretation. Note that I am assuming, for convenience, that a supply shock leaves the level of potential output, Y^*, unaltered. This may or may not be an appropriate assumption, depending on the context. The interested reader should be able to trace through, e.g., what happens if γ and Y^* both change in the same proportion.

region where there is just full employment and pay is exactly competitive. A wage economy is at the mercy of any imbalances between γ, w, M, A, and the other variables or parameters of the system. A trifle more belligerence on the part of labour unions, a slight increase in the cost of imported raw materials, a bit less productivity than expected – may be enough to set off an explosive inflationary spiral, pushing up both prices and unemployment.

If productivity is less than anticipated, and yet workers seek to maintain an inappropriately high level of real wages, even a very small discrepancy between labour's aspiration level and the profit-maximising real wage

$$(70) \qquad\qquad \frac{w}{P} = \frac{\gamma}{\mu}$$

may unleash an accelerating wage-price spiral, abetted by whatever indexation exists, that can ultimately be brought under control only by choking the economy, and the labour force, into submission through restrictive monetary and fiscal policies. When w is pushed up relative to γ, say because productivity has not increased as fast as expected, that just moves up prices in the same proportion, leaving the real wage intact. And unless there is accommodating policy, unemployment results and output declines. Should the monetary authorities ratify the wage hike by increasing the money supply, inflation is created without dampening labour's underlying desire for an increased real wage.

A fundamental problem of the wage system is that prices are set by producers as a markup over wages and neither the government nor anyone else has a *direct* mechanism for changing the price level in the short run. From formula (43), P can only change as w, μ, or γ are altered. And there is no reason to expect a reliable or usable tendency for 'the elasticity of demand, over the elasticity minus one, divided by the marginal product of labour', to vary systematically with business fluctuations.

So the only practical way to moderate prices in a wage economy is to moderate wage costs. Monetary or fiscal policies can slow down wage-push inflation only by throttling the economy into sufficiently low rates of employment to diminish money-wage demands: a very costly, indirect, inefficient and inhumane way of controlling the price level, but the only one available under wage capitalism.

Table 3 displays an interesting contrast that may be relevant for issues concerning cost-push inflation. In a wage economy the pay parameter w influences aggregate output and the price level, but not the real wage. In a share economy, it is the other way round – parameters ω and λ have no effect on output or prices, but do play a role in determining real pay. A cost-push money-wage increase in a wage economy lowers output and raises prices while leaving the real wage intact. But in a profit-sharing economy any pushing up of pay parameters does nothing to aggregate output or prices, while it raises the level of real pay. If the parameters ω or λ are increased, that merely redistributes income in the short run from capital to labour without changing the overall size of the output pie.[20]

8. *Conclusion*

My own conclusion is that a profit-sharing economy has some natural tendencies towards sustained, non-inflationary, market-oriented full employment. A profit-sharing economy can avoid dreaded Keynesian unemployment, even when conducting anti-inflationary monetarist policy. The wage variant of capitalism, on the other hand, does not have built-in stability and so must rely more heavily on skilful discretionary adjustments of financial aggregates in reacting to each unforeseen event as it occurs. Such questions as why wage capitalism is so prevalent and what can be done to change an economy from a wage system to a profit-sharing system must be left for another time.[21] But I

[20] It might be thought, then, that there is a greater temptation for the median worker to attempt to push pay parameters above competitive levels in a profit-sharing economy than in a wage economy. Somewhat paradoxically, the exact opposite is true. See Weitzman (1984), ch. 8, for the details. It turns out that while it may be collectively rational for all workers together in a profit-sharing economy to push up pay parameters above competitive levels, it is not individually rational for a particular worker or union, who will not directly benefit because on the margin the profit-sharing firm will automatically offset artificial pay-parameter increases by hiring more workers and driving down profits per worker, so pay remains at the level prevailing throughout the rest of the economy. In a wage system the opposite is true – it is individually rational for the median worker of a wage firm to push for higher wages no matter what workers in other firms are doing, but it is collectively irrational for the working class as a whole to push for higher wages.

[21] For some preliminary thoughts on these issues, see above, note 13. The welfare effects of changing from a sticky-wage economy to a sticky-share economy should be clear enough, even without a very sophisticated analysis. When outsider unemployed workers are effectively cut out of the wage economy, a significant slice of the national income pie evaporates – resulting in huge first-order Okun-gap losses of output and social welfare. A profit-sharing system stabilises aggregate output at the largest possible national income pie, while permitting only small second-order Harberger-triangle losses

hope it is clear from the analysis of this paper why an economy based on profit-sharing principles may conceivably offer some foundation for a permanent solution to the problem of stagflation.

References

Benassy, J.-P., *The Economics of Market Disequilibrium* (New York: Academic Press, 1982).

Dornbusch, R. and Fischer, S., *Macroeconomics*, third edition (New York: McGraw Hill, 1984).

Dixit, A. and Stiglitz, J.E., 'Monopolistic competition and optimum product diversity', *American Economic Review* 67 (June 1977), 297–308.

Grandmont, J.M., *Money and Value* (Cambridge: Cambridge University Press, 1983).

Hart, O., 'Monopolistic competition in the spirit of Chamberlin: a general model', *Review of Economic Studies* (1985).

Hicks, J. R., 'Mr Keynes and the "Classics": a suggested interpretation', *Econometrica* 5 (April 1937), 147–159.

Malinvaud, E., *The Theory of Unemployment Reconsidered* (Oxford: Basil Blackwell, 1977).

Meade, J. E., *Stagflation. Vol. 1: Wage-Fixing* (London: Allen & Unwin, 1982).

————, 'The macroeconomic implications of monopolistic competition', working paper, 1984.

Solow, R.M., 'Monopolistic competition and the multiplier', forthcoming in *Economic Journal* (1986).

Stiglitz, J.E., 'Theories of wage rigidity', in Butkiewicz, Koford and Miller, *Keynes' Economic Legacy* (Praeger, 1986).

Varian, H.R., *Microeconomic Analysis* (New York: W.W. Norton, 1984).

Weintraub, S., *Our Stagflation Malaise* (Westport: Quorum Books, 1981).

Weitzman, M.L., 'Increasing returns and the foundations of unemployment theory', *Economic Journal* 92 (December 1982), 787–804.

————, 'Some macroeconomic implications of alternative compensation systems', *Economic Journal* 93 (December 1983), 763–783.

————, *The Share Economy* (Cambridge: Harvard University Press, 1984).

————, 'Increasing returns and the foundations of unemployment theory: Reply', *Journal of Post Keynesian Economics* 7 (Spring 1985).

---

to arise – e.g., because a few crumbs have been randomly redistributed from workers in one firm to workers in another, or because the movement of resources in response to firm-specific shocks may be somewhat slowed.

9. Wage Indexation and Macroeconomic Fluctuations

Pierre Dehez & Jean-Paul Fitoussi

1. Introduction

Recent theoretical developments in general equilibrium theory have incorporated the possibility of imperfectly flexible prices, the general consistency of transactions being attained through quantity rationing. The basic contributions along these lines are due to Benassy (1975), Drèze (1975) and Younès (1975).

More recent contributions by Van der Laan (1980), Kurz (1982) and Dehez and Drèze (1984) have questioned both the theoretical relevance and the practical significance of demand-rationing in market economies since such rationing would require a more complex coordination of economic activities and is indeed rarely observed. These authors have therefore proposed an equilibrium concept in which the rationing of supply is sufficient to achieve an equilibrium. In particular Kurz proves the existence of an equilibrium in a framework allowing for a flexible structure of *price linkages* while Dehez and Drèze consider the more specific case of *relative price rigidities*.[1]

The assumption of links between prices is definitely weaker than that of nominal price rigidity. But still the structure of price linkage is exogenous and is, therefore, as vulnerable from the point of view of individual rationality. *Why do rational agents not exhaust their exchange opportunities* is the recurrent question, notably in the rational expectation-market clearing literature. But, quite apart from the fact that 'auction-market clearing' is more an assumption about centralisation and information than about rationality, the question itself could be reversed, as suggested by Olson (1984, 636): *Is there any agent with the incentive and ability to block mutually advantageous transactions among potential buyers and sellers and thus prevent markets from achieving a Walrasian equilibrium?*

The answer to the latter question is 'yes' if one allows for monopoly

---

[1] For applications of this concept within a macroeconomic framework, see Dehez and Fitoussi (1985).

or monopsony power attained through collective actions – but not through individual actions because, otherwise, markets would clear. As suggested by Kurz (1982), price linkages could indeed arise from the fact that some groups of agents succeed in linking their incomes to those of another group, thus reflecting strategic behaviour within the market place. More generally, it is sufficient that some group of agents has in 'good times' some transient monopoly or monopsony power to obtain a structure of price linkages. This suggests that, in a dynamic and non-stationary context, the structure of price linkages will change through time in relation to the state of the economy.

The purpose of this paper is precisely to investigate this aspect in the framework of a simple macro-economic model in which unemployment can be explained by an excessive real wage. We shall indeed assume a perfectly competitive product market, a decreasing marginal productivity of labour and an inelastic labour supply, in which case the excess supply of labour depends only on the real wage.[2]

On the one hand, a falling nominal-wage rate may have adverse effects on the marginal efficiency of capital because it leads to a higher interest rate or simply because it prevents the interest rate from falling. In other words nominal-wage flexibility may be unsuccessful in restoring full employment. This argument, raised by Keynes and substantiated by Hahn and Solow in this book (Chapter One), supports the case for monetary expansion as a means of reducing unemployment. On the other hand, can what is impossible to achieve by way of downward wage flexibility be attained through inflation? It is this question which primarily motivates the present paper.

If the wage rate is fully indexed to the price level, the real wage and thus employment, is unaffected by inflation. But indexation is hardly perfect and, furthermore, the extent to which indexation actually takes place is not invariant but is typically affected by the state of the labour market. Indeed, substantial amendments to indexation clauses have been recently observed in countries experiencing high rates of unemployment. At the same time, in situations of excess demand for labour or low unemployment, the real wage typically rises, which could be considered as a phenomenon of more-than-full indexation[3] in a situation of continuous inflation.

---

[2] When positive, it measures unemployment; when negative, it measures the excess demand for labour.

[3] The relevance of over-full indexation was suggested to us by Arrow in a comment on an earlier paper.

Accepting the fact that indexation is not perfect, but taking into account that it is also not invariant, can inflation act as a regulatory mechanism? Our purpose is to show that it is the case whenever the indexation scheme is not too sensitive to labour-market conditions with respect to the inflation rate. Otherwise, the economy could exhibit fluctuations which are not necessarily convergent.

More precisely we consider a three commodity economy extending over an infinite number of discrete periods with a simple overlapping generation structure. In each period the price level is determined competitively so that the consumption-goods market always clears. In turn the price level determines the wage rate through a linkage function which is fixed at the beginning of each period. Thus, in the short run, the economy can be in a situation either of unemployment or of excess demand for labour (excess capacity). Because an interest rate is paid on money holdings, the stock of money continues to expand from one period to the next, generating a continuous inflation. In this way, we can say that the wage rate is 'indexed' to the price level.

Underlying the linkage or indexation function, there is a bargaining process whose aim is to fix the indexation formula to be applied during the period. The bargaining power of the trade unions which represent the workers and are involved in the negotiations is assumed to be affected by the conditions observed on the labour market in the preceding period: the larger the unemployment, the lower is their bargaining power, and there is a critical rate of unemployment above which less-than-full indexation occurs – i.e. inflation induces a fall in the real wage – and below which more-than-full indexation occurs – i.e. inflation induces a rise in the wage.[4] This can be explained in particular by the assumption that the relative strength of a union critically depends on the proportion of its members who are unemployed. Furthermore, if there are several trade unions involved, it is even more likely that the indexation scheme will be affected by the conditions prevailing on the labour market.[5]

In this framework, the long-run equilibrium or stationary state is not necessarily characterised by full employment. Instead it is defined by the level of unemployment at which indexation is perfect, i.e. by the

[4] Here, a change within a given period in some variable involves a comparison between the current value of this variable and its value at the end of the preceding period.

[5] All this is very much in the spirit of the third part of Hicks (1974). See also Tobin (1980), p. 38.

critical unemployment rate just defined. Hence to say that inflation is stabilising means that the process of indexation is such that inflation will drive the economy (not necessarily in a monotonic way) towards the long-run equilibrium through the process of weakening or strengthening the bargaining position of the unions.

The rest of the paper is organised as follows. The formal model is introduced and the short run equilibrium is defined in Section 2. The dynamics of the economy is then analysed in Section 3 and concluding remarks are offered in the last Section. Finally an Appendix gathers the more technical aspects of the model and also contains an illustration.

2. *The model*

We use the overlapping generation model in its simplest form.[6] The population and its characteristics are assumed to be invariant through time, there are no bequests and the agents live only two periods. For further simplicity we assume that there are only two agents living in every period, one 'young' and one 'old'. This is equivalent to assuming that all agents are identical. There is one *perishable* consumption good which is produced out of the labour which is supplied *inelastically* by the young agent only. A further commodity, 'money', is used as a medium of exchange and reserve of value. We denote by p and w the price level and the wage rate which are both expressed in terms of money.

The production sector is simply described by a production function, $y=f(\ell)$, and there is no production lag. It is assumed to satisfy the following properties:

(a. 1) f is continuously differentiable, increasing and *strictly* concave;
(a. 2) $f(0)=0$ and $f'(0)=+\infty$.

The maximisation of profit, $pf(\ell)-w\ell$, at given price and wage determines the demand for labour. It then only depends on the real wage rate, $q=w/p$, and is simply given by $\ell=f'^{-1}(q)$.

The assumptions (a. 1) and (a. 2) ensure that the demand for labour is well defined and positive for all $q>0$.

We denote by ℓ^*, $\ell^*>0$, the quantity of labour which is (inelastically) supplied by the agent when young. The agent has intertemporal

---

[6] The overlapping generation modelling is convenient and indeed popular. See for example Hahn and Solow in the present volume (Chapter One) or Grandmont (1983, 1985).

preferences over present consumption, c_1, and future consumption, c_2, which are represented by the separable utility function:

$$u(c_1, c_2) = u_1(c_1) + u_2(c_2).$$

It is assumed to satisfy the following properties:

(b. 1) u_1 and u_2 are continuously diffentiable, increasing and strictly concave;

(b. 2) $u_1'(0) = +\infty$.

The last assumption is introduced to ensure that the agent is always willing to consume when young.

The profit realised within one period is distributed entirely to the young agent *at the end of the period*. Hence labour income is the unique source of income for the young agent and the profit is transferred to the next period with the saving, if any.

We shall consider the possibility of interest payments on nominal money balances held by the old agent. If r denotes the interest rate, $r \geqslant 0$, and M_0 is the quantity of money transferred from the preceeding period, $(1+r)M_0$ is then the quantity of money which will be spent by the old agent in the current period. In the sequel we shall use the notation $\lambda = 1 + r$ with $\lambda \geqslant 1$.

Let us consider a given period of time. If p^e and λ^e denote the price level and the interest rate which are expected to prevail at the next period, then $\theta - 1$, with $\theta = \lambda^e p/p^e$, defines the *expected real interest rate*. As shown in Appendix A1, conditionally to a given employment level ℓ, $0 \leqslant \ell \leqslant \ell^*$, the young agent's current and planned demand for consumption good can be written as functions of the real interest rate and real wage rate, i.e.

$$c_1 = c_1 \ (\theta, q, \ell),$$

$$c_2 = c_2 \ (\theta, q, \ell).$$

The assumptions (b. 1) and (b. 2) ensure that these functions are well defined and continuous. Moreover, c_1 and c_2 are positive whenever $q\ell > 0$ and c_2 is an increasing function of θ. An example is given in Appendix A3.

As to the formation of expectations, we assume that $\lambda^e = \lambda$. This is consistent with the fact that we shall restrict ourselves to a *constant interest rate policy*. On the other hand the young agent's price expectation is given by some function ψ,

$$p^e = \psi(p, \lambda),$$

in which the past history of the economy is implicitly incorporated. It is assumed to satisfy the following properties:

(c. 1) ψ is continuous and increasing in p and λ ;
(c. 2) ψ $(p, \lambda)/p$ is non-increasing in p for all $p > 0$ and $\lambda \geqslant 1$.

Hence, the elasticity (if well-defined) of the future price with respect to the current one is positive but does not exceed unity.[7]

It remains to specify how the price level and wage rate are determined in each period. As explained in the Introduction, the price level is determined *competitively* in the consumption goods market and, in turn, the price level determines the wage rate. More precisely, the wage rate is *linked to* the price level through some functional relation ϕ ,

$$w = \phi(p),$$

which incorporates implicitly the past history of the economy. It is assumed to satisfy the following properties:

(d. 1) ϕ is continuous and has positive values for all $p \geqslant 0$;

(d. 2) there exists $b > 0$ such that $\dfrac{\phi(p)}{p} \leqslant b$ for all $p \geqslant 0$.

This last assumption simply requires that the real wage rate remains *bounded*.

At this stage it is not necessary to specify further the linkage function ϕ . This will be done after we have defined the concept of short-run equilibrium and before we proceed to the dynamic analysis.

Let us consider a given period of time. The data consist of the expectation function ψ , the linkage function ϕ and the past history of the economy which includes the stock of money in the preceding period, $M_0 > 0$, and the interest factor $\lambda \geqslant 1$.

A *short-run equilibrium* is defined by a price level $p > 0$, a wage rate $w > 0$ and an employment level $\ell > 0$ satisfying the following conditions:

(i) $w = \phi(p)$;

(ii) $\ell = \text{Min}\left(\ell^*, f'^{-1}\left(\dfrac{w}{p}\right)\right)$

(iii) $c_1\left(\dfrac{\lambda}{\psi(p, \lambda)}, \dfrac{w}{p}, \ell\right) + \dfrac{\lambda M_0}{p} = f(\ell).$

[7] Hence we allow for unit elastic price expectations. This does not prevent the existence of a short-run equilibrium because the young agent is 'forced' to save the profit. See Grandmont (1983) for existence conditions outside such an assumption.

The last condition simply says that (effective) demand and supply coincide in the consumption goods market. By the *Walras Identity* it is equivalent to the following condition:

$$\text{(iv)} \quad \frac{\phi(p, \lambda)}{\lambda} c_2\left(\frac{\lambda p}{\psi(p, \lambda)}, \frac{w}{p}, \ell\right) = \lambda M_0$$

which says that the demand for and the supply of money are equal.[8]

Let us define $q^* = f'(\ell^*)$, the *Walrasian* real wage rate at which the labour market clears. There are two types of *non-Walrasian equilibria* depending on the actual value of the real-wage rate. If, at the equilibrium, the real-wage rate exceeds q^*, there is *excess supply of labour*, i.e.

$$\ell = f'^{-1}(q) < \ell^*.$$

This corresponds to the boundary between 'Keynesian' and 'classical' unemployment in the terminology used by Malinvaud (1977). On the other hand, if $q < q^*$, there is *excess demand for labour*, i.e.

$$\ell = \ell^* < f'^{-1}(q).$$

This corresponds to the boundary between 'repressed inflation' and Keynesian unemployment in the same terminology.

The existence of an equilibrium is proved in Appendix A2 where it is shown that an equilibrium is defined by a pair (p, q) satisfying

$$p = \mu(q, M)$$

$$q = \frac{\phi(p)}{p}$$

where $M = \lambda M_0$ and μ is a continuous function, non-decreasing in q and increasing in M. An example is given in Appendix A3.

3. Dynamic analysis

We shall first specify the indexation scheme in a dynamic context where *deflation does not occur*.

Let us consider the economy at some period t. As indicated in the Introduction, the indexation scheme is fixed at the beginning of the period through some bargaining process in which the relative

---

[8] Benassy (1985) considers a similar definition but with *downward price rigidity*.

bargaining power of the workers depends on the excess supply of labour which was observed in period $t-1$. To capture this idea, we assume that the current real-wage rate q depends on the current price level according to the following indexation formula:

$$q = F\left(q_{t-1}, \frac{p}{p_{t-1}}\right)$$

which defines indirectly the linkage function by $\phi(p) = pF(q_{t-1}, p/p_{t-1})$. The dependence of q on q_{t-1} is twofold. On the one hand, q_{t-1} is the *initial* (or reference) real-wage rate, i.e. $F(q_{t-1}, 1) = q_{t-1}$: in absence of inflation, the real-wage rate does not change. On the other hand, the excess supply of labour in period $t-1$ is given by $\ell^* - f'^{-1}(q_{t-1})$. It depends only on q_{t-1} and therefore it is q_{t-1} which affects the extent of current indexation.

The function F is assumed to be continuously differentiable and to satisfy the following properties:

(e. 1) there exists $\bar{q} > 0$ such that, for all $x > 1$, $F(q, x) < q$ if $q > \bar{q}$ and $F(q, x) > q$ if $q < \bar{q}$;

(e. 2) for all $x > 1$, $F'_x(q, x) \leqslant 0$ if $q > \bar{q}$ and $F'_x(q, x) \geqslant 0$ if $q < \bar{q}$.

Here F'_x denote the partial derivative of F with respect to x. In the same way, F'_q will denote the partial derivative of F with respect to q. Continuity of F and F'_x implies that $F(\bar{q}, x) = \bar{q}$ and $F'_x(\bar{q}, x) = 0$ for all $x \geqslant 1$.

Hence, inflation induces a decrease in the real-wage rate if $q_{t-1} > \bar{q}$ and the larger the inflation, the lower will be the current real-wage rate. And vice versa if $q_{t-1} < \bar{q}$. The level $\bar{q}$ defines the critical level of excess supply of labour above which less-than-full indexation takes place and below which more-than-full indexation takes place. Typically $\bar{q} > q^*$, in which case inflation induces an increase in the real-wage rate if there was an excess demand for labour or if unemployment was not 'too large'; and it induces a decrease in the real-wage rate if unemployment was 'large'. Nevertheless $\bar{q}$ will not be assumed to take any specific value with respect to the Walrasian real wage rate q^*.

We fix from now on the interest rate at some positive value, i.e. $\lambda_t = \lambda$ and $\lambda^e_{t+1} = \lambda$ for all t, with $\lambda > 1$. As to price expectations, we simply assume that $p^e_{t+1} = \lambda p_t$, i.e.

$$\psi(p, \lambda) = \lambda p$$

As we shall see, this corresponds to a self-fulfilling expectation along a sequence of short-run equilibria characterised by a constant real-wage rate, i.e. a sequence of equilibria along which $q_t = \bar{q}$ for all t. Given that we shall restrict our attention mainly to the dynamics in a neighbourhood of $\bar{q}$, this assumption is hardly restrictive. Hence $\theta_t = 1$ for all t and the equilibrium function μ can be written as $\mu(q, M) = M/h(q)$ where $h(q) = c_2(1, q, \ell(q))$. This is a direct consequence of the equilibrium condition (iv) or, equivalently, of equation (2) in the Appendix A2. Therefore along an equilibrium sequence $\{M_t, p_t, q_t\}$ we have for all t

$$p_t = \frac{M_t}{h(q_t)}. \tag{α}$$

Let us now assume that in period $t-1$ the economy was in some equilibrium position defined by $(M_{t-1}, p_{t-1}, q_{t-1})$, i.e. $p_{t-1} = M_{t-1}/h(q_{t-1})$. The initial stock of money in period t is then given by

$$M_t = \lambda M_{t-1} \tag{β}$$

and the new equilibrium position is determined through a tatonnement process starting from (p_{t-1}, q_{t-1}) along which the price level rises continuously until an equilibrium is reached at some $p_t > p_{t-1}$. Hence, p_t is the *smallest* price level in the set

$$\left\{ p \geq p_{t-1} \,\middle|\, p = \frac{M_t}{h(q)}, q = F\left(q_{t-1}, \frac{p}{p_{t-1}}\right) \right\} \tag{γ}$$

In this sense, the short-run equilibrium is *uniquely determined*: we ignore possible equilibria characterised by a price level larger than P_t. Along the tatonnement process, the real-wage rate is rising or declining, depending whether $q_{t-1} < \bar{q}$ or $q_{t-1} > \bar{q}$.

This can be illustrated in the (p, q) plane as in Figure 1 where it has been assumed that $q_{t-1} > \bar{q}$.

Combining (α), (β) and (γ), and using the fact that h is a nonincreasing function of q, it can be shown that the sequence of equilibrium real wage rates satisfies the following equations

$$q_t = \text{Min} \left\{ q \,\middle|\, h(q) \leq \lambda h(q_{t-1}), q = F\left(q_{t-1}, \frac{\lambda h(q_{t-1})}{h(q)}\right) \right\} \tag{δ}$$

which implicitly defines the dynamics of the real wage rate and therefore of employment.

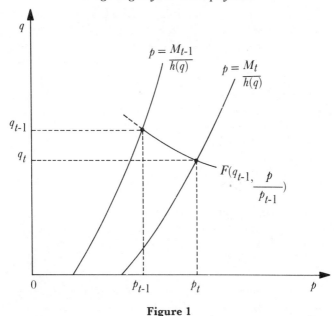

Figure 1

Clearly the sequence of equilibria along which the real wage rate is constant and equal to $\bar{q}$ is a *stationary state* in real terms along which the inflation rate is constant and equal to $\lambda - 1$, and price expectations are self-fulfilling.[9] Indeed, if $q_{t-1} = \bar{q}$, then $q_t = q_{t-1} = \bar{q}$ and $p_t = \lambda p_{t-1}$. Furthermore, by definition of F, if $q_{t-1} < \bar{q}$, then $q_t > q_{t-1}$ while if $q_{t-1} > \bar{q}$, then $q_t < q_{t-1}$. Hence, if $q = 0$ is a stationary state, it is necessarily unstable. On the other hand, there are *at most two* stationary states. Indeed, again by definition of F, $q_t = q_{t-1} \neq 0$ implies $q_t = q_{t-1} = \bar{q}$.

The evolution of the economy in terms of the real-wage rate, and therefore in terms of employment and imbalance on the labour market, need not be monotonic. Indeed if q_{t-1} happens to be above $\bar{q}$, it may be that q_t finds itself below $\bar{q}$, and vice versa. The possibility of such fluctuations is illustrated in Figure 2 where we have successively $q_{t-1} > \bar{q}$, $q_t < \bar{q}$ and $q_{t+1} > \bar{q}$. This does not necessarily correspond to

[9] Actually indexation induces a kind of Phillips curve. Indeed it is possible to construct the locus of short-run equilibrium points in the (q, x) plane as a falling curve passing through the point $(\bar{q}, \lambda)$.

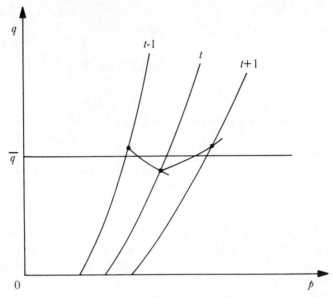

Figure 2

genuine *regime switching*, from unemployment to excess demand for labour or vice versa, except in the particular case where $\bar{q} = q^*$.

The conditions under which such fluctuations may occur can be studied by considering the real-wage dynamics around the stationary state $\bar{q}$. From (δ), the sequence $\{q_t\}$ of equilibrium real-wage rates satisfies the equation

$$q_t = F\left(q_{t-1}, \frac{\lambda h(q_{t-1})}{h(q_t)}\right).$$

Differentiating it and using the fact that $F'_x(\bar{q}, x) = 0$ for all $x \geqslant 1$, a consequence of assumption (e. 2), we obtain

$$\left.\frac{dq_t}{dq_{t-1}}\right|_{q_{t-1} = \bar{q}} = F'_q(\bar{q}, \lambda)$$

In other words, the real-wage dynamics *in a neighbourhood of* $\bar{q}$ is essentially described by the indexation formula, i.e.

$$q_t = F(q_{t-1}, \lambda).$$

On the one hand, by assumption (e.1), we have $F'_q(\bar{q}, \lambda) \leqslant 1$. There remain, therefore, three possible cases, namely:

(a) $$0 \leqslant F'_q(\bar{q}, \lambda) \leqslant 1;$$

(b) $$-1 < F'_q(\bar{q}, \lambda) < 0;$$

(c) $$F'_q(\bar{q}, \lambda) \leqslant -1.$$

In cases (a) and (b), the stationary state is *locally stable*: starting from any q_0 'near' $\bar{q}$, the sequence of real-wage rates converges to $\bar{q}$. In case (a), the convergence is *monotonic* while in case (b) there are *fluctuations* around $\bar{q}$. In the last case, the stationary state is *unstable* and there are *diverging fluctuations*.

Given λ, the difference $1 - F'_q(\bar{q}, \lambda)$ measures how sensitive is the extent of indexation with respect to small change in the real-wage rate away from the 'long-run' equilibrium level $\bar{q}$. Hence instability results from a too high sensitivity of the indexation scheme with respect to the inflation rate $\lambda - 1$. It is to be noticed that $F'_q(\bar{q}, 1) = 1$ and therefore, if λ is close to unity, $1 - F'_q(\bar{q}, \lambda)$ will be close to zero. In other words in response to a moderate exogenous inflationary stimulus, the long-run equilibrium defined by $\bar{q}$ is likely to be stable, at least locally. Otherwise, if the inflationary stimulus is large and/or if the indexation scheme is very sensitive to labour-market conditions, large fluctuations are likely to be observed with the possibility of limit cycles.

We conclude this section by pointing out that, outside the stationary state situation, the real wage rate never falls below the one which would result if indexation had been based on expected inflation. Indeed, when $q_{t-1} < \bar{q}$ inflation is accelerated – i.e. $p_t/p_{t-1} \geqslant \lambda$ and, therefore, by assumption (d.2), $q_t = F(q_{t-1}, p_t/p_{t-1}) \geqslant F(q_t, \lambda)$. Similarly, when $q_{t-1} > \bar{q}$ inflation slows down and $q_t \geqslant F(q_t, \lambda)$. From the preceding discussion we have seen that the two indexation schemes coincide in a neighbourhood of $\bar{q}$.

4. *Directions for further work*

While giving interesting insights into the role of indexation in the employment dynamics of an economy, the above model remains rudimentary and ought to be extended in several directions.

On the labour-demand side, it would be interesting to consider an imperfectly competitive model, a case in which the labour demand is not any more a function of the real-wage rate. Also, this would allow one to consider the possibility of non-decreasing returns to scale.[10]

On the other hand, it would be interesting to make explicit the underlying bargaining process between unions and firms through some game-theoretic approach so that the indexation scheme and the resulting fluctuations become endogenous.

Finally, the way in which inflation is generated is of course *ad hoc.* An alternative way, which we have explored elsewhere, is to generate inflation through deficit spending. It turns out that this does not affect the basic results. It would have complicated the model unnecessarily, therefore. On the other hand, inflation has been postulated essentially because it is the rule, and it is its mere presence which justifies the existence of indexation clauses.

Appendix

A1. Determination of the short-run demand functions

Given some ℓ, $0 \leqslant \ell \leqslant \ell^*$, the optimisation problem of the young agent can be written as

$$\text{Max } u(c_1, c_2)$$

subject to $c_1, c_2 \geqslant 0$, $m \geqslant 0$,

$$pc_1 + m = w\ell,$$

$$pc_1 + p^e c_2 = \lambda^e (m + pf(\ell) - w\ell).$$

It can equivalently be written as

$$\text{Max } u(c_1, c_2)$$

subject to $c_1, c_2 \geqslant 0$,

$$c_1 \leqslant q\ell,$$

$$c_1 + \frac{1}{\theta} c_2 = f(\ell),$$

where $q = w/p$ and $\theta = \lambda^e p/p^e$.

---

[10] See for example Weitzman's paper in the present volume (Chapter Eight). An other example is the paper by Dehez (1985).

A2. Existence of a short-run equilibrium

Let $\ell(q) = \text{Min} \, (\ell^*, f'^{-1}(q))$, the actual employment level as a function of the real-wage rate. We first fix the real wage rate at some value $q > 0$. Then condition (iii) defines the corresponding equilibrium price level as a solution of the following equation

$$(1) \qquad c_1(\theta(p), q, \ell(q)) + \frac{M}{p} = f(\ell(q))$$

where $\theta(p) = \lambda p / \psi(p, \lambda)$ and $M = \lambda M_0$. The existence of a positive solution is immediate and does not require particular assumptions on ψ except continuity. Indeed, when p goes to zero, the aggregate demand goes to infinity. On the other hand, the profit is positive, i.e. $q\ell(q) < f(\ell(q))$, and $c_1 \leqslant q\ell(q)$. Hence, for p large enough, aggregate demand falls below $f(\ell(q))$. By continuity there exists at least one solution to equation (1) and all solutions are positive.

From condition (iv), we know that equation (1) is equivalent to the following equation:

$$(2) \qquad \psi(p, \lambda)c_2(\theta(p), q, \ell(q)) = \lambda M.$$

Unicity of a solution to equation (1) then follows from the fact that the left-hand side of equation (2) is increasing in p. This is a consequence of assumption (c. 2) and of the fact that c_2 is increasing in θ.

Equation (1) then defines a continuous function $p = \mu(q, M)$ which satisfies $\mu(q, M) > 0$ for all $q \geqslant 0$ and $M > 0$, and $\mu(0, M) = M/f(\ell^*)$. Furthermore, μ is a non-decreasing function of q and an increasing function of M. This follows in particular from the fact that real profit, $f(\ell(q)) - q\ell(q)$, and the production level, $f(\ell(q))$, are both non-increasing in q implying that $c_2(\theta, q, \ell(q))$ is itself non-increasing in q.

A short-run equilibrium is then defined by a price level $p > 0$ such that

$$p = \mu\left(\frac{\phi(p)}{p}, M\right)$$

i.e. it is the intersection in the (p, q) plane between the curves defined respectively by $p = \mu(q, M)$ and $q = \phi(p)/p$. Clearly, the properties of μ and the assumptions (d. 1) and (d. 2) ensure the existence of at least one intersection.

A3. An illustration

Let us consider the following specification:

$$f(\ell) = 2\sqrt{\ell}$$
$$u(c_1, c_2) = \sqrt{c_1} + \sqrt{c_2}$$
$$\psi(p, \lambda) = \lambda p$$
$$\ell^* = 1.$$

Then $q^* = 1$, $\theta(p) = 1$ for all p and

$$c_1(1, q, \ell) = \text{Min}(q\ell, F(\ell)/2),$$
$$\ell(q) = \text{Min}(1, 1/q^2).$$

The function μ is then given by:

$$\mu(q, M) = \begin{cases} \dfrac{M}{2-q} & \text{if } q \leqslant 1, \\ Mq & \text{if } q \geqslant 1. \end{cases}$$

Let us now assume that the linkage function ϕ is given by

$$w = \left[1 + \alpha_t\left(\frac{p}{p_{t-1}} - 1\right)\right]w_{t-1}$$

where $\alpha_t = g(q_{t-1})$ is the *indexation coefficient*. The corresponding indexation formula F is then given by

$$F(q, x) = \left[g(q) + (1-g(q))\frac{1}{x}\right]q.$$

The simplest dynamics is provided by the case where $qg(g)$, the slope of ϕ with respect to the current price level is *constant*. Then $g(q) = \bar{q}/q$ and starting from any $q_0 \neq \bar{q}$, the sequence of real wage rates *converges monotically* to $\bar{q}$. Indeed, we have the following equation

$$q_t = \bar{q} + (q_{t-1} - \bar{q})\frac{h(q_t)}{\lambda h(q_{t-1})}$$

which, when applied recursively, reduces to

$$\frac{q_t - \bar{q}}{h(q_t)} = \frac{q_0 - \bar{q}}{h(q_0)} \frac{1}{\lambda^{t}}.$$

Another example is provided by the case where the indexation coefficient depends *linearly* on the real-wage rate, i.e.

$$g(q) = \text{Max}\,(0,\, \beta\,(\bar{q} - q))$$

where $\beta > 0$. Then $F'_q(\bar{q},\,\lambda) = 1 - \beta\bar{q}(1 - 1/\lambda)$ and (δ) defines implicitly a difference equation in q_t whose possible shapes are given in the Figures 3a and 3b, assuming $\bar{q} = q^*$.

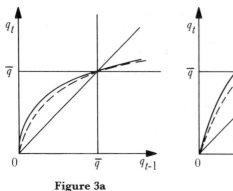

| Figure 3a | Figure 3b |

Figure 3a corresponds to case (a) where $\beta \leqslant \lambda/(\lambda - 1)$ and the stationary state $\bar{q}$ is stable. On the other hand, case (c) where $\beta > 2\lambda/(\lambda - 1)$ is illustrated in Figure 3b. The dotted curves correspond to the graph of the function $q_t = F(q_{t-1},\,\lambda)$.

References

Benassy, J.P., 'Neokeynesian disequilibrium theory in a monetary economy', *Review of Economic Studies* 42 (October 1975), 502–523.
——, 'A non-Walrasian model of employment with partial price flexibility and indexation', in Feiwel, G. (ed.), *Trends in Contemporary Macroeconomics and Distribution* (London: Macmillan, 1985).
Dehez, P., 'Monopolistic equilibrium and involuntary unemployment', *Journal of Economic Theory* 36 (1985).

Dehez, P. and Drèze, J.H. 'On supply-constrained equilibria', *Journal of Economic Theory* 33 (June 1984), 172–182.

Dehez, P. and Fitoussi, J.P. 'Equilibres de stagflation et indexation des salaires', to appear in Fitoussi, J.P. and Muet, P.A. (eds.), *Dynamique et déséquilibres* (Economica, Paris, 1985).

Drèze, J.H. 'Existence of an exchange equilibrium under price rigidities', *International Economic Review* 16 (June 1975), 301–320.

Fitoussi, J.P. 'Modern macroeconomic theory: an overview', in Fitoussi, J.P. (ed.), *Modern Macroeconomic Theory* (Oxford: Basil Blackwell, 1983).

Grandmont, J.M. *'Money and Value: A Reconsideration of Classical and Neoclassical Monetary Theories'* (Cambridge: Cambridge University Press, 1983).

——, 'On endogenous competitive business cycles', *Econometrica* 53 (September 1985), 995–1045.

Hicks, J. *'The Crisis in Keynesian Economics'* (Oxford: Basil Blackwell, 1974).

Kurz, M. 'Unemployment equilibrium in an economy with linked prices', *Journal of Economic Theory* 26 (February 1982), 100–123.

Malinvaud, E., *'The Theory of Unemployment Reconsidered'* (Oxford: Basil Blackwell, 1977).

Olson, M. 'Microeconomic incentives and macroeconomic decline', *Weltwirtschaftliches Archiv* 120 (1984), 631–645.

Tobin, J. *Asset Accumulation and Economic Activity* (Oxford: Basil Blackwell, 1980).

Van der Laan, G. 'Equilibrium under rigid prices with compensation for the consumers', *International Economic Review* 21 (February 1980), 63–73.

Younes, Y. 'On the role of money and the existence of a non-Walrasian equilibrium', *Review of Economic Studies* 42 (October 1975), 489–501.

Index